PRIVATE LIFE IN **NEW KINGDOM EGYPT**

PRIVATE LIFE IN
NEW KINGDOM EGYPT

Lynn Meskell

PRINCETON UNIVERSITY PRESS

PRINCETON AND OXFORD

Library of Congress Control Number 2001096893
ISBN 0-691-00448-X

British Library Cataloging-in-Publication Data is available.

This book has been composed in FrameMaker.

Printed on acid-free paper. ∞

www.pup.princeton.edu

Printed in the United States of America

10 9 8 7 6 5 4 3 2 1

For John Baines

Tʜɪs ɢᴏᴀʟ is, briefly, to grasp the native's point of view, *his* relation to life, to realise *his* vision of *his* world. We have to study man, and we must study what concerns him most intimately, that is, the hold which life has on him. In each culture, the values are slightly different; people aspire after different aims, follow different impulses, yearn after a different form of happiness. In each culture, we find different institutions in which man pursues his life-interest, different customs by which he satisfies his aspirations, different codes of law and morality which reward his virtues or punish his defections. To study the institutions, customs, and codes or to study the behaviour and mentality without the subjective desire of feeling by what these people live, of realising the substance of their happiness— is, in my opinion, to miss the greatest reward which we can hope to obtain from the study of man.
—Bʀᴏɴɪsʟᴀᴡ Mᴀʟɪɴᴏᴡsᴋɪ, *Argonauts of the Western Pacific*

There was a time when archaeology, as a discipline devoted to silent monuments, inert traces, objects without context, and things left by the past, aspired to the condition of history, and attained meaning only through the restitution of a historical discourse; it might be said, to play on words a little, that in our time history aspires to the condition of archaeology, to the intrinsic description of the monument.
—Mɪᴄʜᴇʟ Fᴏᴜᴄᴀᴜʟᴛ, *The Archaeology of Knowledge*

Contents

Illustrations and Tables

TABLES

Acknowledgments

THIS PROJECT began in Oxford in 1998 while I held a Salvesen Research Fellowship at New College, Oxford. I would like to thank the Warden and Fellows for all the support and generosity they extended over the two years I was there. Oxford was a particularly inspiring place to work on Egypt, largely owing to the presence of John Baines. He has been a patient and supportive mentor since my days as an undergraduate in Australia. His intellectual generosity, patience, and constant good humor are just some of the reasons that this book is dedicated to him.

Dominic Montserrat also played an instrumental part from the beginning. The book was originally conceived as a joint project, and many of the themes and ideas presented within are closely linked to that stimulating collaboration. John Baines and Gay Robins carefully read and commented on the manuscript, making it altogether better and saving me from numerous errors. I owe a substantial intellectual debt to Andrea McDowell, whose work on the documents from Deir el Medina is unsurpassed. Lisa Giddy also generously gave permission to include unpublished work from her recent book on Memphis. Richard Parkinson has been wonderfully helpful in many aspects of the project. He read various chapters, shared his own important work, and helped with references.

The book was finished during my first year at Columbia University, and my colleagues here in New York deserve recognition for making this time so rewarding and enjoyable. Lila Abu-Lughod and Sherry Ortner read sections of the book, made valuable suggestions, and gave me enormous inspiration along the way. A Columbia University Arts and Sciences Summer Fellowship enabled me to continue my work in Oxford in 2000. Members of the Oriental Institute in Oxford offered their invaluable expertise and enthusiasm, enduring my constant questions and disruptions, in particular Roland Enmarch, Tom Hardwick, Angela McDonald, Hubertus Meunch, Christina Riggs, and David Wengrow. During that time the Fellows of New College were kind enough to let me return as Visiting Fellow, providing just the right balance of motivation and mischief.

At Columbia, my research assistants Anna Boozer, Karen Holmberg, Scott Kremkau, Aziz Meshia, and Kirsten Olsen have done a great job of seeing the book to fruition. Matthew Palus deserves special thanks for making my life easier and my text more readable. I should also thank the students who took my course on social life in ancient Egypt, and whose excitement and ideas inspired me to rethink many aspects of the book. Maurice Luker and the Media Center for Art History, Archaeology, and

Historic Preservation at Columbia kindly permitted me to use images from their glass slide collection. James Conlon helped prepare those materials for publication. Anne Gout and Vassil Dobrev from the IFAO provided tireless assistance and many of the photographs from Deir el Medina. A number of people and institutions have been similarly helpful and patient: Catharine Roehrig at the Metropolitan Museum of Art, Richard Parkinson and Tanya Watkins at the British Museum, Hugh Kilmister at the Petrie Museum, Tony Leahy and Pat Spencer at the EES, and the staff at the Detroit Institute of Fine Arts.

At Princeton University Press I would like to acknowledge the support and friendship of Walter Lippincott and Fred Appel. Their patience and enthusiasm for the project have been invaluable.

LMM
New York

Conventions

Dates

All dates are B.C.E. (before the common era) unless otherwise noted and are approximate. Dates given for the regnal years of specific pharaohs (abbreviated "reg.") are similarly approximate.

Transcription and Translation

It is difficult to be entirely consistent in transcribing names and words from ancient Egyptian. Royal and personal names are given in a conventional vocalized form. Egyptian terms have, for the most part, been left in their transliterated, purely consonantal forms using diacritics. Egyptian words and texts are italicized to indicate that they are direct translations. Each text is followed by its Egyptological reference, usually an ostracon or papyrus, which appears in a footnote. This convention allows the reader to check a reference in full, without disrupting the flow of the presentation. With respect to translation, glosses are indicated by ( ), restorations by [ ], and omissions from the original text that have been supplied by the translator by < >. Gaps or broken text are denoted by three dots. Most of the Egyptian translations used derive from Lichtheim (1976), Wente (1990), Parkinson (1997), and McDowell (1999). Further details for specific texts can be found in each of these volumes.

CHAPTER ONE

The Interpretative Framework

We had to clear away the brush, stake our claim, and, like archaeologists approaching a site known to contain riches too great to be systematically explored, settle for excavating a few preliminary trenches.
—GEORGES DUBY, *A History of Private Life: From Pagan Rome to Byzantium*

THE MODERN WORLD has a very specific and well-defined concept of *private life*, although it does not maintain a monopoly on the construct. The constitution of our own private lives has been tacitly set against the discourses of the capitalist marketplace, increasing governmental intervention, new technologies, and the forces of globalism. Apprehending a contextual picture of ancient Egyptian *private life* is thus already inflected with Western constructs and cultural baggage, and yet there are threads of commonality that resonate for the archaeologist and interpreter. Endeavoring to craft such a history of private life is problematic, yet no comparable phrase or set of phrases adequately covers the conceptual territory. Despite the semantic disparities and cultural specificities that separate ancient and modern, perhaps there has always been some notion of the private. I am not suggesting that there is an essentialist construct of private life that binds people seamlessly across spatial and temporal boundaries. Yet there are connections worth exploring. Even in cultures where life is more public than is easily comprehensible in Western society, there are private zones of immunity: social networks (often glossed as family or kin), emotional relationships between individuals, the lived experience of the household (not necessarily a physical environment), responses to death, and so on. One can also acknowledge that the boundaries between social spheres—public or private, and living experience and the realm of death, for example—are overlapping and permeable. Ultimately, I suggest that the concept of private life provides one meaningful framework to access ancient social life. And one useful way to approach the Egyptian material is according to its own coherent template: that of the human life cycle, which forms the structure of this book.

High modernity affords us a very specific perspective on locality, authenticity, and belonging and offers an even greater range of self-conscious options for the life project of the individual. What social theorists call the *project of the self* is perhaps the most potent demarcator of our age: the reflexive relationship with the inner self, our construction of self-identity, and our fundamental desires for introspection, analysis, and self-development through the various life stages. The iconic sign of that discursive production is ultimately the body, indelibly connected to the workings of the individual's life project and a visible emblem of our sense of individuality, ethnicity, affiliation, sexuality, and so on. Yet these articulations seem so inherently modern that they may appear unconnected to cultures like New Kingdom Egypt (c. 1539–1075), shrouded in their antiquity and cultural specificity. Examining cultural difference is certainly one aim of this book, and I do not wish to conflate ancient and modern constructions and experience. This theme runs parallel with my desire to strip bare some of the preoccupations and misconceptions that frequently haunt our representations of ancient Egypt. It is not unfair to say that the intellectual colonization of Egypt continues.

Another aim is to present the complexity and sophistication of Egyptian society and to dispel the privileged position we have created for ourselves as primary bearers of culture in the age of post-Enlightenment. New Kingdom Egypt bears all the hallmarks of civilization that we immediately claim for ourselves as inheritors of an intricate Western European lineage. I hope to chart some of those features throughout the book: a substantial corpus of existential writing about humanity and the cosmos, complex mythico-religious systems, a highly articulated sense of embodiment and personhood, evocations of romantic love, eroticism, and sexuality, elaborate social relations, and so on. Some forms of data might offer windows into the personal world, whereas much remains silent. But there are certainly points of connection between ancients and moderns, even though our taxonomies, cultural language and expression, experiences, and outcomes are very different.

Many researchers have to face the eternal hermeneutic dilemma of not being within the culture that they study—of being an interloper with a vastly different language, symbolic system, social setting, and worldview. This is true for anthropologists in the present and all writers of history alike: we are all prefigured in our own setting. There is a great risk of missing the cadences and characteristics of that other culture. It is vital to remain aware of this separation and dangerous to assume too great a certainty and familiarity with others from the past. Various studies of ancient Egypt are perhaps guilty of this normalization, making "them" more like "us" through language and sentiment. Yet it is those very differences that make Egyptian society so mesmerizing and endlessly fascinating. With the insights of social constructionism, it is no longer justifiable to write seamless or isomorphic histories, or to ignore our misunderstandings, the fragmentation, and lacunae (see Foucault 1972). The gaps in the primary evidence are an interpretative space and therefore have a weight of their own in the writing of history.

PRIVATE LIFE AND SOCIAL HISTORY

French historians such as Philippe Ariès, Georges Duby, and others (see Ariès 1962, 1974; Veyne 1987; Duby 1988; Chartier 1989; Prost and Vincent 1991) who pioneered the study of private life from antiquity to modernity have argued succinctly that in all times and places some sense of distinction has been made between the public—that which is open to the community and subject to outside authority—and the private. The private zone, as Duby calls it, is one of relative immunity, where one might relax, take ease, and lie about unshielded. This is where the family thrives, the realm of domesticity; it is also a realm of secrecy and of passions. This private sphere contains our most precious possessions, where we belong only to ourselves. What is divulged here might sometimes be at odds with exterior appearances. In some ways, Egyptian experience does not seem so far from this description. There was a different mode of living within the house or village walls that was at variance with the presentation of the self in formal society or at work. Much of ancient life was probably lived out of doors as well. Textual evidence from the New Kingdom village of Deir el Medina suggests that codes of behavior during work time or outside the village were enacted in ways quite dissimilar from those pertaining to domestic affairs. Levels of tolerance, leniency, and propriety vary greatly across contexts.

> Private life is not something given in nature from the beginning of time. It is a historical reality, which different societies have construed in different ways. The boundaries of private life are not laid down once and for all; the division of human activity between public and private spheres is subject to change. (Prost 1991: 3)

For much of pharaonic society the private zone must have been commensurate with the house, and to some degree the village. However, it would be a cultural conflation to render the house a "home" with all its cozy associations. Like the French historians, when discussing the history of dwellings I hope to avoid using anachronistic terms such as "bedrooms" (contra Kemp 1989), in order to deflect speculation about the history of individualism, or worse, of intimacy. Yet the house and the household remain the principal domain of private experience, thus providing a stable and continuous foundation for this study. Every dwelling shelters a group, a complex social organism, within which inequalities and contradictions present in the larger society are brought to the fore. Throughout this book, I have tried to move across the social demarcations of class and status, attempting to find evidence for nonelite groups, that is, those individuals who made up the bulk of the Egyptian populace. One way of envisaging these designations is to see Egyptian society as crudely divided between those who had servants or "slaves" and those who were in service. I also attempt to unravel the vectors of age and sex to present a range of experiences of social life: there can no longer be nomothetic or broad class treatments for single groups, such as women, children, or foreigners. Clearly, not all individuals in a single category shared commensurate experiences; these would have varied according to rank, status, education, age, stage of life, and a host of other social variables. The new perspectives of feminist theory and ethnic studies have challenged the older reductive and totalizing views, some of which still hold sway in Egyptology and mainstream archaeology.

From New Kingdom Egypt there is more evidence for reconstructing private life than for any other pre-Roman culture, yet little has appeared that exploits this amazingly rich material. The study of Egypt has largely remained impervious to the incursions of theoretical developments in history and the social sciences. Topics such as "finding women's voices" are now regarded as too simplistic and reductive for the writing of a nuanced ancient history, but they still have a niche in Egyptology. These topics are now of primarily historiographic value in other disciplines. In terms of creating a sophisticated access to the ancient data, the *Annales* school of French historians has led the way, perhaps best illustrated by Paul Veyne's seminal article on the Roman family (1978), and followed by the four-volume *History of Private Life* series initiated by Ariès and Duby. Their bold endeavor has yet to be surpassed, and no study of those cultures prior to the Greeks has come close to Ariès and Duby's project. Their encyclopedic scope, empirical rigor, and theoretical sophistication are exemplars of what can be teased out of the ancient materials—although significantly they said nothing about ancient Egypt.

Private life in the classical world has been of interest certainly since the nineteenth century (e.g., Becker 1895; Johnston 1903; McDaniel [1871] 1963); however, the same subject for Egyptian and Near Eastern societies has received much less attention (but see Wilkinson 1841; Erman 1894). This can be explained to some degree by the disciplinary setting for such writing, which was and continues to be predominantly in the field of history rather than archaeology. Moreover, societies such as Greece or Rome have occupied a prominent place in the long history of Western cultural values, whereas the position of Egyptian culture was somewhat ambivalent. Many recent books address in various ways the "daily lives" of the ancient Egyptians with mixed and varied success (e.g., James 1984;

Stead 1986; El Mahdy 1987; Strouhal 1992; Donadoni 1997; Watterson 1997; Wilson 1997; Brewer and Teeter 1999). While some of these books provide very useful and insightful overviews, most fall into the trap of dividing the primary material into discrete Western taxonomies. In this respect they are part of a long tradition of writing about the history of private life but are also part of a genre that was typical of writing in other disciplines in the first half of the twentieth century. It is important to sketch the broader context of such works, as they form the model for these and other books on ancient Egyptian life.

In looking at the historiographical trends in writing about literate, premodern cultures, there is a noticeable progression in thematic focus. This takes into account individual books as well as articles in influential periodicals, such as the *Journal of Family History, Journal of Marriage and Family*, and *Journal of Medieval Studies*. Many twentieth-century studies of ancient cultures outside Egypt drew on documentary evidence, concentrating on kinship, family life, and the dichotomous tensions between public and private spheres. Earlier work was polarized by a familiar range of Cartesian dualities such as male:female, nature:culture, inside:outside. The distinction between public and private seems to have been an essential point of departure for studies in the 1960s. In the following decade, French or French-inspired scholars were fascinated by the relationship between public and private and the concept of the *domus*, most famously formulated in Emmanuel Le Roy Ladurie's *Montaillou* (1980). Also groundbreaking in this tradition was Lawrence Stone's magisterial work *The Family, Sex and Marriage in England, 1500–1800* (1977). Stone's view of the family is not simply structurally defined, but also rests on *histoire des sentiments*, or constellations of attitudes about domestic life. His work, along with that of Le Roy Ladurie, is in some ways the model for this undertaking, though there are fundamental areas where one can disagree with both. Both Stone and Le Roy Ladurie realized the potential of a dialogue between domestic space, historical voices (often marginalized ones that were omitted from conventional histories), and imaginative analysis. The 1970s also saw the first nuanced treatments of woman and sexuality, as women's lives became segregated from the overall project of social life, with the rise of feminism (e.g., Mitterauer and Sieder 1982; Atkinson 1983; Hufton 1984; Nicholas 1985; Millard 1986; Gies 1987). To some degree, the analysis of children's positions and experience followed rather later after initial work by Philippe Ariès (1962) and Lloyd DeMause (1974). Their work on the history of childhood paved the way for scholars researching this largely ignored social group (e.g., Nicholas 1985; Geary 1994). As a corollary, studies on aging also came into vogue (Laslett 1995), thus covering both ends of the life cycle's spectrum.

In the past few decades, gender studies have been interpolated into almost every scholarly discipline. It is important to distinguish between work on gender and women's history, since much of the latter masquerades as a more inclusive gender study. Research on marriage had always been linked to prosopographic work and kinship studies, yet the study of women's lives constituted another somewhat different sphere. From the 1980s onward there has been a vast outpouring of books devoted solely to women's lives in which men are absent (e.g., Hufton 1984; Nicholas 1985; Gero and Conkey 1991; Pantel 1992; Cameron and Kuhrt 1993; Fantham et al. 1994; Herlihy 1995; Leyser 1995; Brooten 1996). Many of these were influenced directly or indirectly by Sarah Pomeroy's groundbreaking *Goddesses, Whores, Wives, and Slaves* (1975). In more synthetic works, traditional areas such as law, demography, inheritance, customs, housing, and religion continued to be foregrounded. Sexuality took center stage in the 1990s after two decades of steadily increasing output (e.g., Boswell 1994; Klingshirn 1994; Brooten 1996). Celibacy, virginity, and religious law have had a long-standing interest for European scholars yet this burgeoning field was closely tied to contemporary sexual politics, the rise of gay activism, and later the development and deployment of queer theory (Lancaster and di Leonardo 1997; Weeks 1997). In the same way, research on medieval marriage was a large part of post-1970s work, suggesting a linkage between Western society's current reconsideration of the institution and its general lack of success. Both of these historiographical trends may reflect European interest in reexamining its own documented history and the possibilities for other ways of constituting relationships. In concert with studies of gender and sexuality, scholarly attention was then directed toward the body, selfhood, self-narration, intimacy, sexual behavior, questions of individuality, and the individual generally (e.g., Duby 1988; Leyser 1995; Nicholas 1985; Sears 1986; Rosenthal 1996).

This necessarily brief survey of private life in Western scholarship shows that a radical shift in subject matter and theoretical approach has occurred in the last two decades. A similar perspective can be gleaned from social anthropology's ethnographic trends in the study of private life. Whereas earlier studies had a clear focus on the family as their foundation, current societal shifts have problematized that particular bedrock. At the heart of this refiguring lies the whole question of what constitutes kin. Anthropologists such as Sylvia Yanagisako and Carol Delaney posit (1995a: 9–10) that in the past "any particular kinship system was thought to be a cultural elaboration of the biological facts of human reproduction, and anthropologists recognized that there were significant differences in how far these genealogical maps extended and how relations in them were classified." David Schneider famously critiqued the reduction of kinship to genealogy, arguing that kinship cannot be conflated simply with a biological infrastructure, since the cultural dimension, terms, and practices vary widely from society to society (see Weston 1995: 88). This is also the case when Egyptian ideas of family and household are examined. If it is difficult to refigure kin outside our own Western terminologies, then consider the modern deconstruction of kinship. Euro-American notions of kinship are being challenged by two powerful domains: new reproductive technologies, and changing gender and sexual relationships (Dolgin 1995; McKinnon 1995). Biological relationships are no longer clear-cut since the inception of in-vitro fertilization (Strathern 1992). Moreover, the increased presence of same-sex relationships and the creation of "new families" is a direct challenge to the familial status quo based on bloodlines. Today, we are effectively rewriting kin in social and legal spheres. This underscores the fragility of "natural" domains, since both science and sexuality have begun to impinge upon what many would posit as the most fundamental of human social relationships at the very nexus of private life.

SOURCES AND PROBLEMS OF INTERPRETATION

Accessing private life in a meaningful way is invariably circumscribed by the types of sources available and their fragmentary, resistant natures. Some have likened the task to an archaeology of the past, as did Georges Duby (1987: vii) in his foreword to the first volume of *A History of Private Life*, which is quoted as the epigraph to this chapter.

This book focuses upon four primary data sources for compiling a history of private life in Egypt. Those sources are documentary, iconographic, archaeological, and what one might broadly call anthropological. Each set of data has its own inherent biases and strengths. For the New Kingdom, the first three sources are particularly rich, and it is not an overstatement to claim that we know more about this period than any other in pharaonic history. For the most part the analyses are restricted to this period, introducing cross-temporal analogies only where they were deemed applicable. Many previous studies of aspects of life, from magical practices to funerary traditions, tend to seamlessly amalgamate examples from distinctly diverse historical periods. Clearly, by focusing on trends and similarities we forget the dynamic nature of Egyptian culture, which was always in contact with its neighbors and regularly borrowed, assimilated, and desired numerous foreign commodities, styles, deities, and so on. While the pace of change in pharaonic Egypt may not be comparable to modern society, it remains axiomatic that cultures are not static—certainly not throughout a period so vast as the Bronze Age.

We cannot simply interpolate data from other periods when the New Kingdom sources are meager, nor assume that socio historic developments have little effect on material culture or belief systems even if some aspects of village life might remain superficially similar. The unbroken thread of pharaonic culture is a fantasy created in the West, part of an imaginary constructed out of romantic and colonial narratives about the Orient—now convincingly exposed and undermined (Said 1979; Mitchell 1990; Bahrani 1998; Bowman and Rogan 1999).

Because of Egyptology's disciplinary history, the traditional area of study has always been ancient language—the translation and interpretation of ancient writings, whether in documents, on monuments, or in other media. This remains the most privileged domain of Egyptology and has resulted in a split between scholars who study texts or iconography and those who undertake archaeological investigations (Kemp 1984a; Meskell 1994a). Few individuals command both, and this disciplinary divide has had serious, negative repercussions for the holistic understanding of Egyptian culture. The resultant downplaying of archaeological materials has meant that fewer, less systematic excavations have been carried out, notably on settlement sites where specialists would derive most of their evidence for social life. Such a predicament has not been lost on Egyptian archaeologists (Bietak 1979; O'Connor 1997), although remedying it is not without significant problems, as discussed below.

Given this situation, it is not surprising that most work in Egyptology is directed toward language and documents. The New Kingdom has yielded the greatest number of personal documents and inscriptions of any period before the Graeco-Roman, many from the settlement site of Deir el Medina. These offer unprecedented insights into historical events, village happenings, and personal histories, giving us a firmer footing from which to discuss private life. In fact, much of what a modern interpreter would deem "private" often became public through the bureaucratic recording of arguments, hostilities, scandals, and court cases, and the custom of reading written documents aloud. These daily, sometimes intimate narratives give their interpreters the impression of being able to "know" the people of the New Kingdom, since many of their sentiments, aspirations, and concerns resonate with our own. The very act of translating the Egyptian language involves a process of making "them" more like "us," using our own familiar words to understand a conceptual system different from our own. The process of translation flattens out difference and diversity, transcribing words and concepts that may have no exact parallel in our own language. The hermeneutic pitfalls of this process are considerable. However, this is not to say that documentary evidence is fatally flawed or unusable—far from it. It provides a connective bridge between the ancient Egyptians and ourselves and gives the sort of background lacking in so many analyses of prehistoric societies. Egyptologists can, with some measure of accuracy, discuss everything from notions of personhood, to attitudes toward women, to fears about death and beyond, from a culturally specific foundation. Many Egyptologists bemoan that they cannot say more. Yet what they can say remains a great deal more than for scholars working on nonliterate societies.

Ancient Egyptian literature is also a central source that allows a specific window onto New Kingdom culture. Didactic texts, poetry, and stories provide vital evidence for many vectors and attributes of society. Unsurprisingly, there is no consensus within Egyptology on the nature of these specific documents. Jan Assmann has frequently characterized such texts as a nonfunctional, residual category where the meaning resides solely in the text rather than its context. Instead he develops the notion of "cultural texts," so that the *Tale of Sinuhe* is likened to a range of ceremonies, dances, festivals, and images that embody knowledge, tradition, and social identity (1999a: 7). This view has been challenged by Antonio Loprieno (1996), who asserts that autoreflexivity and intertextuality must be considered. He argues that Egyptologists need to consider fictionality—the notion of possible worlds constructed within Egyptian writing. Thus one can think of two symbolic systems: topos and mimesis. The first describes the world as Egyptians thought of it, which specifically pertains to didactic or instructional texts. The second relates to the world of the individual author, and this type of literature is best described as realistic narrative (Moers 1999: 45). These are methodological issues that are not resolved easily, yet there are more serious questions of representation.

With the use of written data come additional problems, such as who has access to literacy, and the politics of recording. Research has shown that probably between 1 and 4 percent of the pharaonic population were literate (Baines 1983, 1988), and they were largely the elite, male, scribal class throughout much of Egyptian history. Education was restricted to those boys who were to be trained for official duties and who would eventually be answerable to the government. This meant that women, middle- and lower-status individuals, those of servile status, and probably most foreigners were excluded from the benefits of literacy. Presumably there was little hope of advancing one's social position without such skills. Rather than recording their own voices, these people were the *subjects* of the documents, and this has obvious implications for the politics of writing Egyptian history. However, literacy can be seen as a sliding scale, with many individuals in-between literate and illiterate: some who could perhaps make out symbols but could not write, others who could write to a limited degree, and so on. Women and artisans may have constituted a substantial group of such people. Of the 470 letters from the village of Deir el Medina, only about 14 percent are sent by, or addressed to, women (Sweeney 1993: 525). It was thus possible for women to dictate a letter and have a reply read aloud, which facilitated some level of outside communication. Yet one must reiterate that written histories in all contexts are subjective enterprises. The historian is left only a trace of the original whole and then has to concentrate on specific documents and their lacunae. As with archaeology, there is no total recovery.

Iconography is another major source for New Kingdom life, and it lies at the nexus of textual and archaeological evidence. Word and image were deeply intertwined in Egypt; both were efficacious and could be functionally powerful in this world and the next. Magical texts and images could change an individual's circumstances, and the written name itself was a potent symbol. Yet images had the extra power of being visually evocative. In the case of tomb decoration (the iconographic data set referred to most frequently), this was of special import. The images were the bearers of the owner's identity, personality, and visual likeness and could be called upon as referents in the afterlife. Yet images also had the power to improve upon reality, portraying the tomb owner, for instance, as youthful, beautiful, and without imperfections. We have to remember that these images were created by male artisans specifically for other men, as tomb owners, and were there to serve specific needs (Meskell 1998a: 175–76). They were also there to serve him sexually. Images of young women could also operate as functional pictures to ensure his sexual revivification in the afterlife (as outlined in Chapter 5). The element of male fantasy in the construction of these specific types of female imagery is only now emerging. Too often iconography, especially tomb iconography, has been taken as a literal source of evidence for life experience.

There are other biases inherent in the iconographic evidence. First, a specific world created for the mortuary sphere has only tangential bearing on the experience of daily life. Given the Egyptian aspiration for perfection in the hereafter, funerary art is likely to be skewed toward achieving that goal, rather than being an accurate representation. Second, the images are highly politicized and constructed around the male tomb owner, rather than reflecting the desired reality of those additionally rendered, such as women, children, and workers (Meskell 1998a: 176–78). Even the portrayal of their everyday activities is clouded by the practice of male artisans decorating the tombs and probably having little exposure to the actual details of specific activities (see Samuel 1993). While such scenes are valuable for studying technology and craft, they should not be mistaken for literal recordings of processes that can then be reconstructed step by step. Third, tomb paintings were costly commodities that were only available to the elite or those who were trained artisans, such as the workmen at Deir el Medina. By default, a limited range of socioeconomic strata is represented, reinforcing the elite bias evident with the production of texts.

A major source of evidence for private life, especially for individuals of the middle and lower strata who composed the majority of the population, is the archaeological data. Throughout the volume I draw heavily on both settlement and mortuary archaeology and use it dialectically with the textual sources. Archaeology offers a counter to the documentary record produced by an all-male elite, in that it can shed light on the silent masses—women, children, foreigners, the nonelite, and individuals of servile status. We have material evidence for household activities and domestic life that were not the subjects of written texts. Moreover, archaeological evidence can hint at more subversive trends that explicitly defy the hegemony of the textual record. For example, official records in the Amarna period would give the impression of a pervasive new religion centered on the Aten, whereas the archaeology of the workmen's village to the north of the site reveals that the inhabitants continued to worship the traditional deities in their homes (Kemp 1987) and in their chapels (Bomann 1991: 74), with little or no regard for Akhenaten's (reg. 1353–1336) new religious program. Recent analysis by Verena Lepper (1998: 58–69) indicates that this pattern may have been even more widespread throughout the city, given the significant number of objects featuring traditional deities. Here material culture is a source for counterevidence and can provide additional strata of information for the complex workings of private life.

The main problem with using archaeological material—apart from the obvious questions of subjectivity and interpretation common to all sources—is the standard of fieldwork done in the last century or so of excavation. Current excavations at Amarna or Memphis will be more reliable than those conducted in the nineteenth century at Gurob for instance. Most of the evidence for domestic life and the funerary sphere stems from Deir el Medina, excavated over the first half of the twentieth century by Bernard Bruyère. Some Egyptologists claim that this material was not excavated to a standard that is readily usable, yet his methodologies were more advanced and less ethnocentric than those of his contemporaries at Amarna. The material from Deir el Medina is clearly substantive and has the potential to yield important insights into living experience and the constitution of inequalities based on age, sex, status, ethnicity, and so on (Meskell 1998b, 1999a, 1999b). For this reason, coupled with the abundant textual evidence, Deir el Medina forms the basis for much of this volume. Egyptologists are generally reticent to do the sort of analysis that archaeology requires or to incorporate this type of work. More seriously, important Egyptian settlement sites like Deir el Medina and the Roman period town of Karanis have not received due archaeological analysis, since the wealth of documentary data has overshadowed the richness of the nontextual material.

The fourth methodological source is best described as anthropological and cross-cultural. This primarily consists of case studies drawn from a wide temporal and geographical range, utilized so as to accentuate the possibilities for difference in the ancient record. Too often scholars have presumed a seamless extrapolation from our own contexts to the Egyptian situation, which is untenable and misleading. Restoring the cultural difference that Egypt possesses for the Western viewer is an explicit part of the current project. If we make the ancient Egyptians more like us, we circumscribe the richness of their historical specificity. This is intellectually irresponsible and also undermines the raison d'être of our own fascination with Egypt.

EGYPTIAN EXPERIENCE

Egyptian history is written from an elite perspective, using the sources generated by pharaohs and their officials. From these predominantly textual sources Egyptologists have constructed the frameworks for a social history. But how does one characterize the specificities of elite culture? As John Baines (1991: 132) remarks:

> In most periods, the elite who ran affairs of state were a close-knit group of a few hundred. They were all men, and they were the fathers of the next generation of the elite. Although no rule required that positions be inherited, elite children stood an altogether better chance of reaching high office than others. The core elite with their families numbered two or three thousand people. There were perhaps five thousand more literate people, who with their families would have brought the total ruling and administrative class to fewer than 50,000, of whom perhaps one in eight were literate officeholders. They might have formed 3 to 5 percent of the population, which, in the Old Kingdom was perhaps one to one and a half million.

Their experience was very different from that of the vast majority of the Egyptian populace. By virtue of their wealth and station, the elite constructed monuments that have survived to a greater degree than those of the middle or lower strata. Their aspirations and connections reached levels of society unattainable, perhaps almost unimaginable, for the rest. Elite and non-elite hoped to have many children (Baines 1991: 132; see Chapter 2). This was a necessity if they were to increase or even reproduce themselves, because only a minority of children survived to become adults. Adults could not look forward with confidence to long careers. Evidence from Roman Egypt suggests a life expectancy at age fourteen of 29.1 years, whereas research at the cemeteries of Gebelen and Asyut suggests 36 for the Dynastic period (Nunn 1996: 22). At birth, average life expectancy must have been much less than 20. These figures may seem startling, but their plausibility for all but the elite is corroborated from a number of sources (Baines 1991: 133; see Chapter 3).

The majority of society lived in relative poverty and simplicity. Agricultural laborers formed the backbone of Egyptian society, yet we know little of their lives other than that they struggled through a life of penury, privation, and toil and died leaving little trace in the world. Such people undoubtedly lived "without the least hope of better days, inexorably chained to the very bottom of the social scale, shackled for life, that was the most distressing circumstance of their tormented existence—but did they ever in the least perceive it?" (Caminos 1997: 28). While these descriptions are vivid, the appropriate terminologies for particular social categories have eluded scholars. Egypt's agricultural laborers have been referred to as "peasants," "rural poor," and the "lower classes," and yet all terms have problematic European associations. Other diverse professions that were associated with this lower socioeconomic group include soldiers, minor officials, tenant farmers, peasants, and slaves (Trigger et al. 1983: 193–94). A major source for the New Kingdom agricultural economy, the Wilbour Papyrus, documents a large tract of land in Middle Egypt. Here the local rural population consisted of five thousand, and the text indicates that 60 percent were cultivators, while the remaining 40 percent were part-time farmers (O'Connor 1995: 319). There were other groups of workers we might classify as artisans, including higher-status foremen and supervisors and lower-ranking craftsmen and laborers, like those from Deir el Medina. In the New Kingdom, the barriers between the lowest and middle social strata were probably more permeable (Valbelle 1997: 46). As a general rule, professions in Egypt corresponded with specific social groups, and individuals were largely identified with the work they did (Loprieno 1997: 188); this classification offers the most contextually accurate way of discussing social structure. Despite the ambiguities, I have used "elite" to describe officials of high status and "non-elite" for those people who formed the middle and lower strata of society, being more specific when possible. I also tend to use the word "strata" rather than "class" with the recognition that all such terms undoubtedly elide important cultural specificities.

Since the beginning of Egyptology's emergence as a subject, there have been numerous books that recreate an overarching social history of ancient Egypt, usually portraying daily life in contemporary taxonomic frameworks (e.g., Wilkinson 1841; Osburn 1854; Budge 1891; Erman 1894; Scott 1944; Sameh 1964, James 1984). Scholars tended to dwell upon the elite, refraining from substantive work on the middle and lower social strata (Meskell 1999a), and very few concentrated on the mortuary record as a possible source for life experience and inequality. Later works focused on macroscopic accounts of Egyptian society, economy, politics, and religion (e.g., Trigger et al. 1983; Kemp 1989; Grimal 1992). Those interested in social issues have tended toward a nomothetic approach, focusing on classes or groups of individuals. For instance, there has been a recent proliferation of books in English devoted to women (e.g., Watterson 1991; Robins 1993a; Tyldesley 1994; Capel and Markoe 1996; Lesko 1999). The majority of such studies (with the exception of Robins) take a simplistic and monolithic approach, thus failing to account for the rich variability in women's lives relating to social class, age, ethnicity, and experience. They also tend to reuse the same set of data, with few new insights. The core of this work remains indebted to P. W. Pestman's 1961 study of marriage and the legal position of women. Issues of gender have hardly been addressed at all: for writers on Egypt, gender is still synonymous with finding women. As a result there have been no studies focusing on men's lives and very few on children (see Janssen and Janssen 1990; Feucht 1995) or minority groups. To date, sexual experience for the pharaonic period has been examined only in one book (Manniche 1987).

Egyptian life experience often tends to be interpreted in these books as a uniform category and ancient life compartmentalized into inherently Western classifications: economics, legal system, love and marriage, the family, dress and adornment, and so on. Methodologically, it is unhelpful to partition Egyptian experience into contemporary categories; it should be seen in relation to the cultural system in which it operated. Such an approach consciously sets out to contextualize the data in ways that would have been meaningful in ancient times. This particular volume, however, is structured according to the dynamics of category and the cycles of life as perceived by the Egyptians themselves, so that the link between life cycle and cyclical time is more clear (see also Meskell 2000a).

Notions of time in Egypt are complex and revolve around several conceptual frameworks. One construction of time, *nḥḥ*, was associated with cyclical time, like the repeated dawning of the new day, which parallels the conceptual cycle of rebirth, in which time is a spiral of patterned repetitions and a coil of countless rebirths. Creation was not a single past event but a series of "first times" of sacred regenerative moments recurring regularly within the sacred space of temples through the media of rituals and architecture (Shafer 1997: 2). Operating in tandem was the concept of *ḏt*, which we might translate as linear time and which occurs in references to the night and to the ruler of death, Osiris. Together they determine and embody the spatial structure of the created world and constitute its temporal shape (Hornung 1992: 68–69). *Nḥḥ* is often characterized as dynamic and _dt_ as static, connoting "flow" and "duration" of time, respectively. However, they can be used interchangeably, which complicates our desire to categorize them discretely. Divine time is eternal and constituted from two aspects, endless repetition and linear continuity. _Dt_ and _nḥḥ_ reinforce each other, the former being associated with Osiris and the latter with Re (Bochi 1994: 56).

The Egyptians did not have a general word that can be glossed as _time_. A number of terms denote various units of time. It was primarily divided into human or divine time, what might be called "here-time" and "there-time." Earthly life could be broken into increments of years (_rnpwt_), months (_3bdw_), days (_hrw_), hours (_wnwt_), and moments (_3wt_) (Bochi 1994: 56). Two calendars were operative in Egypt. The lunar calendar was religious in function whereas the civil calendar was dominant, being used consistently in daily life (Depuydt 1997: 2). The civil calendar consisted of twelve months of thirty days and five additional days, making a total of 365 days. This was a cycle that simply repeated itself. The cyclical nature of the Nile itself probably played an important role in the creation of the civil calendar: the first season refers to the inundation. Apart from agricultural events, astronomical events such as the heliacal rising of the star Sirius in July in conjunction with the rising Nile also heralded new beginnings (Depuydt 1997: 14). The Egyptian calendar was independent of both sun and moon, and consequently the civil year slowly rotated through the natural year. Days were divided into twenty-four hours, twelve for day and twelve for night, while hours were not divided.

The ancient Egyptians had a concept of the lifetime, called ' _ḥ'w_, and in many instances measured it with the utmost care (Hornung 1992: 58). The optimum human life span was some one hundred years plus ten or twenty extra years to attain ultimate earthly knowledge and wisdom. Although this was the ideal, the corporeal realities of life were usually very different. Egyptian ideology may have stressed the wonders of the next life, yet the sentiments expressed in didactic texts among others were inflected with fear and dread at the realization of bodily death. Generally, the wisdom texts tend to stress the importance of living a full life, a life of moral worth, pleasure, and material success. The identity of each individual was accumulated through life and was used to determine the deceased's fate at the pivotal day of judgment. This was marked by the weighing of the heart ceremony: the just individual was allowed to proceed to the next life whereas the unjust was consigned to a second death and ultimate damnation. One's earthly identity and character were somatic entities or aspects of the individual that persisted after corporeal death and, as such, were part of a cyclical process.

In this book, my intent is to try to uncover the rich strata of private life from the matrix of Egyptian social history, sifting through the archaeological, historical, textual, and iconographic sources and piecing together the fragments from which one might write narratives. Since the inception of the postmodern there can be no single, unilinear history but rather a mosaic of different narratives based on the context and situatedness of our ancient sources and those individual voices from the past (see Shanks and Tilley 1987a, 1987b; Knapp 1996; Hodder 1999). The foundations of academic authority have been eroded, as can be seen in the writings of "alternative" histories of Egypt: Afrocentric, millenarian, New Age, and even fascist (Montserrat 2000: 108–38). One could argue that while much of the necessary evidence for a social history has been present, the interpretative approach and willingness for interdisciplinary conversation have not been at the forefront of Egyptology. I hope that my own diverse interests—archaeology, anthropology, gender studies, and social theory—will cohere in contributing something new to the study of New Kingdom Egypt. That particular perspective might offer scholars of Egypt new ways of looking at the remarkable material they claim as their own.

CHAPTER TWO

Locales and Communities

THE CHRONOLOGIES and titles given to ancient time periods are our own construction. The New Kingdom is a case in point. Egypt was called by various names such as the Black Land, *kmt*, or the Two Lands, *t3wy*, which included Upper and Lower Egypt. This chapter explores the historical and geographical settings for New Kingdom life from a localized perspective. It considers how the Egyptians themselves may have viewed international and national spheres, including evidence for regionalism and local traditions, and moves to questions of ethnicity, authenticity, and issues of citizenship. Textual data give us insight into feelings of local pride, veneration of place, and even nostalgia for one's place of birth. Narratives of travel, both biographical and literary, provide further clues about the importance of locality, genealogy, and identity. Egypt was geographically diverse, and the archaeological record demonstrates that local conditions materially affected life experience. As today, life in larger cities was very different from that experienced by people living in villages and rural settings. It is also important to briefly outline the excavated settlements—Amarna, Deir el Medina, Tell ed Daba, Gurob, Memphis—and the exact nature of their archaeological remains. Here I suggest that new information can illuminate the social perspective that might be retrieved from archaeological sources. A rich stratum of evidence for urban, village, and domestic life can be employed to highlight different living experiences at the household level. Finally, settlement evidence is linked to discussions of the family as the major structuring authority of social life.

HISTORICAL SETTING FOR NEW KINGDOM EGYPT

The New Kingdom is conventionally supposed to start in 1539, with the accession of Ahmose, and to finish in 1075 with the end of Ramesses XI's reign. Inevitably, such a term smoothes over the huge political and social changes that took place during such a long period of time. But there is some evidence that the Egyptians themselves looked back upon the New Kingdom as a differentiable period of time with a distinct beginning and end. The reigns of Ahmose at the beginning of the Eighteenth Dynasty, and the successors of Akhenaten at the end, certainly seem to have been regarded as historical turning points. This is hinted at in tomb paintings

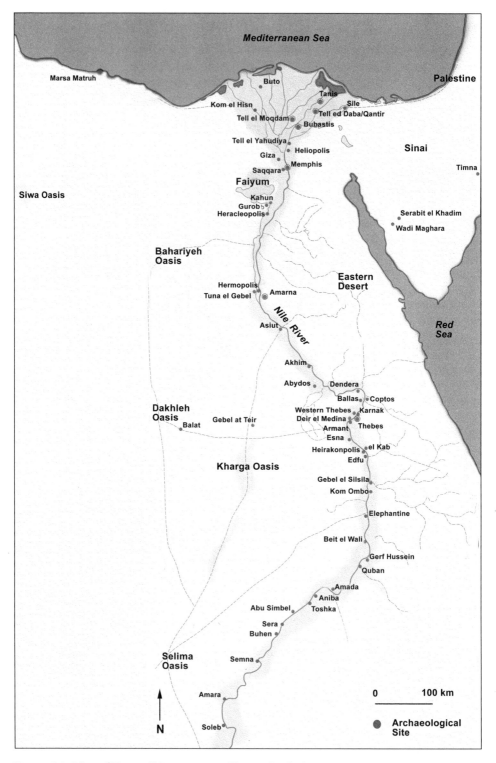

Figure 2.1. Map of Egypt. (Map courtesy of James Conlon)

from the early Nineteenth Dynasty. In the Theban tomb of Amenmes, the tomb owner and his relatives make offerings to the succession of pharaohs from Ahmose (reg. 1539–1514) to Seti I (reg. 1290–1279), excluding Akhenaten and his successors. Similarly, the military turmoil and struggles for power during Ramesses XI's (reg. 1104–1075) reign were seen as marking the end of something: during the last decade of his reign a new system of era dating was introduced that apparently acknowledged the end of one cycle and the beginning of another one. In view of the evidence, it is justifiable to think about Bronze Age Egypt between 1539 and 1075 as a specific historical era.

The determining historical event that inaugurated the New Kingdom was the victory of the pharaoh Ahmose over the Hyksos—ethnically foreign kings from Syro-Palestine who ruled from Avaris in the Delta. This proved to be more than an affirmation of Egyptian power; it can be viewed as an example of the changing beliefs and behaviors that were to characterize the following dynasties. Ahmose mounted a series of military campaigns to rid Egypt of the Hyksos. The battle centered on the Hyksos capital Avaris, modern Tell ed Daba, itself located in a strategic position in the eastern Delta (Bietak 1995; Davies and Schofield 1995). Evidence suggests that after defeating the Hyksos, Ahmose built his own city on the ruins of their settlement. In the following years, Hyksos elements were effectively removed from Egyptian culture, to be replaced by an influx of other foreign objects. In fact, Bowman and Rogan (1999: 6) have pointed out that from the Hyksos through to the British Protectorate, the ordinary laborers of Egypt were predominantly ruled by foreign sovereigns.

Control of trade routes and resource networks was of primary importance throughout the New Kingdom. Ahmose and the pharaohs after him were aware of the need to situate Egypt not in isolation, but as a powerful player in the Mediterranean basin and in parts of northeast Africa. Control of strategic areas, whether for trade or particular resources, was usually accomplished through conquest and colonization in areas close to the Egyptian heartland, rather than through diplomatic ties or reciprocal trading alone. This was particularly apparent in the strategy used to control Nubia, where an Egyptian viceroy was installed to oversee the large amount of tribute expected from each region. Areas further from Egypt, such as the Near Eastern and Mediterranean polities, retained their self-governance but were still expected to provide tribute (Baines and Málek 2000: 43). Diplomatic and trade envoys are presented to the pharaoh in many reliefs and wall paintings at Thebes and Amarna.

The influence of this more intensive contact could be seen in a number of ways. Artefacts from New Kingdom sites show a greater number of foreign prestige goods than ever before, and foreign motifs were incorporated into many domestic items. Excavations at Tell ed Daba have revealed a large number of vessels from foreign lands immediately following the reign of Ahmose (Bietak 1995: 70–72). Mural paintings in one section of the royal palace were of a style traditionally associated with Minoan Crete. Alternatively, art historians have argued that this is a "palace style" common to the larger Mediterranean–Near Eastern koine. Reciprocally, Egyptian goods from this period—although proportionally fewer—have been found throughout the Mediterranean basin. This increase in trade was facilitated by innovations in transport and ship-building technology that made Mediterranean sailing less hazardous. Bronze Age shipwrecks off the Turkish coast, such as the Cape Gelidonya and Ulu Burun wrecks (Bass 1987), show the dangers faced.

During the New Kingdom, many words of Semitic origin entered the Egyptian language, highlighting the degree of contact that the two areas maintained (Hoch 1994). Apart from the influx of goods and ideas, there were also significant numbers of foreigners living in Egypt, particularly in urban centers such as Thebes. One important continuity in Egyptian history is that of Egypt's attitude toward foreigners. The Egyptians saw themselves as culturally superior to all other peoples, a belief supported by their expansionist policies (Trigger et al. 1983: 194). Craftspeople were brought in or captured during war to work on Egyptian state projects. For archaeologists, this situation presents problems in attribution. As with the wall paintings at Tell ed Daba, there is controversy as to whether such work was the result of foreign craftsmen or trained Egyptians (Davies and Schofield 1995). Equally problematic is our inability to determine whether an artefact is of foreign manufacture, reaching Egypt via trade or tribute, or if the object was made in Egypt, using materials that were brought from elsewhere.

As Egypt expanded its territory, contacts, and trade networks throughout the New Kingdom, the military became larger. Military prowess and strength were expected personal characteristics of the pharaoh. What we might term "political propaganda" was central to artistic regimes and monumental architecture, the pharaoh being shown smiting opponents and conquering foreign enemies, although the term fails to problematize the concept of audience and multiple readings. Notions of contextualization and decorum are perhaps more pressing concerns (Baines 1996: 344–60). On a pragmatic level it is doubtful, however, whether many pharaohs actually led their armies, especially when battles were fought so far from the Egyptian heartland. Armies were now capable of journeying the long distances that were needed to traverse the extent of Egyptian territory. Under Thutmose I (reg. 1493–?), Egypt reached its largest area, extending from the Euphrates in the north to Kurgus upstream from the fourth cataract in the south (Baines and Málek 2000: 42). The Egyptian adoption of the chariot was one of the factors that aided Ahmose's defeat of the Hyksos (Shaw 1991: 40). During the reign of Thutmose III (reg. 1479–1425), a formal Egyptian chariotry division was introduced in the Battle of Megiddo. Subsequent additions of boats to transport the Egyptian army, coupled with Egyptian-controlled harbors in the Near East, suggest concerted strategies by Egypt's military planners. These military ventures were essential in securing tribute for Egypt and for augmenting national pride. Nubia was of prime importance to the Egyptian economy because of the large amount of gold that was extracted in the form of tribute. The Egyptian concern for securing these resources can be seen in the continued construction of settlements and fortresses well into Nubian territory, which had already begun in the Old Kingdom.

Another outcome of the Hyksos interlude was a new vision of religion. The main god of the Hyksos had been identified with and incorporated into the Egyptian god Seth, the deity associated with chaos and warfare. Throughout the New Kingdom, gods from conquered areas were incorporated into the Egyptian pantheon, although the Egyptians continued to identify with a principal god associated with a ruler and world order—Amun-Re, the patron god of the Theban rulers. Extensive building programs were undertaken at Thebes, Amun-Re's cult center, reaching their height in the reigns of Amenhotep III (reg. 1390–1353) and Ramesses II (reg. 1279–1213). In addition to Amun's preeminence throughout most of the New Kingdom, allegiances to local gods were extremely important. The priesthood of Amun was actively involved in the government, and new rulers would seek support from the oracle of Amun to legitimate their reign. The priesthood came to assume greater importance, although the extent to which priests were really able to challenge the pharaoh's authority is difficult to assess (Trigger 1981). At the same time, religion became increasingly personal, with more ways for ordinary people to communicate with the gods—through worship at local chapels and community shrines, "pilgrimages" to great temples at festival times, and maintenance of statuettes of deities in domestic settings (Baines 1987). The reign of Akhenaten attempted to curtail multiplicity in Egyptian religion and assert the dominance of a new god, the Aten or divinized sun-disc, which was directly associated with the pharaoh himself and members of the royal family. One of the reasons for the failure of Akhenaten's religion may have been its exclusion of other gods; however, the social base of the Aten cult was probably narrow, perhaps largely confined to the royal family and its close associates. After the death of Akhenaten, the worship of Aten effectively ceased. Most of Akhenaten's monuments were destroyed by subsequent pharaohs, though his memory remained potent. In subsequent periods his reign was referred to as *the rebellion* or *the time of the enemy* (Murnane 1995: 241).

The increase in the military, the priesthood, and the extensive building programs required the expansion of bureaucracy. The Egyptian government became increasingly centralized, with power no longer residing in the hands of nomarchs, the governors of the "nomes," or provinces, of Egypt. Yet as Eyre (1999: 33) suggests, pharaonic society was not a socio-cultural unity based on the notional efficiency of centralized bureaucratic norms. Tribute was being received and redistributed on a larger scale than ever before. For instance, the temple of Amun at Karnak was in charge of receiving the huge quantities of gold that were brought in from Nubia. With the large amount of wealth that was flowing into Egypt and the large number of people depending upon governmental rations or payment, there were increasing opportunities for corruption and mismanagement. Numerous edicts have been preserved, notably from the reign of Horemheb (reg. 1319–1292), that tried to correct governmental policy (Trigger et al. 1983: 194). These measures may have been successful for a short time, but by the end of the Ramesside Period most of the bureaucracy and governmental organization had broken down. Texts from Deir el Medina mention strikes over rations that had not been received (Eyre 1979; Frandsen 1990). At the end of the Ramesside Period, corruption and probably a drought led to grain shortages and economic inflation, and control shifted into the hands of government officials and priests.

GEOGRAPHY AND DEMOGRAPHY

In the New Kingdom, the basic areas constituting Egypt were the Nile Valley, the Delta and the Faiyum, as well as regions which the Egyptians controlled beyond the borders of Egypt proper, such as Nubia and mining operations in various deserts. Control of peripheral areas fluctuated, but generally we can say that the area up to the line of oases running from Siwa in the north to Kharga in the south, roughly parallel to the Nile and about 200 miles west of it, was controlled by Egypt throughout the Dynastic period (Baines and Málek 2000: 12).

Ancient Egypt was a riverine culture often referred to as the gift of the Nile. The arid Saharan environment restricted the area that could be used for permanent habitation and agriculture. After flooding, the Nile deposited a fine layer of rich, fertile silt on the fields adjacent to the river. When the waters receded, the sowing of crops could begin in October and November; these became ripe between January and April, according to variety. Agriculture was possible throughout much of the Valley and the Delta except for sections of swamp. The total cultivable area has been estimated at about 34,000 square kilometers but was probably less in antiquity. While there have been major climatic changes in the Valley over a longer time period, there has been relatively little change in the last five thousand years, so that agricultural activity provided the stable base upon which Egyptian society could flourish.

Without the Nile and its annual inundation, Egyptian society would not have been able to reach the size and complexity witnessed throughout pharaonic times. Our knowledge of the climate during the pharaonic period, however, is fairly limited (Hassan 1997: 55). Several major studies have looked at the environment during the end of the last ice age and the beginning of the Holocene era (Butzer 1976; Wendorf and Schild 1976; Peters 1988; Brookes 1989; Gadfelter 1990), but fine-grained studies examining the climate during Dynastic times are few. Climatological research in relation to settlement patterns is also limited, since relatively few settlement sites have been located and excavated. Because of the Nile's slow migration and its annual deposition of alluvium, many sites have been buried under meters of silt and sand. Numerous sites are now below the current water table and would have been largely destroyed (Jeffreys and Tavares 1994). The Nile has slowly moved eastward through time, so that sites once situated on the East Bank have gradually been engulfed by the river. Those settlements that have survived the ravages of Nile movement would naturally be located on higher ground. For several thousand years people have been repeatedly targeting those same locations for security, resulting in meters of successive settlement debris. This presents a problem for archaeologists who might be interested in the New Kingdom levels of a particular area. As much as three or more meters of sediment have collected in the Valley since the New Kingdom, which has hindered settlement recording and retrieval. Only relatively recently has serious work been undertaken on Egyptian settlements (see Bietak 1979). In addition, the limited methodologies of early archaeological excavations have resulted in a substantive loss of information.

By some accounts, the climate of the Nile Valley during the New Kingdom was fairly stable. Although the general drying conditions that appeared during Predynastic times still continued, and many lakes either dried or became saline (Butzer 1976), the Nile itself seems to have remained reasonably predictable. It is important to remember, however, that much of the information on the level of the Nile derives from reports made in pharaonic times, the apparent consistency of which may be due to the altering or embellishing of records for ideological reasons (Nicholson 1996: 62). In more detailed analyses, climatologists have shown that much of the New Kingdom was subject to periodic, severe low Niles (Hassan 1997).

Catastrophic low inundations occurred repeatedly over the last ten thousand years, usually on the order of once every five hundred to thousand years. Research into more recent periods shows that even during periods of high annual floods, such those between 1735 and 1800 c.e., there were still several severe low Niles. During the New Kingdom, it seems that the most severe period of low floods was during the Twentieth Dynasty.

Throughout the Delta the situation was similar to the Valley, but because of the numerous swamps and lagoons resulting from the proximity to the Mediterranean Sea, this land must have been a more difficult area to reclaim. According to climatological studies, at about 3600, and again from 3200 to 2940, the ocean levels dropped and changed the channel of the Nile (Hassan 1997: 64). This led to an increase in siltation and the closing of many channels in the Delta. It is believed that some early channels in the Delta existed during the New Kingdom, but that they were probably of limited use because of low Niles. However, the agricultural richness of the region dominated Egypt's political and economic life from New Kingdom times onwards—the amount of available land in the Delta being twice that in the Valley. In addition, the Delta was closer to the Near East, and thus had higher degrees of trade and contact than did the Valley.

In the Faiyum, the water level may have dropped several meters through the accumulation of silts in the main channel of the Bahr Yusef, the channel of the Nile that flows into the Faiyum depression to supply the Birket Qarun with water. The level of the Birket Qarun had been artificially lowered in the Middle Kingdom, and much later in the Ptolemaic Period, as a means of reclaiming land for settlements and agriculture. However, its natural lowering around the end of the Eighteenth Dynasty probably made the area less popular.

The main crops Egypt produced were generally similar to those in the ancient Near East, namely emmer wheat and barley. The staple Egyptian foods were therefore bread and beer—the latter drunk by everyone, including children. There were also pulses like lentils and chickpeas. Vegetables—including lettuces, onions, and garlic—and fruits such as dates were common (Baines and Málek 2000: 16). Animals provided meat, dairy products, hides, and transportation. Meat, however, was an expensive product: beef was considered premium (Ikram 1995: 199), but there was also pork (Miller 1990, 1991), mutton, goat, and desert game. Numerous bird species were caught or bred as a source of protein, including pigeons, ducks, geese, and wild game birds. The Egyptians did not have chickens before the New Kingdom, and they only became common in Greek times. Honey was an important sweetener and used for winemaking, so beekeeping must have been an active business. Grapes were grown primarily in the Delta and Oases and were made into wine, as

FIGURE 2.2. Agricultural Fields around Saqqara Village. (Photo courtesy of the author)

were pomegranates and dates. However, Egypt was not completely self-sufficient, and various products such as oil and wine were extensively imported from the Mediterranean and the Near East. Finally, flax and papyrus were important all-purpose crops from which clothing, sails, ropes, and writing materials could be made. Date palms provided another source of fiber that could be made into roofing, matting, or baskets.

Diet was dependent on wealth and status. There are significant disparities between the food included in the tombs of the wealthy and that provided to poorer individuals in their graves. At Deir el Medina chief workmen were buried with meat, game, and poultry, whereas ordinary workmen and their families were simply furnished with bread and dom nuts. The basic source of calories for the entire population was grain (Miller 1991). One *aroura* of land (2,735 m^2) yielded approximately 750 liters of grain each harvest. Extrapolating this into calories, one *aroura* would provide 5,300 calories for each day of the year. If half of that produce was lost to taxes or vermin and some more was designated for re-planting, then this could still sustain one adult for the year. In theory, one agricultural worker could work twenty *arouras* of land

and thus provide for twenty adults (Nunn 1996: 19). This explains the rich agricultural base Egypt offered and the mechanism by which numerous other trades and professions could be supported, as shown in Table 2.1.

In terms of overall population, the Nile Valley seems to have experienced periods of substantial population growth. It has been suggested that between the third and second millennia the population of the Valley more than doubled, from 850,000 at the start of the third millennium to over 2 million by 1800 (Andreu 1997: 2). Although Kemp (1989: 10) states that population growth was slow and steady during early periods, numbers may have been approaching 4 to 5 million people by the late New Kingdom. According to Hassan (1997: 56), the population of the Valley alone during the New Kingdom was approximately 2.1 million, but population growth may have been as slow as 0.057 percent annually.

Settlements from the New Kingdom show that some demographic reorganization was taking place in both Egypt and neighboring lands. Several settlements found in the Delta seem to have no pre–New Kingdom components, but it is quite possible that earlier sites have been lost because of shifting river patterns and sediment deposition. Work in Nubia, present-day Sudan, shows that typical Nubian traits disappeared quickly after its reconquest by Egypt in the early New Kingdom. Many interpretations of this are possible, but it seems most likely that the Nubian population became increasingly Egyptianized through the new civil administration imposed by ruling pharaohs, as well as through contact with settlers from Egypt. From the start of the New Kingdom, and even before the Hyksos were expelled, Egypt had already begun to launch raids to the south. Nubia was a vital source of finance for Egypt, and its mercenaries were highly valued recruits for the Egyptian army. It is not surprising, therefore, to find many large, imposing New Kingdom monuments such as Abu Simbel built well upstream from the first cataract of the Nile.

To the west, there were changes in the population structure of desert oases. In the Dakhleh Oasis, much of the area seems to have been abandoned by Egyptians in the New Kingdom. Documentary evidence points to this being an area where exiles were sent or where criminals could go to escape from Egyptian authorities (Giddy 1987: 92–3). The inhabitants of these peripheral areas developed distinctive local traditions and may have considered themselves to be quite different from the people of the Nile Valley. The Oases were very fertile regions that linked the western Nile Valley with areas to the south in Nubia, as well as areas farther west in Libya. Although it was extremely important for Egypt to occupy the Western Oases as a means of controlling nomadic Libyan groups who raided the Valley, it seems that for parts of the New Kingdom this area was out of direct Egyptian control.

TABLE 2.1
Grain Rations at Deir el Medina

Individual Designation	Daily Calorific Values
Chief workman	48,195
Scribe	48,195
Workman	35,343
Guardian	28,917
Female servant	19,278
Boy	12,852
Porter	9,639
Doctor	8,033

CONDITIONS OF LIVING

When discussing private life, it is fundamental to recognize the different experiences of those living in urban centers as opposed to rural settings. New Kingdom Egypt was divided into town districts, which consisted of a major town surrounded by satellite towns and villages and a rural hinterland (O'Connor 1995: 321). Archaeologists are thus confronted with a variety of settlement types. Major urban centers such as Memphis have only recently become targets for systematic fieldwork. Excavations at Memphis by the Egypt Exploration Society have been small in scale, but the rigorous and systematic methodologies employed and material retrieved are potentially very telling in terms of living experience. On the other hand, the city of Amarna, ancient Akhetaten, has been excavated sporadically since the 1820s, with rather mixed success. The unique nature of the site, its desert location, and its subsequent abandonment have preserved much in the way of archaeological materials, making it an important source of information on urban living. Both Memphis and Amarna were capitals in the New Kingdom. Lesser-known sites such as Gurob, which functioned as a provincial palace town, offer another view of city life beyond the capitals.

To understand fully the specific character of Egyptian urbanism, it is perhaps most useful to employ a multiscalar framework. This begins with the larger urban aggregations and works down to discuss regional centers and villages, followed by a closer examination at the household level, as far as this is possible. This seems to be a valid way of looking at the archaeological data, because the Egyptians themselves had a variety of terms for different sizes and kinds of settlement. However, this terminology was fairly elastic: the same Egyptian word, *niwt*, can be used to designate a provincial town or nome capital, a capital city such as Thebes or Akhetaten, or a subdivision of a larger place. Cities could be regarded as composed of accretions of smaller settlement units, *dmi*, which exactly fits the layout of Akhetaten. The texts from Deir el Medina usually simply call it "the village" *p3 dmi*, suggesting that it was seen as a component of the larger city unit of Thebes (Černý 1973: 85). Terminology was therefore locational and relational to the person using it rather than being fixed, especially since the official names of places could be equally fluid. *St m3ʿt*, the official name for Deir el Medina, also covered other places at different times (Černý 1973: 37, 40, 64–7). Outside the major cities, the elite perception of Egypt was of a country visibly divided into villages or towns, and small settlements that were parts of the large estates, referred to as *ḥwt* (Eyre 1999; Moreno Garcia 1999).

In older Egyptological scholarship, the debate revolved around the question of whether Egypt was a civilization without cities (Wilson 1960). More recent studies have focused on the particular profile of Egyptian urbanism, and how the impact of the Nile affected its specific trajectory. Urban planning underwent drastic changes between the Middle and New Kingdoms. Urbanization in the Middle Kingdom may have been characterized by intensively planned settlements that some see as mirroring the highly controlled and ordered bureaucracy of the time (Kemp 1989: 155). Those settlements featured rigid, highly organized layouts, usually in square grid patterns. However, our sites from this period—namely the Nubian fortresses and the workmen's community at Kahun—are hardly representative. In the New Kingdom, with a more varied set of sites preserved, the pattern appears to shift. Urban renewal was more or less organized around the rebuilding of temples and the construction of new ones, such as at Luxor. Towns and cities were apparently left to grow more organically out from the central temple precincts.

This brief general survey of the New Kingdom settlements begins with Amarna, since it offers the widest spectrum of urban life—from elite villas to residential zones, poorer housing, and workmen's villages. In some respects, it is an ideal place to study Egyptian urbanism. It is situated in Middle Egypt near the modern town of el Minya, on the East Bank. Amarna was built on new ground by pharaoh Akhenaten from about 1347 as a religious and political statement reflecting his radical break with the status quo. Accordingly he chose a new desert location without evidence of previous occupation and somewhat remote from other centers. The main site was also occupied for a short period of time, approximately twenty years, so there is

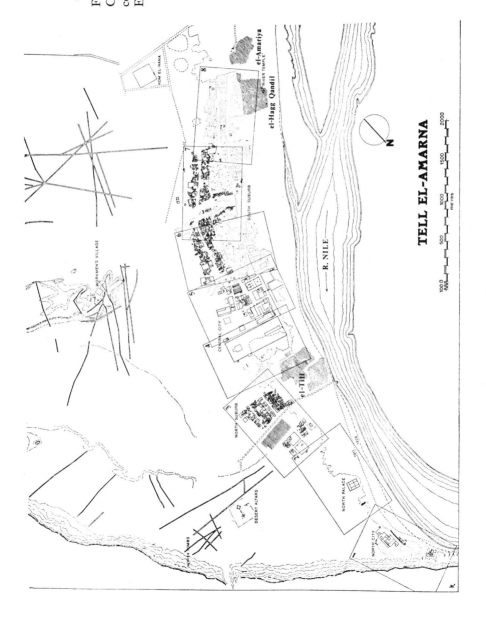

FIGURE 2.3. Plan of the City of Amarna. (Plan courtesy of the Egypt Exploration Society)

only a single phase of habitation—although some parts of the site continued to be used in later times. Akhenaten's religious ideologies were played out in this vast desert landscape surrounded by a bay of cliffs perhaps representing the symbolic domain of the Aten, his chosen deity. The surrounding cliffs are reminiscent of the hieroglyph for horizon, and Akhetaten literally means "Horizon of the Aten." Since Akhenaten instigated a "new" religion and broke with some older, entrenched traditions, the site was later seen to evoke negative associations in official Egyptian sources. Much of the city was dismantled, with the stone being reused as architectural fill in later pharaohs' monuments.

Because of this unique concatenation of events at Amarna, the foundations from the majority of structures were still visible when archaeologists began surveying and excavating the site. Some buildings were extremely well-preserved—the pylons of the small Aten temple were still standing seven meters high at the beginning of the nineteenth century. Given the history of Amarna, archaeologists can be relatively certain that the excavated material largely belongs to a single, circumscribed period and that all the buildings are contemporaneous. The excavators claim it is the most complete city or town left from ancient Egypt (Shaw 1996: 92). However, its unorthodox history, brief occupation, and construction on virgin soil limit the degree to which we can argue it represents a typical city in ancient Egypt.

At Amarna there were two main residential areas north and south of the so-called Central City. They are much more haphazardly planned than the Central City precinct and display patterns of organic growth. Unlike settlements from the Middle Kingdom and earlier, such as Kahun, much of the city seems not to have been planned. Instead of separate neighborhoods, or residential areas for different social groups, the so-called South Suburb appears to be a collection of several different communities. The wealthy houses of officials like Pawah and Panehesy were situated alongside the houses of poorer people. The sculptor Thutmose also lived in the South Suburb: in his workshops the famous bust of Nefertiti was uncovered in 1911 by the Deutsche Orient-Gesellschaft (Arnold 1996: 41ff; Kemp 1989: 295). The South Suburb was the largest residential part of the site and held over 50 percent of the city's population. The total population of the city was perhaps as high as fifty thousand but more likely to have been between twenty and thirty thousand. The city's main suburbs held about 90 percent of the population. In reality the word "suburb" is slightly misleading, as these areas were the core residential areas of the city. The use of this word reflects the preoccupations of the British archaeologists who dug the site in the 1920s and 1930s and were keen to present Amarna as the most up-to-date urban site of antiquity, a sort of proto-London complete with suburbs (Montserrat 2000: 73–77, 82). The rest of the population was spread out into several smaller areas.

Analysis conducted by Tietze (1986) suggests that there are eight types of household that were occupied by members of the three basic strata of society at Amarna. The lowest level comprises almost 60 percent of the population, leaving a middle stratum of 34 to 37 percent and an upper stratum of 7 to 9 percent. Approximately 65 percent of the population lived in houses below 100 m^2, whereas the next interval—houses between 100 and 200 m^2—accounts for about 21 percent, and the third 100 m^2 interval accounts for as little as 8 percent (Shaw 1992: 156). There was a tendency for smaller households to cluster around larger ones. This seems to fit the analysis of granaries and their spatial relationship within communities (Shaw 1996: 100). Many of the granaries were associated with the larger houses, and Barry Kemp suggests that smaller households were supplying the elite with labor and finished products in return for food and grain supplies. The spatial patterning in the South Suburb shows interdependence, with workers supplying each other with most of their needs, rather than large groups of workers taking part in a redistributive economy. Most of the households exhibit small-scale local production, although they undoubtedly undertook work of the elite as well. In other parts of the suburb, small houses with only a few rooms grouped together (e.g., houses O47.2, 3, 4, 6, 7). In house O47.4 there was a long courtyard, probably unroofed, running parallel to the street. This led into a main central room, with two smaller rooms leading off to the right and another straight ahead, making a total of five interrelated spaces (Borchardt and Ricke 1980: 74–75). The dwelling abutting this one also had a central room and two side-rooms, making only three in total. This presents a very different scenario than in other residential areas of the South Suburb, suggesting a level of variation of living conditions in the main city that is often downplayed.

The North Suburb had smaller houses than those in the South and fewer elite houses. It appears that an expansion of the North Suburb was planned but never completed. It is possible that some people living in this area were working in the large-scale manufacture of wood fittings and implements, not necessarily on a state-run basis. The suburb was also quite differentiated, housing a variety of workers, fishermen, and people preparing food, as well as scribal and clerical workers. In the South Suburb, an average-sized house (M50.2, dug in 1911) had a number of standard features: a wide hall measuring 7.4 m by 3.8 m, with a central column to support the roof of this first room. It had side doors leading off to two small rooms. There was a square room which served as the main room, the most important in the house, with the customary supporting column and middle door. The middle door led to other rooms, some of which may have been more private areas, what early excavators referred to as sleeping rooms with bed niches (Borchardt and Ricke 1980: 282–83). Additional processing and cooking spaces were located to the rear of the house.

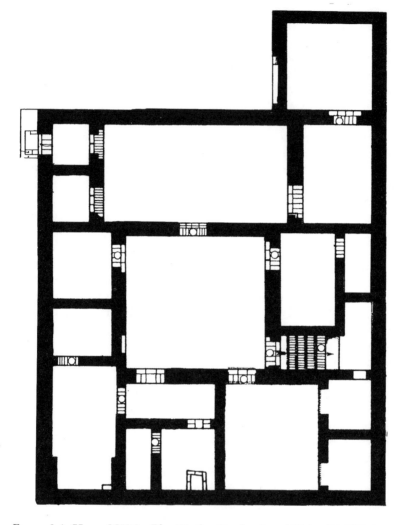

FIGURE 2.4. House M50.2—Plan 94 after Borchardt and Ricke, *Die Wohnhauser in Tell el-Amarna*—1980.

Amarna was an atypical site, since it had large tracts of available space and was not subject to the limitations at older settlements. The layout of the city is its striking feature, but ultimately its unrepresentative character limits fruitful extrapolation to other settlements. If, for example, some older towns were abandoned to make way for new settlements in wide-open areas, then Amarna may provide more of a pattern for New Kingdom urban contexts. However, its situation is sufficiently different from Memphis and Thebes, which had long-term habitation. Kemp (1977a) argues that Amarna represents a copying of existing city layouts that would have been found in Thebes and/or Memphis. This would explain why Amarna seems to be constituted in such a disorderly manner. A good comparison can be made with the workmen's village to the north of the site. This settlement may have been similar to the site of Deir el Medina near Thebes, which was the home for the workers who built and decorated the royal tombs in the Valley of the Kings. The two sites are somewhat different, both in terms of their layout and their occupants, yet both villages were planned settlements initiated by the state.

Thebes was an important center through much of Egyptian history, although the evidence of residential life there is severely limited because of the extent of possible excavation. Known as $w3st$, or "the southern city," in pharaonic times, it was not the country's capital in the sense of an administrative center but rather a focus of religious and ideological life. By the end of the Middle Kingdom, the center of the city covered around 0.5 km^2 (Kemp 1989: 201), with residential structures spreading out into the surrounding area. Kemp (1977b: 196, 1989: 202) argues that the city expanded substantially in the New Kingdom, especially in the areas near the main temples. These sectors were built on slightly higher ground, so that much of the new settlement was in the floodplain near the Nile. David O'Connor (1995: 320) has estimated that New Kingdom Thebes covered an area of 2.7 km^2 and was occupied by about ninety thousand people. Owing to the Nile's gradual movement and subsequent sedimentation, the New Kingdom extension of the city is now below the water table. This effectively prohibits secure identification, much less excavation, by archaeologists. The majority of the city extended out to the east, perhaps occupying the area between and surrounding the temples of Karnak and Luxor, encompassing a total of around 3 to 4 km^2. There have been a series of small excavations in and around Thebes, some still continuing (Kemp 1989: 201); however the published results are insufficient to create a picture of urban life in the New Kingdom.

We can only envisage what living in the sprawling city of Thebes was like. Many of the houses excavated appear to be shantylike and often abut the temple precincts. Evidence from Old Kingdom times onward reveals that supposedly "sacred" areas were not spared from residential encroachment. This can be witnessed at Giza at the Khentkawes complex and the Valley temple of Menkaure (Kemp 1989: 144–48). Housing at Thebes would have run the gamut from elite villas to small shacks erected haphazardly wherever space was available. Thebes was undoubtedly a cosmopolitan city with a substantial foreign population and Egyptians drawn from the length and breadth of the country. It must also have been a mixed community, with a large scribal bureaucracy, priests, a workforce of builders and artisans, and the usual assortment of tradesmen and producers. Agricultural laborers would have lived in or at the outskirts of the city, which was bounded on both sides of the river by fields, some possibly privately owned but many controlled by the state through the operation of temple estates and the like. As with any urban site, Thebes was also a place of opportunity, and therefore of crime, at every level. When Panehesy returned to Thebes in the reign of Ramesses XI with his mercenaries from Nubia, all chaos erupted as his troops ran riot in the city. This frightening episode in the history of Thebes was subsequently recorded in the letters of the Deir el Medina workmen (Wente 1990: 171–204) .

Memphis offers the same relatively limited data as Thebes. The majority of this important site is now buried below meters of alluvium. Thanks to the work of the Egypt Exploration Society's Survey of Memphis team we have a good idea where most of the city may be, although we know almost nothing of its layout. Memphis was the de facto capital of Egypt through most of its history, so it undoubtedly had many more administrative areas and a larger population than other settlements. Excavation shows that it probably had a quite different general shape than Thebes. From what we can tell of the layout, the city seems to have been a massive sprawl, partially as a result of its size and importance as a capital, but also because it followed the Nile as it loosely meandered through the Valley. Memphis was a city that aggregated over time and shifted throughout its history in attempts to accommodate the Nile's movement. According to Kemp (1977b: 194), New Kingdom Memphis was similar to Amarna in layout, with unwalled residential sectors, but this theory could be confirmed only through further survey and excavation.

The Egypt Exploration Society excavated a small residential area of Memphis, known as Kom Rabi'a, with levels dating to the Eighteenth Dynasty, Ramesside Period, and Third Intermediate Period. A number of small domestic units and courtyards were carefully excavated and have produced a vast amount of material culture. The houses were of modest dimensions with narrow walls and clay floors. Material remains suggest that craft activities took place alongside a range of domestic practices. Giddy (1999: 9–11) suggests that these households may have been reliant on an institution such as a temple or administrative complex. Over 3,000 objects were recovered, ranging from ritual items, processing tools, craft items, jewelry, and ceramics. The sheer volume of material found in such a limited space, 500 square meters, suggests a high degree of material diversity and prosperity. However, textual evidence was negligible, which fits broadly with the profile of an artisan class. Rigorous excavation suggests that even among the urban nonelite, people of the New Kingdom had substantial numbers of household goods and items of personal adornment. This commodified aspect of ordinary life has not been addressed in the interpretive discussions of previous excavations. Data from Memphis might shed further

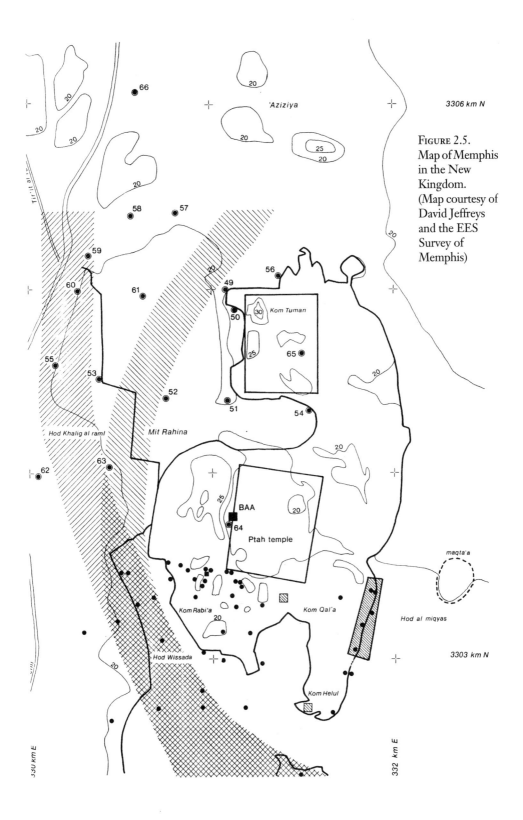

3306 km N

FIGURE 2.5.
Map of Memphis
in the New
Kingdom.
(Map courtesy of
David Jeffreys
and the EES
Survey of
Memphis)

66

'Aziziya

58   57

59

56

60   61   49   Kom Tuman
                50   30

                      25   65

55

53

52

51   54

Hod Khalig al raml   Mit Rahina

62   63

                        BAA
                        64

                        Ptah temple

Kom Rabi'a   Kom Qal'a   maqta'a

Hod Wissada   Hod al miqyas

                                3303 km N

Kom Helul

330 km E   332 km E

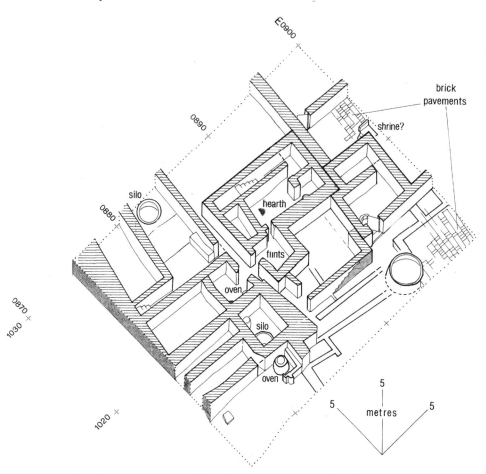

FIGURE 2.6. Excavation Area of New Kingdom Memphis, EES. (Plan courtesy of David Jeffreys and the EES Survey of Memphis)

light on the urban masses who populated other cities such as Thebes and Amarna, suggesting a richer material life than previously thought.

REGIONAL CENTERS

Regional centers were also an important part of the Egyptian state. Gurob, at the neck of the Faiyum, is one example of how Egyptian planning affected these settlements. Created in the reign of Thutmose III, the town was occupied until at least the reign of Ramesses V (reg. 1150–1145), although most of the site had been deserted during the reign of Merenptah (reg. 1213–1204) (Thomas 1981: 4). The town shows clear evidence of planning; its original structured town wall is in the form of a square, common to many settlements throughout the New Kingdom. Yet, after this initial show of order, there seems to have been very little planning in additions and rebuilding, and the character of the town becomes much more irregular and haphazard. As is typical with such settlements, Gurob grew by accretion. It was divided into three parts, what the excavators termed the South Town, the Main Town, and the North Town. There is little to be extracted from the domestic arrangements of the town, as Petrie's excavations there in 1889 were rather confused. His field notes were lost, and when the Gurob material was later taken to England, some of it was mixed up with that excavated from Amarna. However, Petrie described houses that appeared to lack the granaries, colored dadoes, or stairs leading to the roof that are present in other houses typical of the period from Amarna or Deir el Medina.

Mi-Wr, as Gurob was known in ancient times, was ostensibly built to house the royal "harem." However, this is a term loaded with problematic Orientalist notions. In the Egyptian context this refers to the private quarters of the queen mother, the royal wives, the princesses of different generations, and their entourage (Feucht 1997: 336). At Gurob it was probably associated with a temple dedicated to the crocodile divinity Sobek and economically linked to textile manufacture. On the basis of ethnic names identified at the site, this major industry may have employed significant numbers of foreign women (Thomas 1981: 6). Influenced by this idea, Petrie, who discovered several pits with burned debris, apparently within the temple, interpreted them as funeral pyres. A more recent examination, however, suggests that they were simply pits for burning refuse (Thomas 1981: 13).

The town may also have been initiated to provide a royal retreat and stopping point for pharaoh on his travels up and down the Nile (Kemp 1989: 222). Gurob's location on the edge of the desert near the Faiyum was also ideally situated to take advantage of fishing in the area, which was clearly important for the town, and for trading with people occupying the nearby desert. The remains of kilns and glass factories, as well as stone and metal workshops, were found at the site, indicating that Gurob had a substantial industrial function. The main cemetery was located northeast of the town, and the majority of its tombs, with few grave goods, belonged to the lower and middle social strata. Another cemetery, Cemetery D, was southwest of town and apparently reserved for higher-status individuals. There were also elite rockcut tombs located outside the town; all were looted but yielded some high-quality funerary statues (Kozloff and Bryan 1992: 258–60).

Moving down into the Delta, it is worth briefly examining the site of Tell ed Daba, ancient Avaris. In the New Kingdom it extended about 4 km north to south, and was about 3 km^2 in area. It owed its importance to its favorable geographic position: it was located on the Pelusiac branch of the Nile in the

Delta and on a lake harbor, and also was protected from the eastern frontier by a huge drainage system consisting of a series of lakes, one of them over 10 km long. The site was the link between the waterway leading to the Mediterranean, Palestine, and the Near East. At Tell ed Daba, after the fall of its Hyksos rulers, the last stratum suggests that the town was abandoned. There is a little evidence for burning, but it is localized and not sitewide. For the most part, the settlement appears to have simply ceased.

There is firm evidence that the main citadel was reoccupied in the early Eighteenth Dynasty, with palatial installations forming a new royal citadel. Of special significance is an enormous platform, made of mud-brick walls about 70 m long and 47 m wide, dating to the reign of Ahmose at the beginning of the Eighteenth Dynasty (Bietak 1995: 68). To the east of this platform there was a settlement with workshops. The house-type is typical of the New Kingdom, and the stratigraphy confirms that the houses were constantly changed and rebuilt. Within the settlement numerous royal scarabs were found: they document the names of pharaohs from Ahmose to Amenhotep II. During the reign of Horemheb, the site of Pi-Rameses was founded on roughly the same site as Tell ed Daba. This city formed the political capital of Egypt until the end of the Ramesside Period. The settlement was oriented to the cardinal points, a change from the earlier, non-Egyptian Hyksos settlement built during the Second Intermediate Period. The site was demolished in the Twenty-First Dynasty and its architectural blocks removed.

VILLAGE LIFE

Given the paucity of excavated settlement sites, one cannot really discuss rural villages, where much of the farming population would have lived. Archaeologists are then left with sites with other nonagricultural functions that have survived in arid desert zones. The best-preserved residential site of the New Kingdom, the village of Deir el Medina, offers evidence for how domestic life was experienced in such a settlement. Most writing about ordinary life in New Kingdom Egypt has been gleaned from the archaeological and textual sources recovered from Deir el Medina. Despite this major scholarly focus, most Egyptologists regard the site as so anomalous as to be unrepresentative in terms of daily life. While the professions of the workers and their levels of literacy might be unusual, the ways in which ordinary life and social relations were enacted were probably quite representative of village life more generally (Meskell 1994a; Eyre 1999). For example, the Deir el Medina houses and their fixtures were relatively modest, in contrast to the elite villas present at Amarna. I would therefore suggest that daily life and domestic conditions in the village were similar to many other nonurban sites.

Figure 2.7. Photo of Deir El Medina. (Photo courtesy of the author)

The purpose of Deir el Medina was to house the scribes and workmen who designed and constructed the royal tombs, and their families, in close proximity to the Valley of the Kings. This fact was revealed by Jaroslav Černý's translation of textual data in 1929, although objects from the site were discovered much earlier. The first settlement was probably constructed at the outset of the Eighteenth Dynasty under the pharaoh Thutmose I. It was expanded during the Nineteenth and Twentieth Dynasties when the team of workmen was increased as the scale of the royal tombs grew more and more ambitious. The official role of the village came to an end during the reign of Ramesses XI, when civil unrest made the occupants gradually leave the site. However, the site continued to be an important religious and mortuary locale over the following centuries into Christian and Islamic times (Montserrat and Meskell 1997). There are substantial archaeological remains at Deir el Medina today, and it is possible to see individual residence units within the enclosed village, various chapel complexes, and the Hathor temple, as well as remnants of some four hundred tombs scattered in various necropoleis. More information has been gleaned from this community than from any other in pharaonic history. Its highly literate occupants left a wealth of documentary data and the favorable desert conditions have preserved both houses and tombs. While the textual data have received much scholarly attention, the material remains of Deir el Medina have only recently been analyzed systematically (Meskell 1997, 1999a). Both sets of data are necessary before a fuller picture of village life can emerge.

Deir el Medina settlement history encompasses at least twelve phases of construction (Valbelle 1985: 442). In its final phase, the enclosed village took on a subrectangular format some 5600 m^2 in area. The extension to the south had covered the Eighteenth Dynasty dumps and a portion of the earlier cemetery. Architectural evidence from the village compound affords a specific picture of daily village life. For instance, the dimensions of the major street or the minor alleyways are such that space must have been cramped and movement restricted. This suggests that people may have used areas of contiguous roofing to facilitate movement across the settlement, possibly affording another entrance to the house. Contiguous roofing also reduces the surface area exposed to the sun, thus lessening the interior temperature within houses. The majority of residence units have a staircase that permitted roof use and mobility across blocks. At the northeast corner, Bonnet and Valbelle (1976: 444) identified a passage and stairway that permitted roof access across the precinct and probably led to the south. Numerous activities undoubtedly took place at roof level, much as they do in Egypt today. The roof was a space for keeping birds, hanging the washing, drying crops, storing goods, or sleeping during summer. Some roofed areas, however, may have been on different levels, while others were separated by open courts. Roof heights have been interpreted from the placement of supporting columns, and numerous house models of the period also indicate this convention.

The conditions present in individual residence units at Deir el Medina are reminiscent of those in the mud-brick domestic dwellings of Egyptian villages and provincial towns today. Houses were intermittently added to, amalgamated. partly demolished and reconstructed, divided and partitioned—according to family considerations, pressing domestic and financial concerns, and the limitations of the material environment. While the documentary data reflect the supposed authority exercised by the state, contemporary settlements such as Amarna also show individual modification of domestic structures to suit the requirements of particular inhabitants (Kemp 1980). The professional knowledge of the Deir el Medina villagers would have enabled them to build and remodel their own dwellings. Documentary evidence of such activities survives in records of absence from necropolis duties: *Year 3, third month of summer, day 16. What the workman Paneb gave to the draughtsman [...] ... for the construction work he did in my house: a workroom and another wall makes 1...sack.*[1] The sixty-eight houses at Deir el Medina were divided and partitioned into a number of rooms ranging from three to ten, the most common numbers being between four and six rooms. These strip houses had total residential areas ranging from 40 to 120 m^2, the average being 72 m^2 (Valbelle 1985: 117). The first room of the house averaged an area of between 8 and 24 m^2, whereas the second room was larger, ranging between 14 and 26 m^2. It was usually at a higher elevation, which allowed light to filter through window grilles high in the upper walls. A series of smaller rooms lay toward the back of the house, between 3 and 6 m^2. These have been designated as cooking and processing areas because of their archaeological emplacements: ovens, grinders, basins, and querns. It was in this area of the houses that almost all of the staircases that allowed for roof access were located (Meskell 1998b: 234–7). Some have presumed a second story for these dwellings because of this staircase. However, this seems unlikely given the rather thin walls and the lack of extensive debris that would have fallen from upper levels when they collapsed.

Perhaps the closest contemporary parallel to Deir el Medina was the workmen's village at Amarna (see Kemp 1979, 1984b, 1985, 1987a, 1987b; Shaw 1988; Loose 1992; Samuel 1999), another walled settlement with only limited means of entry. The presence of a wall should not be read as a defensive measure at either site; rather it should be seen as the typical Egyptian predilection for the enclosure wall in domestic architecture. The workmen's village is a perfect square, completely planned and arranged, unlike the rest of Amarna. There were approximately seventy houses, of which forty have been excavated (Kemp 1987a; Shaw 1988). The site was designed originally to fit neatly into a natural hollow; however, owing to the poor placement of initial construction, an extra row had to be placed on a higher level. Each house block was built in a series of L-shapes up against the enclosure wall, and internal partitions were constructed at a later date. Those partitions did not bond to the main walls. Overall, there was complete uniformity in house type, and all the houses, except one, were of the same size. The excavators suggest that the larger house belonged to a foreman (No. 1 East Street). Entry to the settlement was from the south, through a gate with a wooden pivot-bloc and a stone threshold; this led to a broad street or square. Within the settlement's lifetime, the whole of the southwestern corner of the village became a midden area, with animal droppings and straw (Kemp 1987a: 27).

Householders regularly encroached onto the village streets: brick mangers were built, water pots cemented into the street area, and awnings stretched across the streets. Pegs sunk into blank walls suggest they were used for hanging out thread or weaving. While the state was undoubtedly responsible for the initial construction, the inhabitants thereafter made their own arrangements and continued making modifications when they were needed (Kemp 1989: 225). Houses were made of sun-dried bricks, and the excavators noted occasional rubble foundations and lower courses. Given the thinness of the walls (35 cm thick) it is likely that dwellings were single story, although light superstructures, such as mud-and-wattle constructions, may have been added. The high proportion of finds relating to food production, storage, and textile production suggests that the villagers actually supplied a great deal of

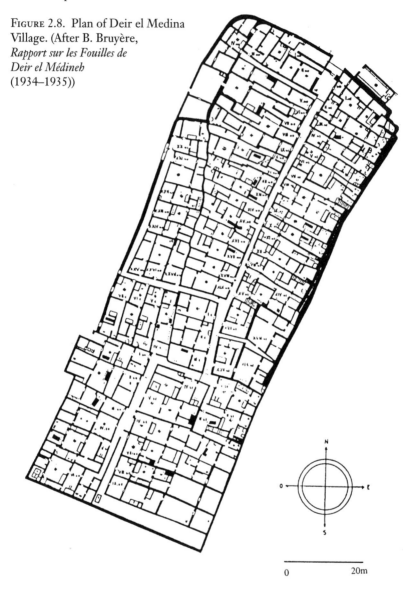

FIGURE 2.8. Plan of Deir el Medina
Village. (After B. Bruyère,
*Rapport sur les Fouilles de
Deir el Médineh*
(1934–1935))

0   20m

their own needs. Ikram's analysis of faunal remains shows a range of domesti-
cates, wild game, fish, and birds. However, pig farming was the predominant
industry (Ikram 1995: 211). This again reinforces a certain sense of autonomy
at Amarna that can be paralleled at Deir el Medina.

Houses were simple constructions partitioned into four to five rooms.
Each frontage onto the street was about 5 m, followed by rooms of unequal

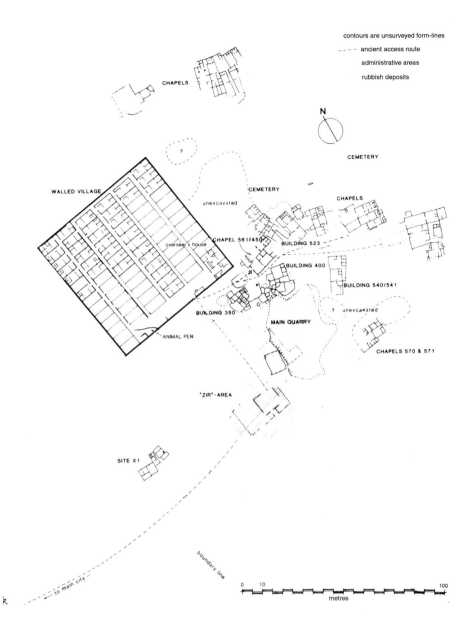

contours are unsurveyed form-lines
–––– ancient access route
administrative areas
rubbish deposits

CHAPELS

N

CEMETERY

WALLED VILLAGE

unexcavated

CEMETERY

CHAPELS

CHAPEL 561/450

BUILDING 523

overseer's house

BUILDING 400

BUILDING 540/541

BUILDING 350

? unexcavated

ANIMAL PEN

MAIN QUARRY

CHAPELS 570 & 571

"ZIR"-AREA

SITE X1

boundary line

to main city

0   10   100
metres

FIGURE 2.9. Plan of Amarna Workmen's Village. (Plan courtesy of the Egypt
Exploration Society)

size cut by two main walls (Peet and Woolley 1923: 55). The back areas of houses were further divided into two rooms by brick partitions. The first room was a type of entrance hall, the second a main living room and reception, the third another room, followed by a staircase, a kitchen, or both combined. The front rooms originally stood about 2.3 m high, although the walls remained only to 1.8 m at the time of the original excavation, and there was no sign of windows (Peet and Woolley 1923). The second room was elevated, with windows still higher up—perhaps to front and back, overlooking other rooms, as envisaged for Deir el Medina. Animal dung, straw, and tethering stones show that animals were kept within houses. In other cases these spaces were utilized as workshops. For example, four houses in Main Street had socket emplacements for weaving in which the upright loom was used. In 3 Main Street the excavators found the wood from the loom itself and a "warp spacer" used in the weaving process. Other houses contained wooden sticks, known as "beaters-in," in conjunction with numerous pottery bowls also used for spinning. Square hearths or open fireplaces were also found in the front rooms. One can assume that a significant amount of industrial activity took place at this site: there is evidence of smelting in the form of furnaces, crucibles, and molds for metal objects, and of other minor trades such as stone-bowl production. Picks, adzes, and winnowing fans were also excavated, suggesting that the inhabitants of the Amarna village were significantly different from those living at Deir el Medina—the lack of evidence for literacy at the former is notable, indicating that they were not of a scribal background.

At Amarna the second room, often named a "living room" by the original and later excavators, had a divan, a high ceiling supported by posts or a column, and wall paintings that find parallels at Deir el Medina. There was a hearth near the divan and a water supply for ablutions or drinking near the adjacent wall. Other vessels undoubtedly stood on ring stands in these rooms, while some were buried, and each contained water, food, and so on. Additional rooms, often termed "bedrooms," might more appropriately be called multifunctional spaces. In three cases (Main Street houses 6, 7, 9) there were "sleeper-walls," which were supports for wooden shelves. However, there was no evidence to suggest that beds were placed there: the only example of a wooden bed was found in a street.

Locales, Authenticity, and Place

From the foregoing survey of residential sites, it is clear that the general setting for life experience varied considerably from place to place. It is also important to consider the evidence for Egyptian notions of local versus both "national" and "international" spheres. The concept of borders and boundaries is key here, whether natural, geographical, mental, or material. They are the devices by which groups define and delineate spheres of continuity or disjuncture. Ethnicity in our own culture represents a mode of action and representation involving decisions people make about themselves and others symbolically, as the bearers of a certain cultural identity (Cohen 1994: 119). Whether such terms of reference are usefully applied to antiquity is debatable, and an Egyptian notion of ethnicity would perhaps be significantly different from our own. Yet the Egyptians were keen to set themselves apart from other groups in the Mediterranean and Africa, and this concept of cultural distinction between individuals and groups is a salient feature of ethnic identity (Eriksen 1993: 12). Indeed anthropologists have argued that the capacity to locate identity by means of the prototypical in order to determine a sense of distinctiveness and separateness represents a crucial component of human understanding (Fernandez 2000: 134). The Egyptians were certainly guilty of what we would term today as ethnocentrism and saw themselves at the center of the known world. In the *Hymn to the Aten*, it is the Aten who is responsible for setting *every man in his place*, and as a result *their tongues differ in speech, their characters likewise*, and *their skins are distinct*.[2] Language, disposition, and skin color are all set as demarcators of difference. Moreover, the *Tale of Sinuhe* connotes that the customs and traditions of Egypt's neighboring countries were immediately perceived as distinctly different and inferior: *How like am I to a bull of the roaming cattle in the midst of another herd?... Can an inferior ever be loved as a superior? No barbarian can ever be ally with a Delta man.*[3] Sinuhe yearns for his native Egypt, especially when faced with the threat of being buried in a foreign land, perhaps the most salient aspect of one's identity as an Egyptian. The thought of being buried in a ram's skin without the elaborate funerary preparation of Sinuhe's own culture would be anathema to any Egyptian. His return home is marked by a number of significant corporeal changes effectively removing foreign enculturation: shaving, hair combing, changing to clothes of fine linen, anointing the body with oil, and finally being able to sleep in a bed.

Concepts of the foreign may have been portrayed in the literary sources as distinctly different and unappealing, but the iconographic and archaeological evidence suggests a certain desire for foreign luxury goods and even people. Theban tombs of the period evince the desire for prestige items from Africa, the Near East, and the Mediterranean. Desirable commodities included wine, leopard skins, ostrich eggs, metals, gold, prestige ceramics, and so on. There is a vast amount of evidence—textual, material, iconographic—for an extensive pan-Mediterranean trade network. Ships traversed the Mediterranean, possibly originating in the Aegean and stopping off in Crete, then Marsa Matruh on the Egyptian coast, and moving on to Levantine and Near Eastern ports including Cyprus. Each port would have had access to the various materials on board, whether copper, tin, terebinth resin, oil, wine, scrap metal, glass, ceramics, and so on. Shipwrecks such as those at Ulu Burun and Cape Gelidonya off the hazardous Turkish coast attest to the array of goods and raw materials carried on these vessels in New Kingdom times. Parallels to the ships' cargoes can be found in various New Kingdom Theban tomb paintings, the best known being those of Rekhmire. Mediterranean archaeologists have actually used the images of the boats depicted on the tomb walls to reconstruct visually the Ulu Burun ship (Bass 1987). Many of the commodities shown in Rekhmire's tomb, as well as the ethnically diverse people depicted, reflect the types of transactions and desire for luxury foreign goods during this period.

There was a long-standing tradition of procuring exotica from sub-Saharan Africa—leopard skins, ostrich eggs, monkeys, ivory, and people. Cypriot and Aegean ceramics have been found at various New Kingdom settlement sites (Kemp and Merrillees 1980; Bell 1982; Bourriau 1991), mostly containing imported oils, perfumes, wine, and so on. That they were packaged in decorated foreign vessels such as Mycenaean pilgrim flasks probably only added to their prestige. Ships also traversed the Red Sea carrying foreign exotica, as attested from the Middle Kingdom onward. In the *Tale of the Shipwrecked Sailor*, a boat traveling along the Red Sea from Punt is said to *carry a cargo of myrrh and malabathrum, terebinth and balsam, camphor, shaasekh-spice, and eye-paint, tails of giraffes, a great mound of incense, elephant tusks, hounds, and monkeys, apes and all good riches.*[4] Foreign elements were often represented in depictions of dress (see Figure 2.10), specifically in Egyptian tombs such as those of Rekhmire, Sobekhotep, and Qenamun. Garments such as the leather loincloth are generally seen as Nubian imports, whereas the use of tapestry ornamentation is likely to be the result of Syrian or Hyksos influence (Vogelsang-Eastwood 1993: 7; 1999).

Something secret is in fine linen. You are clad in red cloth. The Cypriot is there with wool (?). The Hittite is there with moringa oil. What is mine? These transport ships have moored. <Their> products are delivered. The imports from Syria and before those of Kush at the head [...] The gold of the king is what is placed at the neck. You are the one who gives the grain wages to Memphis, and my clothing <for> Heliopolis. My Syrian woman...[5]

Throughout much of Egyptian history the population would have been composed of native Egyptians and foreigners alike. However, official sources tend to suppress this fact. Dynastic culture is often portrayed by Egyptologists as a single culture consisting of a single ethnic group with a single language and a homogeneous set of cultural values. This assumed uniformity is a result of the dominance of the elite's record and their particular perspective, and this bias is partly mirrored in the research agendas of Egyptologists today. But in the end we are left with the paradox that on the one hand the state presented an image of ideological unity, and on the

FIGURE 2.10. Wall Painting from Tomb of Sobekhotep. (Photo courtesy of the British Museum, EA 37991)

other, Egypt was open to the immigration of foreigners in all periods, and its neighbors were of great significance (Baines 1996: 362).

Regional and local difference was also potent. From textual evidence it appears that traveling to distant areas, whether the Delta or south of Elephantine, elicited rather specific responses. When one traveled there was an opportunity to worship local gods, specific gods tied to potent locales. One well-attested traveler was Thutmose, scribe of the necropolis in the reign of Ramesses IX–XI. A series of letters written from his various travels, to Nubia and so on, were sent home to his family in Western Thebes. *Every single day I am calling upon every god and every goddess by whom I pass to keep you alive, to keep you healthy, and to let me see [you] when I return and fill my eyes [with] sight of [you].*[6] Deities associated with particular regions were very much tied to geographical specificity. Horus of Kuban was linked to adjacent mountains, as was Meretseger, who resided in and was the personification of the Western Peak above Deir el Medina (see Figure 2.11). The importance of landscape, specifically the western mountains, was also reflected in the frequency of the female names Meretseger and Hathor at Deir el Medina. Place and personal piety were inextricably linked: *Every*

FIGURE 2.11. Stela dedicated to Meretseger. (Photo courtesy of the Petrie Museum London. UC 14439)

single day I am calling upon [Horus of Kub]an, who dwells in this mountain, to give you life, prosperity, and health. Thutmose then asks about the well-being of his relatives, urging them to call upon the gods of their place, the Theban West Bank, to ensure his safe return: *Call upon Amun of the Thrones of the Two Lands, Meretseger, Amenophis, [Nofretari, Amon of the] Beautiful [Encounter], Hathor, mistress of the West, Amun, Holy of Place, and the great and [august] Ogdoad to bring me back prospering and let me arrive back home down [in] Egypt from the far off land (Nubia).*[7]

Part of these discourses of travel was a real participation in local shrines, a practice that continued through later history (Foertmeyer 1989). Visits to shrines were valued for three main reasons, as is made clear by the Late New Kingdom letters. First is the desire to honor local deities so as to secure safe passage in their territory. Second, praying to a range of deities was seen as more effective than to a single god. Last, there was a professed love of travel and seeing sights, with all the attendant status associations. As Pinch suggests (1993: 350), the second and third reasons may have encouraged women to visit shrines outside their local area as well as within it. Festivals may have been the optimum time to do this and similarly to visit local temples (see Chapter 6), although it is unlikely that ordinary people would have been allowed inside the temple precinct. Personal piety on this level effectively meshed "official" temple religion and private concerns and practices. Prayers and libations may have peaked when relatives were absent: such practices were not onerous in terms of time or resources (Baines 2001). However, my own view on the possibilities of travel has to be set against that of other scholars who have argued that travel and the notion of pilgrimage applies in only a limited way to ancient Egypt. For example, Traunecker's (1979: 23) work at the temple of Karnak suggests a strong tendency toward local religious participation rather than a tradition of pilgrimage to the major sites. Pilgrimage may in fact be an inappropriate term for New Kingdom Egypt, yet this does not rule out that other forms of limited travel were possible and similarly reinforces the importance of locality more generally.

Archaeological evidence in the form of cultic stelae suggests a strong tendency toward localism. Local gods pertinent to the place of one's birth might accompany the individual or family as they moved into new communities. Clear examples of this occur at Deir el Medina. Deities were associated with specific locales, as can be seen from inscriptional data, material culture, and patterns of naming. In the Amarna chapels minor deities such as Shed and Renenutet were favored. At Deir el Medina the snake goddess Meretseger was the prominent local deity, yet there was also evidence for the cults of Seth of Ombos, Montu of Armant (McDowell 1994), and the triad from Elephantine: Khnum, Satis, and Anukis. Evidence for the latter is represented on the naos shrine of the workman Kasa, now in the Turin Museum (Valbelle 1972). The prominence of this triad on such an important funerary monument indicates that the family of Kasa probably originated in Elephantine and brought their local deities and devotional practices with them to Deir el Medina. However, this triad was found elsewhere at Deir el Medina (Valbelle 1981), and its occurrence may reflect a trend in New Kingdom ritual practice. Other stelae were offered to the Asiatic deities Anat, Reshep, and Qadesh (Bomann 1991: 73). We know that skilled workmen were transferred from various institutions to the site when the team needed to be increased in order to complete a royal tomb as a pharaoh neared death. McDowell cites three such individuals and their families taken from Karnak in the time of Ramesses II: Pashed, Qen, and Ramose. She also states that the scribe Amenopet seems to have had links with Kush (1994: 42–43). These individuals brought not only their families, but their expertise, customs, and personal wealth—all adding to the character of the community. We cannot rule out the possibility that there were intranational and international members of the village, and though much of the diversity might often be masked by the homogeneous nature of the material culture, such variations must have been felt (more noticeably) in the social relations of the community.

As Appadurai argues (1997), locality is an inherently fragile social entity. Even in the most intimate, spatially confined, geographically isolated situations, locality must be carefully maintained. Much of what has been considered local knowledge by anthropologists is actually knowledge of how to produce and reproduce locality under conditions of anxiety and entropy, social flux, ecological uncertainty, and cosmic volatility, and the ever-present instability of one's kin, enemies, spirits, and so on (Appadurai 1997: 179, 181). The importance of place, and its obvious associations with lineage and authenticity, was often emphasized in elite Egyptian writing. Being out of place was also a significant concern. Again in the *Tale of Sinuhe* this disjuncture was framed in terms of geographical specificity: *It was like the nature of a dream, like a Delta seeing himself in Elephantine, a man of the marshy lagoons in Southern Egypt.*[8] Upper and Lower Egypt are often polarized in this way as two locales inherently out of sync with each other. This could also be characterized in terms of dialect: *mixed up when heard, so no interpreter can untie them, they are like a speech of a Deltaman with a man of Elephantine.*[9] Being born in a relevant place, such as Thebes, was often stressed when questions of power and control were at issue. Such claims were intensified when one's descendants were also born in the same place. There are various examples of elite inscriptions emphasizing the connection between place, power, and citizenship. The Abydos stela of Wepwawetaa[10] encapsulates this desire for connectivity with all the associations of time immemorial—stretching back to the primeval itself. Whether such claims were grounded seems secondary, and while it could be argued that such statements are largely formulaic, the sentiment and conviction remain in the forefront: *As for this tomb which I made in the Western desert of Tadjeser amongst (my) forefathers who created my flesh, (being) nobles of the First Occasion, possessors of monuments, ancient ones of office, primeval ones who commenced at the making of the Bank of Heqet since the time of Geb, I made it to embellish (my) place amongst them, it being my nome also.*[11]

A well-attested genre that developed in the New Kingdom was what Egyptologists have termed the "praise of cities," which similarly recounts a form of local pride, connections to specific local gods (see Parkinson 1998), and citizenship. Paralleling the contemporary growth of urbanism, these poems celebrate the character of the city alongside the author's feelings of belonging: *Behold, I do not want to depart from Thebes. Save me from what I abhor!* There is also a sense of comparison that only comes about with journeying, and the importance of travel is an important feature of much Egyptian literature.

> *Every time I leave on a journey,*
> *I travel North*

with the City beside me,
with the Temple of Amen on my path (may I reach it!),
Medamud before me,
and Tenet Khonsu together with me
in the boat of my mission.
Bring me to your city, Amen!
Because I love it;
it is your city that I love,
more than bread and beer, Amen,
more than clothes and oil.
(I) love the soil of your town
more than the ointment of another land.[12]

Amennakhte, a well-known scribe at Deir el Medina, wrote a similar, perhaps more personalized account of his relationship to Thebes. Central are comparisons with other towns or cities, coupled with the superior produce and commodities of Thebes, which are the envy of all others. Thebes was eulogized in this way, perhaps competing with the rival centers of Memphis or Pi-Rameses (McDowell 1999: 157). Feelings about certain regions of Egypt could be quite intense, as exemplified in references to a dire situation in the Delta in the Heqanakhte letters (James 1962). At one point the author describes the local inhabitants as so hungry that they were eating one another!

What do they say to themselves
in their hearts every day,
those who are far from Thebes?
They spend the day
dreaming (?) of its name, (saying)
"If only its light were ours!"
Its windows are for
the clothesless,
its boat-seats are for the notables.
The bread which is in it is more tasty
than cakes made of goose fat.
Its [water] is sweeter than honey;
one drinks of it to drunkenness.
Behold, this is how one lives in Thebes!
The heaven has doubled (fresh) wind for it.[13]

It is a common misconception that ancient people were completely tied to their community or village, unable to travel or seek other experiences, and reflects our own prejudices about traditional lifeways. In much Egyptian literature tales of travel are prominent, the *Tale of Sinuhe* and the *Tale of the*

Shipwrecked Sailor being evocative examples (see Moers 1999). As Parkinson notes (1997: 89), voyaging is a common metaphorical device for conjuring a person's journey through life. In the *Shipwrecked Sailor*, the storyteller *had gone to the Mining region of the sovereign . . . in a boat 120 cubits long, in which there were 120 sailors from the choicest of Egypt,*[14] only to be stranded on an island in the Red Sea and faced with numerous trials and disasters. Various other literary texts have at their core notions of travel, perhaps in both literal and metaphorical senses, as it provides the vehicle for self-reflection. In the *Tale of the Eloquent Peasant*, the central character travels from Wadi Natrun west of the Nile Delta to Heracleopolis. In the late Ramesside *Report of Wenamun* we read of an official from the Temple of Amun who travels in search of Lebanese cedars (Lichtheim 1976: 224). Leaving aside the narrative plot, Wenamun's experiences impel him to question what constitutes Egyptian identity and authenticity in the face of the strife he encounters in Byblos and Alasia. We can detect the underlying importance of place and belonging, as well as differentiating concepts of home and other. Wenamun asserts the belief that Egyptian supremacy, specifically that of the god Amun-Re, permeated even these far-flung places: *His is the sea and his the Lebanon of which you say "It is mine."*[15] However, this is not to overstate that in ancient times all people, irrespective of gender, class, or status, traveled freely and according to whim. Rather, for some groups travel was either necessary or vital to their occupation and the general maintenance of empire. Author and anthropologist Amitav Ghosh (1992) remarks on similar circumstances in his ethnography of a small village in modern Egypt, where certain individuals traveled extensively to find work, both within Egypt and abroad. Indeed every man was a traveler. He lyrically writes that on arrival in that quiet corner of the Nile Delta he had expected to find on such ancient and settled soil a settled and restful people; that view was quickly dismissed.

FAMILY CHARACTERISTICS

Archaeology provides a framework from which to discuss the material conditions of life, but what of the occupants of the houses? We have some insight into this question for Deir el Medina households, through a census-like document termed by Egyptologists the Stato Civile. Unfortunately the document remains unpublished in full, but from the thirty households for which information is available, we can identify one couple with four children, five couples with three, one man with three offspring from two wives, six couples with two children, seven with a single child, four couples on their own, and six single men (McDowell 1999; Toivari 2000: 175). It has been noted that about 42 percent of that population is made up of children, but since ages are not given, we must allow for the possibility that many of these individuals were adolescents or older.

House of [Amennakhte son of Bu]qentuef, his mother is Tarekhan
His wife, Tenetpaip, daughter of Khaemhedje, her mother is Tenetkhenu <emheb>
His mother Tarekhan, daughter of Neferhotep, her mother is Khaty
His sister Kaytmehty, daughter of Bukentuef, her mother is Tarekhanu
House of Paankha son of Hormose, his mother is Nebuemheb
House of Thutmose son of Kha[emhedje, his mother is Te]netkhenuemheb
House of Penpare son of Nebnefer [...]
House of Inherkhau son of Seti[...]
House of Pawaamen son of Hor[...]
House of Pennesettawy [...] son of Pashed [...]
House of Monthuhatef son of Khon[...]

House of Qedakhetef son of Qenymin, his mother is Dua[nefer]
His wife, Merutmut, daughter of Neferhor, her mother is [...]
His son, Paankheriautef son of Qed[akhetef ...]
His daughter Wenher, the (one of) Qedakhet[ef ...]
House of Amennakhte son of Khay, his mother is Henut[meteret]
His wife, Tahefnu, daughter of Nakhteemmut, her mother is [...]
House of A'opatjau son of Sawadjyt, his mother is Mer[...]
His wife, Wabet, daughter of Neferher, her mother is Dua[...]
His daughter Meretsger, daughter of A'opatjau, her mother is [...]
House of Hornefer son of Qenna, [his] mother is [...]
His wife, Hutiyt, daughter of Hay, [he]r mother is [...]
His son, Qenna son of Horinefer, [his] mother is [Hutiyt]
House of Ipuy son of Neferhor, her (sic) mother is Merutmut
His wife Henutmire daughter of Nakhte(em)mut, her mother is Hathor
His daughter Henutnetjeru daughter of Ip[uy], her mother is Henutmire
His daughter Duanefret [daughter of Ipu]y her mother is H[enutmire]
His daughter Hathor daughter of Ip[uy, her mother is Henut]mire[16]

The text provides some evidence of kinship ties between households. The first list shows Thutmose, son of Khaemhedje, living two doors down from his sister Tenetpaip, who is married to Amennakhte. The house lists were evidently compiled at different times, and where enough survives of both to compare the occupants of a single house, McDowell (1999: 51) has demonstrated the natural waxing and waning of families. For instance, Penpare, son of Nebnefer, who was included in his parent's household in an even earlier list, is shown acquiring his own house in the above text. Moreover, Tarekhan had been living in her husband's house before, then moved into the house of her son and daughter-in-law. Despite the detailed information it contains, this fragmentary text presents us with several problems of interpretation. First, the exact purpose of the document is unknown, and if it is a form of census, it may be that the workmen had a vested interest in keeping the numbers somewhat limited. Given that the state supplied their rations (Janssen 1997: 1–11), workmen may not have wanted to appear to be supporting numerous family members and other lodgers. Second, it may simply report immediate kin at a specific time, rather than the fluid composition of the household and the other members who constitute the domestic unit, such as servants, slaves, even possibly newborns, and so on. Given the notorious inaccuracies of modern census documents, we must factor in a significant amount of indeterminacy.

As John Baines has suggested, the basic family unit was large, encompassing parents (sometimes more than one wife), children (sometimes with their own children), unattached or widowed relatives, misfits, and the incapacitated (1991: 134). In modern Egypt bedouin camps and hamlets include a number of families or individuals who have attached themselves to the group, some living there for decades. Sometimes there is a distant kin relationship with the main family, and other times not (Abu-Lughod 1986: 63). Again we might reconsider the work of Le Roy Ladurie, since it may prove more fruitful to employ the *domus* as our social and material framework of analysis. We should think of these households, both modern and ancient, as generational. Marriage marks a new household, yet this does not necessarily entail the construction of a new house. Newly married couples may have moved in with parents initially due to financial constraints or social pressures, a situation hinted at in the New Kingdom love songs (Mathieu 1996: 153–5, see Chapter 5). One might gloss this by saying that Egypt was basically patrilineal.

Men are denoted by the hieroglyph *s* with a male determinative, whereas *ḫ3y* stood for husband. Women are referred to as *st*, *ḥmt*, or *t3y ḥmt*, the latter two meaning woman or wife in specific contexts. The term for child is either *ꜥḏd* (male) or *ꜥḏdt* (female). By adding the feminine ending *t*, the word for brother *sn* can be transformed into *snt* or sister. Yet such terms are deceiving, since *snt* can also mean half sister, mother's sister, mother's sister's daughter, sister's daughter, and spouse's sister (see list below). Gay Robins argues (1979: 203) that in the New Kingdom the term also extended to the father's sister and brother's daughter. Egyptian kinship terms behave differently according to generation and cover a wide range of relationships. Moreover, *sn* and *snt* are used in love poetry for the relationship between lovers and in tomb contexts for conjugal relationships. At Deir el Medina the pair could be used to refer to siblings, cousins, nephew/niece, and brother/sister-in-law, as well as to one's peer group (Willems 1983: 159; Toivari 2000: 31; see also Whale 1989: 255). The word *mwt* generally referred to mother and *it* to father but could also denote grandparents or even ancestors (Robins 1979: 200; Bierbrier 1980: 100). Similarly *s3* and *s3t* refer to son and daughter respectively. Combinations of these terms could specify nonnuclear kin relationships more precisely: for example, *sn n mwt.f* is "brother of his mother," or maternal uncle (Whale 1989: 239, see below). Filiation is often key to understanding the context of terms.

Basic Kinship Terms

mwt   mother, mother's mother, mother-in-law

it   father, father's father, mother's father, father-in-law

s3   son, son's son, son's son's son, daughter's son, son-in-law

s3t   daughter, daughter's daughter, son's daughter, daughter-in-law

sn   brother, mother's brother, father's brother, father's brother's son,
        mother's sister's son, brother's son, sister's son, brother-in-law

snt   sister, mother's sister, father's sister, mother's sister's daughter, sister's
        daughter, brother's daughter, sister-in-law

In a rather unusual case, five generations of an extended family are depicted in the tomb of Paheri at el Kab. McDowell's analysis at Deir el Medina suggests that no more than two past generations were usually depicted on tomb walls, suggesting that generational memory was limited. Only occasionally are grandparents depicted in tombs, sometimes on both maternal and paternal sides. In the tomb of Paheri at el Kab (Tylor and Griffith 1894) a great deal of genealogical material is included: the tomb owner, his wife, sons and daughter, grandchildren (names lost), father and mother, brothers and sisters, grandmother and grandfather, grandmother's sisters, mother's brothers, wife's father and mother, wife's sisters and brothers, and even his wife's cousin (Whale 1989: 70–71). Another two generations of this family are known from the tomb of his grandfather, Ahmose, son of Ibana. Iconographically, some of Paheri's female relatives take precedence over their male siblings: his eldest daughter taking precedence over some of the sons represented. Also included in the banqueting scenes are family "nurses," illustrating that the *domus* extended beyond biological kin. As is typical of Egyptian tombs and other "official" art, specific life stages and the inevitable signs of aging were represented schematically. It was also customary for all forms of familial breakdown to be conveniently smoothed over.

The gendered ratio of relatives represented in the tombs is also instructive. In the case of Inenni (TT 81)[17] nineteen "brothers" are shown but only one "sister," together with nine wife's "sisters." This is a recurring pattern in Egyptian tombs, but it has received little attention. One can only surmise what would have been the religious repercussions for the omissions of women in these familial tombs, specifically in respect to attaining a full afterlife. As a rule small children are not shown, so that families were not depicted in full. However, in an unusual tomb (TT A11) recorded by Manniche (1988: 50–52, Fig. 8), nine women were depicted nursing small children. Other examples of babies, as opposed to small children, are shown in the tomb of Inherkhau (see Figure 3.11), or in scenes of agricultural life where women work with babies wrapped to their bodies.

Gendered postures and gestures of couples might also offer additional insights. Sheila Whale's (1989) typology of forty-five poses for couples in Eighteenth Dynasty tomb scenes demonstrates that only two display any semblance of reciprocity between spouses. Most of these images of partnership display the centrality of men and the servitude of women, who libate for them, offer ritual food, drink, or flowers to them, or show them some form of deference through pose or gesture. The two examples cited do not reflect any obvious hierarchical ordering in their composition, although whether this absence can be read as something meaningful is unknown. Gay Robins has conducted an analysis of private stelae and tomb painting in relation to this issue. On stelae she suggests that men, who are identified by their titles, are generally placed forward, assuming the dominant position. Women, by contrast, are situated via their marital relationship. Sometimes a man is depicted in the upper register and the woman below, again reinforcing his dominance (Robins 1994a: 36). Women were restricted in the forms of monuments they could own in the New Kingdom, yet they sometimes appear as the owners of funerary stelae, and more often votive stelae. Robins points out that it is surprising that so few women had funerary stelae, owing to the incidence of death in childbirth. Given the representational dominance of men in such monuments, it is impossible to tell if and when they were erected for such women, since men continued to assume primacy. In this way the monument served both male and female dedicant. One way around this was to avoid representing one's husband altogether, which occurs in a few instances. Perhaps for this reason, the number of votive stelae portraying women on their own is far greater.

Thus far I have sketched the basic arenas within which private life was played out from the macro level—the nation, the locality, and the immediate environment—to the micro, namely the house and the family. Now I turn to more private and embodied spheres of life that operated at an individual level—the social self.

CHAPTER THREE

Social Selves

THIS BOOK ADOPTS a cyclical format, paralleling the passage of life from birth to death and beyond, which is in keeping with the Egyptian preoccupation with cyclicality. I examine various aspects of life experience throughout the life cycle: pregnancy, birth, childhood, adolescence, adulthood, old age, and death. These embodied aspects of life may have material correlates in the archaeology of settlements and cemeteries; we can also apprehend these sensuous stories of life and the progression of the life cycle, as it was experienced by specific individuals, through the rich textual data. While various groups were often excluded from official narratives—children, women, slaves, nonelites, or outcasts—texts such as those from the village of Deir el Medina document a wide range of people and their corresponding activities. Reading between the lines may reveal more about those very different perspectives on life. And the silences of the texts can to some extent be counterbalanced or checked by the archaeological sources.

PERSONHOOD

Although an integral aspect of social life, the conceptualization of personhood in ancient Egypt has received limited attention. Concepts of personhood have received considerable treatment in anthropology and the social sciences (e.g., Midgley 1984; Carrithers et al. 1985; La Fontaine 1985; Strathern 1988; Morris 1991, 1994; Cohen 1994; Porter 1997; Douglas and Ney 1998; Harré 1998), largely influenced by Mauss's seminal essay (1938 [1985]). Apart from Jan Assmann, John Baines, and Herman te Velde, few Egyptologists have explicitly tried to tease apart the various aspects of the living self and embodiment, whereas the self in death has prompted an enormous scholarly outpouring. We cannot assume that either this latter manifestation or our own culturally specific interpretations parallel the Egyptian understanding. For instance, the Egyptians tended to personify various aspects of the body and the natural environment, as well as abstract concepts—a situation very different from the Euro-American context.

While much of this could be seen as part of a metaphorical process rather than an isomorphic relationship, it is characteristic of an Egyptian way of seeing and must be studied accordingly.

In terms of human categories the Egyptians referred collectively to "mankind" or "people" as *rmt*. From the New Kingdom onwards this term extended to non-Egyptians as well. It has the existential punning reference to humans as coming from the tears, *rmit*, of the creator god's eye. As such they were made of the same substance (Nordh 1996: 66–67). *Nds* and later *nmh* are additional terms that demarcated ordinary citizens and could refer to both literate and nonliterate individuals. Elite Egyptians perceived different taxonomies of people, based on the criterion of career. In the Middle Kingdom *Satire of the Trades*, a sage named Khety extols the virtues of being a scribe, as opposed to a range of other occupations, which are described for their negative aspects (see Parkinson 1999: 273–83). This text, which was well known in the New Kingdom, may give us some indication of the types of people who comprised Egyptian society, from a specifically elite perspective: sculptor, goldsmith, metalworker, craftsmen, corvée land-worker, jewel worker, barber, reed cutter, maker of pots, wall builder, carpenter, gardener, field worker, mat maker, arrow maker, courier, stoker, sandal maker, washerman, fowl catcher, and fisherman. Khety underscores the features of specific jobs that were abhorrent to the Egyptians, namely physical trauma, poor working conditions, deplorable smells, and sheer exhaustion.

The Egyptians did not embrace the Cartesian dichotomy of body and soul as separate and distinct spheres. They did not subscribe to a rationalization, comparable to the Western concepts of internal and external, in respect to the origins of thoughts and emotions, spirituality or self-determination. Jan Assmann's work (1982, 1999b) on concepts of personhood and being is central here. He divides the investigation of personhood into two spheres— the public manifestation and private experience. I focus here on the latter. The private dimension of personhood can be best described as the fundamental form of existence for the individual, together with people's experience and understanding of themselves. This dimension includes what we could term self-consciousness or the intersubjective domain where thoughts, intentions, sensations, personal characteristics, and self-reflection are processed. This is not to say that a universal consciousness exists, since individuals are shaped by their cultural context and specific constructions of embodiment and being. Egyptologists might be able to apprehend aspects of this private sphere through personal letters, whereas archaeologists have practically nothing of a residual nature that could capture this personal dimension. Writing was not a mirror of the inner world, since it was destined for consumption by others, probably to be read aloud, and thus had a public aspect. We do not know whether Egyptian people wrote for themselves alone, since nothing like a private diary survives. Individuals in their tomb biographies make clear the desire for personal distinctiveness and a unique character, setting themselves apart from their contemporaries. This suggests a strongly contoured notion of the individual and his or her place in the world. Yet there was an underlying tension, as in any society, between this expressed desire and the need for conformity within one's cohort group or society at large.

The private experience of the self lay at the intersection of a number of vectors, such as the body, sociality, consciousness, and self-experience. The Egyptian concept of personhood was multidimensional and was constituted of parts, not all of which were operational during life. Of all the components of the self integral to individual being—the *ba*, *ka*, and others—it is likely that two played an important role in life, rather than fundamentally coming into existence at the point of death. The first was the name, or *rn*, which had powerful associations during life: one is a name, just as one is a body (Milde 1988). Names had ritual potency, and the writing or reading out of a name was an efficacious act. Similarly, destruction of the name meant a loss of self, especially in terms of survival in the hereafter. An individual's name powerfully encompassed bodily, social, spiritual, and intellectual spheres. It was a means of presenting one's identity in this life and became even more potent in the transition to the next world. The second was the heart, the seat of intelligence, from which one speaks, one's center for feelings, memory, and understanding (te Velde 1990: 93). One is called upon to follow one's heart, the constant companion that provides the right path in life. The heart was considered the seat of knowledge, rationality, and emotion and was one of the most important aspects of the self in the spheres of life and of death. It guided the individual in all forms of action, emotion, and moral discourse. The heart could also abandon the embodied self, since it was unsteady and susceptible to strong emotions, through the experiences of erotic desire, terror, and yearning. By contrast, the brain, which we see as the seat of the mind, was not considered a potent part of the body, often being discarded at the point of embalming. In the living world the unity and cooperation of these various components of selfhood presented no problem, whereas in death this interior community was dissolved. The Egyptians remedied this situation through rituals to ensure an even more powerful state of the person through renewed assimilation, allowing these different constituents of the self to initiate new forms of interaction. As Assmann argues (1999b: 384), death and immortality were founded on the idea that the person, as a community, is threatened with dissolution and yet is capable of reintegration.

Another important constituent of the self, the *ba*, seems to have retained the character of the individual, although it depended on the physical body for existence. Scholars still debate whether translations as *self* or *soul* are appropriate (Assmann 1999b: 388). In the sphere of death the *ba* had material needs as well—bread, beer, and everything else that a body requires (Hornung 1992:181). The *ka* also required nourishment and both were important for the living. The *ba* was known to leave the body in cases of extreme terror such as social isolation. It was a freely moving agent, representing the person and supplying a link between the earthly world, heaven, and the afterworld. In the *Dialogue of a Man and his Ba* the living man and his *ba* discuss their respective and opposing views about death. While the man longs for death and all it promises, his *ba* warns that the agony of death should be avoided till the last. The protagonist urges his *ba* to stand by him—a common wish found also in funerary texts—on his journey to the otherworld (Parkinson 1999: 152). Indeed, the boundaries between the concepts of identity and existence often appear to be imperceptible (Nordh 1996: 52). One can say that the pluralities of the person covered several facets: the materiality of the body, bodily being, spiritual associations, and, in death, divine aspects.

Finally, the living person was embedded in a number of foundational social matrices: one's immediate family and kin group, those sharing the same title and rank, one's social role, and one's general position in the divine, royal, and human order of things, that is, the idea of *Maat*. On a broad societal level the concept of the person and his/her role in the worldly schema was an important existential issue. As John Baines (1999: 24) has stated:

> Human lifespans and concepts of the person are essential components of the individual's role in any society. Egyptian written texts can be only very partial windows onto the society's negotiation of these matters, and their presentation is affected by such factors as genre and decorum. . . . The person is a moral entity that balances self-interest with social participation in widely varying ways. With personhood comes the sense of a shape proper to a life, including expectations, goals, achievements, and its end. Most societies attach a positive value to a specific and personal life trajectory, possible exceptions being where ideals are strongly communitarian or where the individual's ultimate aspiration is extinction of self in some impersonal or cosmic whole, as in some Asian belief systems. Such does not seem to have been the case in Egypt. The positive value of a person can tend toward unique achievements that changed someone's world, or toward their full and harmonious embodiment of the ideals and aspirations of their social group. In the former case the focus is upon the individual, but positive achievements also must embody group values in some way. Conversely, exemplification of those values is significant only if it is focused in a particular individual. In either case, there is a tension between the individual and the group, between the dynamic and the static.

Linked to personhood is the specific understanding of the body in New Kingdom culture. Some scholars have suggested that the Egyptians perceived the human body as "being constructed and functioning not as a single organism but more as a corporation, a loose association, of separate anatomical entities" (Walker 1996: 283). Concepts of the person were inextricably linked to the corporeal self, especially as both persisted after death. The body's integrity had to be guaranteed in order to ensure one's existence in the afterlife. Reflecting this, the word $ḥ'$, commonly rendered as "body," can also refer to the more existential concepts of "self," "person" and "own" (Walker 1996: 3), reinforcing this important link between selfhood and corporeality. According to Walker, in some cases $ḥ'$ is more than just the physical matter or substance of the body: it is the physical aspect of a person or one of their "states of being." Another word, $ẖt$, written with a sign representing an animal belly, has a wider meaning as the locus of inner life, the location of thoughts, feelings, and memories (te Velde 1990: 89). Throughout pharaonic times, the body was considered more than a corporeal entity: it was a fundamental dimension of the person.

Egyptian writing on the concept of *mtw* is illustrative here, since it links corporeal and esoteric aspects and has no direct equivalent in Western medical understanding. In the Papyrus Ebers the *mtw* is described as including blood vessels, ducts, tendons, muscles, and perhaps nerves, although we are unsure whether the Egyptians identified them separately (Nunn 1996: 44). A number of substances can be transported by the *mtw*, such as blood, urine, air, semen, and disease-carrying entities, as well as benevolent or malevolent spirits. Semen and poison were often linked, as detailed in the mythological accounts of Seth impregnating Horus with poisonous semen, and were similar in written and phonetic form. In one text there was a total of 22 *mtw*, and it states that *all come to his heart. They distribute to his nose and all unite at the anus.*[1] Nunn proposes that this statement accords with Egyptian concepts of the circulation of noxious substances. For instance, the breath of life was thought to enter through the right ear, whereas the breath of death enters through the left. Illness was often considered to be the work of demons penetrating the borders of the body, threatening its integrity. In Ebers paragraph 854 some 52 *mtw* are described linking various parts of the body, some relating to the vascular system. Those *mtw* named for the arms and legs perhaps relate to pulse points, while those located in the testicles, which give semen, probably relate to the vas deferens, which can similarly be felt through the skin (Nunn 1996: 49). Some of these readings fit with modern medical understanding, others do not, and whether or not the Egyptians understood the circulatory system remains inconclusive. They believed that one's heart could speak through the *mtw* in all the limbs. Egyptian medical knowledge reflects the locus of embodiment as they knew it and at the same time shows an understanding of some key concepts. It is also important to remember that these medical texts were essentially learned but not necessarily practiced as we might envisage.

BECOMING A PERSON

Egyptian cosmology may be informative for ideologies of conception and birth, both of which were directly and explicitly linked to sexual beginnings. According to the Heliopolitan Theology, the origin of the world was phallic. Ra-Atum, the original father, brought the world into being: *he took his phallus in his fist and made sweet ejaculation from it, and the twins, Shu and Tefnut, were born.*[2] Other texts erase this primeval act of masturbation, suggesting that Atum sneezed or spat his offspring into being. Hare argues (1999: 112–3) that from this early date we can see an ambivalence surrounding male sexuality and desire. Atum's purpose, in the first account, is pleasure, not parenthood. His act is one of desire, without need of a partner, and his progeny are accidental: they are a supplement to his autoerotic intent. In this account, his semen produces the air god Shu and the moisture goddess Tefnut. Brother and sister have sexual intercourse and thus create Nut, the sky goddess, and Geb, the earth god. Nut and Geb embraced so tightly that nothing can exist between them, and their own conceived children cannot be born. Shu forced Geb and Nut apart, holding the sky goddess high above the earth, so that her body became the starry heavens. She then gave birth to Osiris, Isis, Seth, and Nephthys (Pinch 1994: 24–25). According to this narrative, the universe came into being through autoeroticism and was sustained through sexuality. Other creation myths developed at regional centers such as Hermopolis and focused on the god Thoth, Khnum, or Amun.

By the Eighteenth Dynasty the goddess Hathor was linked to the myth of creation in her epithet and role as the "Hand of Atum," literally the one who stimulated the god into orgasm, and thus creation. Hathor became central to all aspects of women's lives and personified female sexuality, yet she was also linked to male sexuality (Robins 1994–95). She was also known as Lady of the Vulva, Lady of Drunkenness, Goddess of the Western Mountain, and so on. A woman in labor could be identified with Hathor (P. Leiden I 348, spell 28) or clasp a Hathor amulet ring during the delivery (spell 31, see Borghouts 1971). She was an important deity at villages such as Deir el Medina, where she featured in shrines, tomb paintings, stelae, papyri, votive cloths, and domestic items. There were more votives dedicated to Hathor than any other deity in the New Kingdom: according to her epithet she was *the one who listens*. She was important for both royal and private funerary religion and provided a key

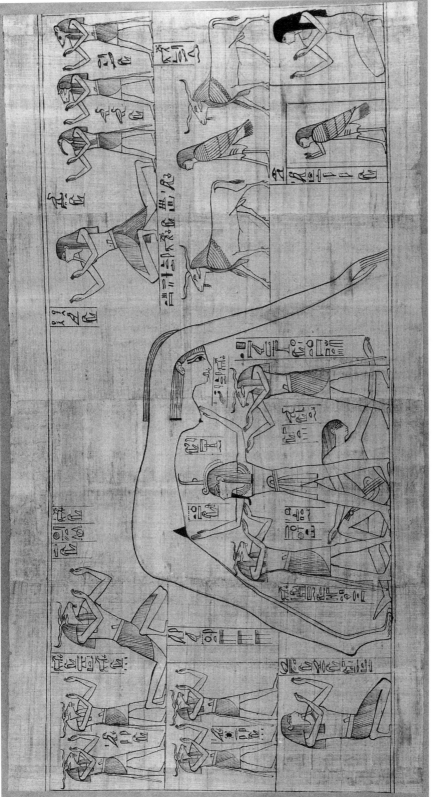

FIGURE 3.1. Image of Creation Featuring Geb and Nut. (Photo courtesy of the British Museum, EA 10554-87)

focus for personal piety. Offerings to Hathor discovered at her various shrines included models of breasts, female genitalia and phalli (Pinch 1993). At Deir el Bahri on the Theban West Bank, most of the votives can be dated to the early Eighteenth to the early Twentieth Dynasty. Many of the votive cloths found at the site name women and tend to depict family scenarios. Since the dedicants were primarily women (all male donors were priests), one might infer that they were petitioning for help and protection during the fertile phase of their lives. A similar pattern is seen for the votive stelae. Some textiles depict specific shrines and/or festivals, reinforcing the notion that their function was votive rather than funerary

FIGURE 3.2. Votive Head of Hathor in Faience. (Photo courtesy of the Petrie Museum, UC 29145)

(Pinch 1993: 134). However, votive phalli may have been offered by men, as in the documented case of Ramose, seeking a cure for male sexual problems, impotence, or infertility: this does not rule out the possibility that women donated phalli as well.

The desire to have children was central for the Egyptians, not simply for emotional reasons but because their social system relied on the support of parents by children in the later years of life and their maintenance of the funerary cult. Those who were without offspring often sought magical intervention, such as offering votives to Hathor or invoking spells, or possibly divorce. Others were publicly derided for their infertility, as in the case of the scribe Nekhemmut who was berated by a colleague: *You are not a man since you are unable to make your wives pregnant like your fellowmen. A further matter: You abound in being exceedingly stingy. You give no one anything. As for him who has no children, he adopts an orphan instead [to] bring him up.*[3]

The Egyptians saw the fertile earth as masculine and believed that men played a greater part than women in the formation of the child. Fertility may therefore have been regarded as a male responsibility (Roth 2000: 190). Desire for children was often gendered, and the great hope always appears to have been for a male child. As Gay Robins remarks (1994b: 234), if a child is named on an apotropaic wand, it is always a boy, and representations of children with their mothers on clay bed models generally depict male children. Medical prescriptions required the milk of a woman who has borne a male, ensuring its added potency. Overall the picture presents us with a normative desire to give birth to boys rather than girls. And Robins correctly stresses that as a result we know more about the lives of boys growing up than girls. If there was a genre of advice from mother to daughter, corresponding to the literary one for males, it would have to have existed in spoken form only.

Egyptian gynecological knowledge was relatively sophisticated, and some of it survives in written texts. The obstetric and gynecological writings preserved in the Kahun Papyrus, dated to 1820, the Ebers Papyrus, 1500, and elsewhere are often presented as exemplifying the Egyptians' concern over women's reproductive lives. Men were interested in women's fertility possibly because of the centrality of children in old age and in terms of the mortuary cult. These texts belong to a mainstream medical tradition transmitted by priests and scribes, which thus assumes that the medical practitioner will always be male. The Ebers Papyrus has a section devoted to women's conditions, such as those of the uterus, her milk, or the process of birth: *If you examine a woman who experiences pain in one side of her vulva, you should say concerning her: It is an irregularity of her menstrual period.*[4] The text also provided help on matters such as *to recognise good milk* and to *loosen the child in the belly of a woman* (Robins 1994–95: 26). An extensive range of ingredients was supposed to aid in contracting the

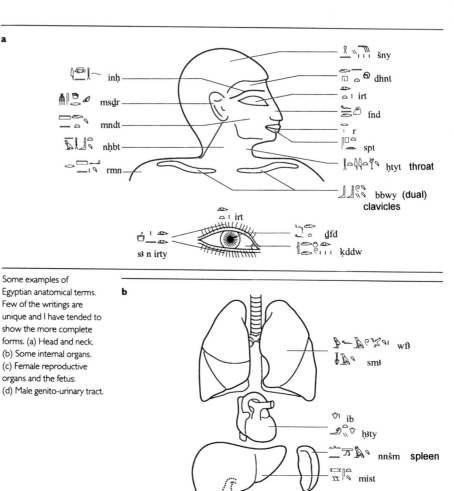

Some examples of Egyptian anatomical terms. Few of the writings are unique and I have tended to show the more complete forms. (a) Head and neck. (b) Some internal organs. (c) Female reproductive organs and the fetus: (d) Male genito-urinary tract.

b

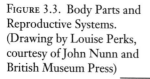

FIGURE 3.3. Body Parts and Reproductive Systems. (Drawing by Louise Perks, courtesy of John Nunn and British Museum Press)

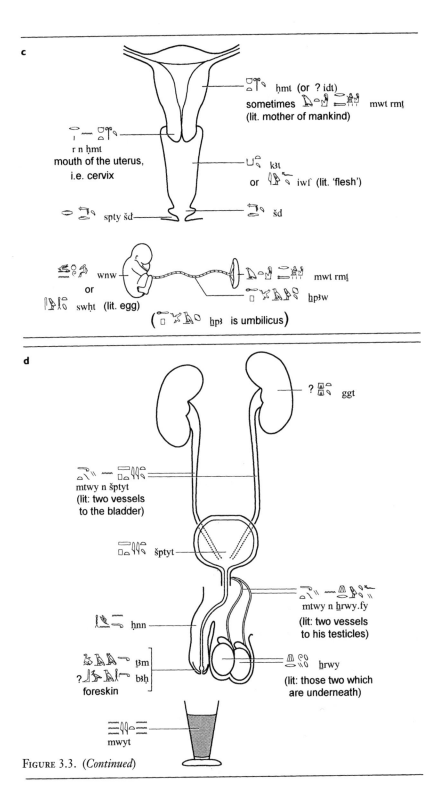

c

ḥmt (or ? idt)

sometimes ... mwt rmt (lit. mother of mankind)

r n ḥmt
mouth of the uterus,
i.e. cervix

k3t

or iwf (lit. 'flesh')

spty šd

šd

wnw

or

swḥt (lit. egg)

mwt rmt

ḥp3w

(ḥp3 is umbilicus)

d

? ggt

mtwy n šptyt
(lit: two vessels
to the bladder)

šptyt

mtwy n ḫrwy.fy
(lit: two vessels
to his testicles)

ḫnn

ḫrwy
(lit: those two which
are underneath)

3m

b3ḫ
foreskin

mwyt

FIGURE 3.3. (*Continued*)

uterus, such as honey, milk, date juice, ground celery, ground hemp, juniper berries, resin, excrement, and various oils. Some were to be ingested, others were inserted into the vagina, applied to the abdomen, or sat upon (Nunn 1996: 195). They also had a clear familiarity with the linkage between insemination and pregnancy, which is evident from texts such as the Ebers Papyrus. They knew that the production of sperm, *mw*, was connected with the testicles, *inswy*, and believed that the child received all its hard tissues from the father and its soft ones from the mother (Strouhal 1992: 12). The embryo was referred to as a *swḥt* or "egg," in both humans and animals. Some people may also have believed that nongenital sex, particularly oral sex, could lead to conception, as several myths suggest. There was certainly a fear that penetration of any of the bodily orifices by the sperm of a demon—even the ear—could ultimately lead to conception (Nunn 1996: 98).

The level of interest in gynecological matters illustrates the Egyptian concern with the human body and perpetuating the family. Ascertaining pregnancy was of particular interest, characterized by specific checks on the complexion or state of the breasts. For instance, a type of pregnancy test existed that entailed a woman urinating on young plants. If she was pregnant (*iwr*), the plants would grow and if not they would perish. Germinated barley meant a boy, while sprouting emmer meant a girl. This prognosis is based on the grammatical gender of the Egyptian words for barley and emmer, being masculine and feminine, respectively. If a woman wanted to check her fertility she would drink the milk of a woman who had borne a son, and if she vomited she either was or would soon be pregnant (Pinch 1994: 82). Papyrus Berlin 3207 makes clear the numerous hazards of birth and disease (Robins 1994–95: 26). Magical incantations make clear that deceased individuals could be responsible for miscarriage: *To repel (evil) activity (?) of a dead person or of a god.*[5] Demons were also an ever-present threat. Numerous spells to ward off miscarriage were said over pieces of knotted material that were then placed in the vagina like a form of tampon: *Anubis has come forth to keep the inundation from treading on what is pure—the land of Tayt. Beware of what is in it! This spell is to be said over threads of the border of yaat-fabric with a knot made in it. To be applied to the inside of her vagina.*[6] This makes sense if we consider that *the inundation* referred to here paralleled the blood flow from a possible hemorrhage; Tayt was the goddess of weaving. The knot was a powerful symbol that both bound together positive forces and blocked out malevolent ones. Items of jewelry, such as knotted bangles and the cowrie shell girdles that protected the pelvic area, acted as both decoration and protection for sexually mature women. In tomb 8 at Deir el Medina a woman named Merit was buried wearing a gold girdle across her hips, which probably functioned to highlight her sexuality and fertility in the next life (Meskell

2000b). It is not surprising then that these issues were so salient during women's lives—the continual cycle of conception, pregnancy, and birth preoccupied women from puberty to menopause—and spilled over into the mortuary realm.

COMING INTO THE WORLD

While in the womb the unborn child was considered a living being and as such required protection in the social realm (Feucht 1995: 94). The newborn was named at birth (Hornung 1992: 178), since without a name the individual could not exist. We know little of the moment of birth itself, and representation of such a liminal event was probably taboo in Egyptian culture, as were the general depictions of pregnancy and child rearing. There was concern for the mother's and child's welfare, which was guarded ritually by the recitation of potent spells, some intended to separate the child from the womb, others to speed up the delivery process: *His wife was nearing her time. I made the calling one stop his weeping. The wife of the man cried for a statuette of a dwarf of clay: come, let somebody betake himself to Hathor, the lady of Dendera. Let her amulet of health be fetched for you that she may cause the one in childbirth to give birth.*[7] Births fell into three categories: satisfactory, *ḥtp*, difficult, *bnd*, and protracted, *wdf*. The process could be speeded up by burning resin near the abdomen or massaging with saffron powder steeped in beer to reduce the pain (Strouhal 1992: 18). The realities of this dangerous time would have been ever-present, either in the form of personal experience or by the presence of cemeteries of infants. Using cross-cultural statistics, Robins (1994–95: 27–28) estimates that perhaps 20 percent of recognized pregnancies spontaneously failed, another 20 percent of all newborns died within the first year, and a further 30 percent did not survive beyond the age of five. This high rate of infant and child mortality accords to some degree with the mortuary data from sites like Gurob, Matmar, Mostagedda, and Deir el Medina (see below).

As a general indication of the risks, the Cairo Calendar shows that there were more unlucky days to give birth than lucky ones—a ratio of 21:13. This calendar was a type of handbook detailing predictions and injunctions for each day of the year and, in some cases, for each part of the day. It would suggest that the day and hour of the birth be recorded (Leitz 1994: 67–71). The birthday had serious ramifications and moral repercussions in later life and ultimately decided one's fate: one recorded date of birth signified that the person would die in debaucherous circumstances (Leitz 1994: 68). At Deir el Medina the workmen sometimes recorded births by the absences of the respective fathers. For instance, we know that Menneferemheb's child

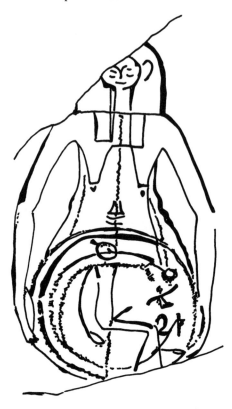

FIGURE 3.4. Ostracon Depicting a
Pregnant Woman. (Redrawn by
the author. After A. Piankoff, *Bulletin de la Societe d' Archeologie
Copte* 16 (1962): 261, Figure 1)

was born at night, since it was recorded in the necropolis journal (P. Turin
2044 in Toivari 2000: 159). Fathers evidently took time off to be with their
families, yet whether this was only in dire circumstances is unknown. While
the idea of gender segregation may be closer to ethnohistoric or anthropological accounts of birth in Egypt, the fact that the workman Kasa took time
off work to be at home during the birth of his child challenges such preconceptions: *Second month of inundation, day 23. Those who were (with) the scribe
Pashed working for the vizier: Ipuy, Nakhtemmut. Those who were with the chief
workman Khay: Khamu, Sawadjyt; and Qaha was ill. Those who were with the
chief workman Paneb: Kasa, his wife being in childbirth and he had three days off.*[8]
While we are unfamiliar with the exact preparations, one likely scenario
is that when birth was imminent "the expectant mother was isolated from
the rest of the household, or at least its adult males, . . . to the pavilion in
which the birth [wa]s taking place. Painted ostraca show women suckling
children in an airy pavilion whose columns are wreathed with columbine or
bryony" (Pinch 1994: 126–27). If these birth arbors were material, rather

than symbolic, they might have been specially constructed outdoor buildings. Other scholars have suggested that they were constructed on rooftops (Loose 1992: 23). To date, no archaeological examples from either context have been discovered, which is not surprising given the materials of construction. Representational evidence shows women either squatting or kneeling to give birth, ideally over birthing bricks, with female attendants offering assistance. In the votive stela of Neferabu, dedicated to the goddess Meretseger, he claims: *I sat on bricks like the woman in labour*.[9] Royal and mythical relief scenes from Deir el Bahri and Luxor temple show pregnant queens aided by female attendants. In the Middle Kingdom tale of Papyrus Westcar, Meskhenet was one of the goddesses who assisted with childbirth in conjunction with Heqet (the frog goddess), Isis, and Nepthys. However, the evidence for midwives is sketchy, and no word for midwife has been identified from New Kingdom sources (Nunn 1996: 132). If complications arose, we can be fairly certain that most doctors would have been male.

The magico-medical text Papyrus Leiden I 348 (Borghouts 1971) makes mention of the experience of giving birth. There were a host of spells for the woman's pain as well as the husband's anguish and for the dispersal of the amniotic fluids. There was also a spell for the delivery of the placenta, which was recited over a four-day period. Both the umbilical cord and placenta were thought to have magical potency, and in the Eastern Necropolis at Deir el Medina excavators discovered placenta burials and the materials associated with birth (Bruyère 1937; 11; see p. 81).

Iconographic sources from settlement contexts depict women suckling infants while seated on stools or reclining on beds postnatally. At Deir el Medina it is likely that births took place in the first room of the houses, which have been preserved with fixtures and wall paintings in situ (Meskell 1998b: 219). These rooms were loaded with iconographic images relating to the lives of mature women; more specifically, these images related to sexuality and birth. Parallel examples have been noted at the New Kingdom worker's village at Amarna, suggesting this was not an isolated phenomenon. Excavations at Amarna in the 1970s revealed several wall paintings featuring Bes and Taweret (Kemp 1979). Bes was a male deity with a leonine head and tail the stocky body of a dwarf, bowed legs, a distended stomach, and genitals that were often exposed (Robins 1994–95: 29). Taweret was a composite being like Bes; she was depicted as pregnant, with the combined features of a hippopotamus, crocodile, lioness, and human shown standing upright on her back legs carrying protective symbols such as the magic knife and *s3* sign. In the main city of Amarna, Peet and Woolley earlier had found domestic altars similar to those at Deir el Medina houses. There were also cultic cupboards, and in one was discovered a stela showing a woman before Taweret, a female figurine, and two

FIGURE 3.5. Statue of Bes with Tambourine. (Photo courtesy of the British Museum, EA 20865)

model beds (Peet and Woolley 1923: 24–25; Pinch 1983: 414). Taweret and Bes also feature prominently on more informal sketches; for example, women on beds with carved legs depicting Bes were very popular.

From Deir el Medina alone there are scores of figured ostraca of women breastfeeding, women on beds—some with children—women with female attendants, and women with toiletry objects. The specific hairstyles of many of the women portrayed in the domestic iconography closely resemble erotic representations and fertility figurines (Brunner-Traut 1955: 25–27), stressing the sexual associations surrounding childbirth. Particular wigs and

FIGURE 3.6. Ostracon Showing Bes. (Photo courtesy of the Petrie Museum, UC 33198)

clothing may have marked the end of the mother's and baby's period of isolation (Pinch 1983: 405). There are also marked similarities between this iconography and that represented on New Kingdom bed models: they usually depict a nude female wearing a heavy wig and accompanied by a child, both reclining on a bed. Both these contexts feature images of grooming such as unguent cones, toilet items, or mirrors, suggesting notions of purification and more generally female eroticism. The children are often male or of indefinite sex and shown as miniature adults, which makes it impossible to estimate their age (Pinch 1983: 408). So-called fertility figurines and bed models were found in both settlement and cemetery contexts at New Kingdom sites such as Memphis, Deir el Medina, and Gurob. At Deir el Medina molds for these figurines were excavated from the settlement (Bruyère 1939: 214).

At least six Deir el Medina houses (NE10, 12, 13; SE9; SW6; C5) preserved images of the deity Bes, who was a potent force in all aspects of women's private lives, primarily in regard to sexuality and protection during childbirth (Meskell 1999a: 225). In house SE1 was a painting of a woman breastfeeding in the first room; other paintings showed scenes of female grooming. Young females depicted with the mother might be midwives or women who aided with the birth, physically or symbolically. Imagery of this nature was not present throughout the rest of the domestic space at Deir el Medina. Iconography, ostraca, and figurines not only assisted with the successful production of offspring, but with sexual conception and childbirth as well. Desire for children should not be separated from sexual desire (Pinch 1983: 413).

There is no evidence for particular social events surrounding the moment of birth. Scattered textual evidence from the Papyrus Westcar (11, 18–19) suggests that there was a seclusionary period after birth: *Rudjedet purified herself in a cleansing of fifteen days*. Wilfong cites ostraca from Deir el Medina that give a list of supplies for festivals, one called *the purification of his daughter*.[10] Possible time frames of seclusion range from fourteen to forty days in total. Since births seem to have taken place in the home, in the first room off the narrow Deir el Medina laneways, we need to discard our own notions of privacy for such an event. Women typically had many children during their lives and their houses were probably home to a large number of people: male and female, elite and servile, young and old (Meskell 1998b). Prosopographic studies at Deir el Medina show that it was not unusual for couples to have at least ten children, as in the case of Baki, Neferronpet, Kasa, and others and that it was certainly the norm to have as many as six or seven (see Davies 1999).

Women were responsible for the rearing of children, some with the assistance of female servants. At Deir el Medina, men—whose occupation was the construction of the royal tombs in the Valley of the Kings—were

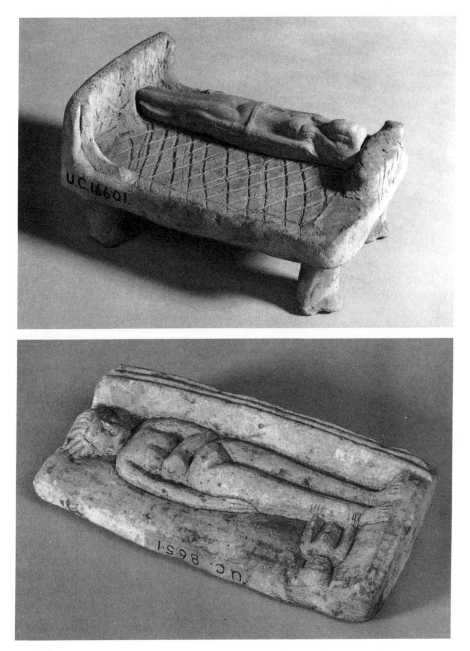

FIGURE 3.7. Two Clay Bed Models. (Photo courtesy of the Petrie Museum, UC16601, UC8651)

away for ten days at a time, leaving women dominant in the domestic sphere. Time and space conjoined to produce a very specific experience of domestic life. Archaeologically, women as a group could be almost described as invisible. Here we must rely on the documents relating to men's lives to illustrate the life cycle of the house. A well known instruction text states that it was a child's mother who did most for it during life and who, in turn, had to be looked after as she approached old age: *Double the provisions your mother gave you, support her as she supported you; she had many burdens in you, but she did not abandon them to me. You were born after your months, (but) she harnessed herself, still, her breast in your mouth for three years while you flourished. Your excrement disgusted, (but she) was not disgusted, saying: "What shall I do?!" She sent you to school, when you were taught to write, and she waited for you daily, with bread and beer in her house.*[11]

The whole process of growing up was fraught with dangers, both explicable and mysterious. There is a considerable body of material culture in the form of amulets, apotropaic items, figurines, and inscribed spells to protect children at this liminal time. Ivory clappers, amulets, necklaces, or jewelry in the form of knots all functioned in this way. The deities depicted most often on these items of material culture were Bes, Taweret, and Hathor. The first two were deployed in their protective roles, warding off demons; their unpleasant appearance as composite beings itself had apotropaic value. Clappers in the shape of hands were carved from wood or ivory and were used in music and dance. In some instances the hands incorporate the mask of Hathor (e.g., Figure 3.8), evoking her protective and sexual roles. Performing with cymbals, rattles, and castanets and performing lively dances was also thought to ward off demons and hostile forces (Pinch 1993: 84–85). Ensuring the survival of their offspring was obviously of great importance to most parents, and many sought magical practices to guarantee their children's safety. Specific amulets were worn, usually as jewelry, in crisis situations such as childbirth, and spoken magic was probably recited at the crucial moments. There were spells to protect the newly born from being stolen by demons in the night. The Ebers Papyrus offered ways of ascertaining a child's fate: if on the day of birth it said *"ni,"* it would live; however, if it said *"mebi,"* it would die. One papyrus gives instruction for making an amulet for a baby, the spell being said over gold and garnet beads and a seal with images of a crocodile and a hand. These images were there to destroy or ward off dangerous spirits. Both seal and beads were strung around the infant's neck, and many examples have been found archaeologically (Pinch 1994: 115) at sites such as Deir el Medina. An amuletic necklace from under a house floor at Gurob may have been worn by the mother during pregnancy or in labour.

Even after a successful birth there may have been problems for the infant if an inadequate supply of milk was available. There was no substi-

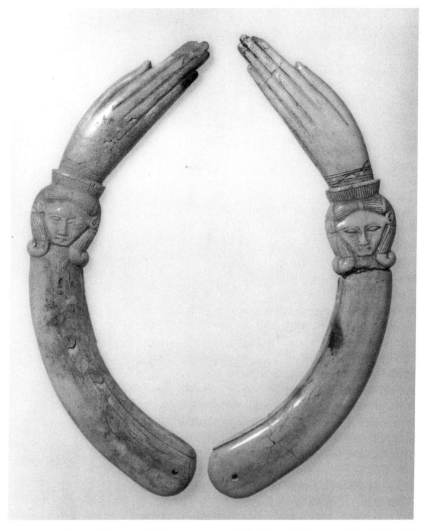

FIGURE 3.8. Ivory Clappers. (Photo courtesy of the British Museum, EA 20779.80)

tute for breast milk, so mothers made use of wet nurses. There was also an aspect of social convention to this practice, and Robins notes (1994–95: 29) that high-status women of the Eighteenth Dynasty acted as wet nurses for royal children. But there were other more pressing instances when a mother relied on another woman, owing to her own limited supply or possibly her untimely death during the birth. There are numerous containers in the form of a woman, with or without a child, holding her breast, which may have been designed for breast milk. Their cubic capacity is roughly

FIGURE 3.9. Vessel in the Shape of Mother and Child. (Photo courtesy of the British Museum, EA 24652)

equivalent to the amount one breast produces at a single time (Janssen and Janssen 1990: 19). This may signify the importance of wet-nursing or simply reiterate how mother's milk was a potent ingredient in medico-magical prescriptions. While various specific interpretations are possible, these vessels testify to the importance of the birthing process in the life of both mother and child.

The principal deity for pregnant women and during childbirth was Taweret, who bore all the markers of magical protection. Taweret featured commonly in wall paintings at Deir el Medina and Amarna. Even during the religious upheaval of the Amarna period, the villagers did not relinquish their need for Taweret and Bes in paintings and amulets alike. Such protection was vital since the dangers surrounding childbirth and child rearing were great.

> You will break out, you who have come in the darkness, who have entered stealthily—his nose turned backwards, his face averted, having failed in what he came for! . . .
> Have you come to kiss this child? I will not let you kiss it.
> Have you come to hush it? I will not let you do your hushing with it.
> Have you come to do it harm? I will not let you harm it.
> Have you come to take it away? I will not let you take it away from me.
> I have ensured its protection against you with clover—that means, use of force—with garlic which harms you—with honey—sweet to people, but bitter to those there.[12]

The above text addresses several commonly held fears and offers a form of protection. Many Egyptians believed that demons regularly attacked at night and portrayed them as visitors from the darkness or from a world turned upside down. Dead individuals were also to be feared: they existed in spirit form, and their jealous tendencies could rob a mother of her newborn child.

MORTUARY MATERIAL

Egypt offers a remarkable environment for the preservation of physical remains. Excavated bodies attest to the frequency of women dying in childbirth owing to severe complications, usually a narrow or deformed pelvis (Strouhal 1992: 18). These risks meant that women had a shorter life expectancy than men, as is borne out both in cemetery data and from analysis of bodies now held in museum collections. For the newborn, the highest death rate occurred in the first few days, decreasing over the next month and then again after the first year. Disease and infection claimed many. The goddess Seshat was considered responsible, since she accorded

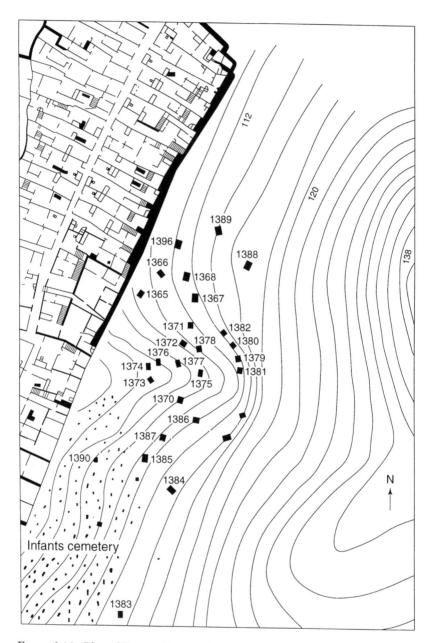

FIGURE 3.10. Plan of Eastern Necropolis, Deir el Medina. (From L. Meskell *Archaeologies of Social Life*, 1999, figure 4.11)

the designated length of life, at the moment of birth. In her sevenfold human form Hathor also pronounced the fate of the newborn (Pinch 1993: 222).

The scores of infant burials at the base of the Eastern Necropolis at Deir el Medina demonstrate the difficulties of life. The lowest part of the slope was assigned to very young children. This region was a mass of small pits, circular, square, or rectangular, cut 40 to 90 cm deep into the rock without any internal or external masonry (Bruyère 1937: 11). The excavator Bernard Bruyère discovered infants, neonates, fetuses, placentas, and organic residues among bloody cloths, and the remains of viscera. Adolescents of both sexes were assigned to the middle section of the hill and adults to the upper portion, with women being more numerous than men. Thus, the cemetery was spatially stratified along age-determined lines, a distribution that was probably linked to marital status as well.

The Eastern Necropolis burials demonstrate that children of all ages were given meaningful burials, rather than simply being disposed of expeditiously. Yet anthropologists, demographers, and sociologists have often been eager to suggest that many ancient cultures did not consider the child a person, or that they did not achieve personhood till a particular age. The mortuary evidence at Deir el Medina challenges such a view. Excavation revealed various modes of burial for very young children: in ceramic amphorae, baskets, boxes, and coffins (Bruyère 1937; Meskell 1994b). Associated grave goods such as beer or ceramics do not belong to the world of the child but to a fully developed adult world and were symbolic of adult styles of provisions for the afterlife. Moreover, the burying of the placenta, which was known to represent the twin self and a powerful spiritual force (Pinch 1994: 130), lends weight to the argument that children were already perceived as embodied individuals. Perhaps the physical body itself was all that was necessary to constitute a person whether it survived birth or not. In most cases, a sharp flint, probably used in the delivery operation, accompanied the burial (Bruyère 1937: 12). We know that items that had such close contact with the body of the individual were ritually important and integral to the burial.

I worship your ka, O Lord of Gods
Though I am but a child!
Harm is what befell me
When I was but a child!
A faultless one reports it.
I lie in the vale, a young girl,
I thirst with water beside me!
I was driven from childhood too early!
Turned away from my house as a youngster

Before I had my fill in it!
The dark, a child's terror, engulfed me,
While the breast was in my mouth![13]

The bodies of children were also placed in baskets of various types (tombs 1373, 1374, 1378, 1383, 1385, DX1, DX2, DX4) and were usually wrapped in a piece of linen, having a small number of funerary goods such as plates of food (Bruyère 1937: 12–13). These assemblages were more akin to those of standard adult burials, even though often on a smaller scale, but they did not constitute a specific funerary vision of "childhood" in any Western sense. The same could be said of box burials (tombs 1384, 1390). These boxes were either reused domestic objects or specifically created for burial. Funerary goods and small items of jewelry accompanied these children to the next life. They often wore small necklaces and bracelets, some with faience beads, others with scarab amulets. In keeping with the standard iconography of children, several of the bodies (both of boys and girls) had their heads shaved, some with the traditional sidelock of hair. Coffins were used for small children and adolescents alike, some coarsely hewn from a tree trunk, others in anthropoid form. While all the manufacturing techniques evidenced were rough, some coffins had a coat of whitewash and others had yellow painted figures and inscriptions that were then varnished. An example of this extensive provisioning is the case of three children who were found together in tomb 1372, two in anthropoid coffins and one in a casket coffin, surrounded by numerous tomb goods (Bruyère 1937: 161–4). In the Eighteenth Dynasty children were also often buried on their own, connoting that they were considered individuals who warranted their own tombs.

At Deir el Medina in the Eighteenth Dynasty, many of the villagers' children were buried in the Eastern Necropolis. The child of a wealthier individual named Sennefer (tomb 1159A), who commissioned a decorated tomb in the Western Necropolis, was placed in that tomb alongside the woman Nefertiry. The child was wrapped in linen and placed in a wooden box, much like contemporaneous burials in the Eastern cemetery. There were thus various burial options for infants, as there were for adults at this time. During the Nineteenth Dynasty the community moved from the burials of individuals and couples to lineage-based burials in larger, multivaulted tombs, all located in the Western Necropolis (Meskell 1999b: 189). Some tombs contained at least three generations, as in the case of Sennedjem (tomb 1). Later on, New Kingdom children and adolescents were placed in the tombs of their families, drawing on the benefits of magical tomb goods and wall paintings. At this time the Eastern Necropolis largely fell out of use, with the possible exception of poorly preserved pit burials. It is likely that the methods of burial for the poor have left no visible trace in the archaeological record. Some scholars suggest that the bodies of poor children were left exposed at the desert edge or thrown into the Nile; however, these suppositions cannot be substantiated. While such practices are conceivable, we have to be careful how we ascribe them to other cultures.

Twin or multiple births were accorded great significance, as were their burials. *Qenherkhopishef addresses the woman Inerwau: What means your failing to go to the diviner on account of the two infants who died while in your charge? Inquire of the woman diviner about the death of the two infants, whether it be their fate or destiny . . .*[14] It is tempting to see these twins as those represented by the exceptional "burial" DX3 in the Eastern Necropolis, which contained two wooden boxes and grave goods, yet in which no bodies were found. The tomb was intact and covered with undisturbed stones. Each box contained a wooden statue wrapped in linen, suggestive of some magical practice. The burial assemblage consisted of some eighteen ceramic vessels, two baskets, and a wide variety of foodstuffs (Anthes 1943: 55). Taken together, the evidence indicates a purposeful and somewhat expensive substitute burial.

Other sites of approximately the same period reveal a high degree of infant mortality. Diana Craig Patch has calculated the percentages of infant burials in the cemeteries of Gurob, Matmar and Mostagedda. Some 50 percent of the 276 graves at Gurob, 48 percent of the 233 at Matmar and 42 percent of the 31 burials at Mostagedda contained the burials of infants (cited in Robins 1994–95: 28). At Gurob there was a cemetery reserved for children, much like the lower slope of the Eastern Necropolis at Deir el Medina. Here too burials consisted of shallow pits cut into the rock, and individual infants were placed in pottery jars.

Children as Individuals

Surviving infancy was perilous, and the bioanthropological evidence, as well as that from the Ebers Papyrus, confirms that the hazards of childhood were significant. Children suffered from stomach infections, skin troubles, tonsillitis, anemia, and poor nutrition. Poor hygiene would have caused or exacerbated these illnesses.

According to archaeological and iconographic data and ethnographic parallels, from a very early age children of the non-elite were involved in work. At the site of Abydos the footprints of small children have been found in the mud plaster around the mortuary complex and tomb of Khasekhemwy, suggesting that they worked alongside adults during construction (David O'Connor, personal communication). Young boys scattering seed in the fields and young girls tending animals or looking after younger siblings all contributed to lower socioeconomic households. Girls probably also assisted with field labor, as is commonly seen in modern Egypt. The notion of a carefree childhood where one's only duty is to play is a very recent Western invention. Moreover, in recent history European children worked down in mines, in factories, and on the streets to earn a living. In New Kingdom Egypt there was not a sharp divide between adult experience of the world and that of many children. Boys often adopted the professions of their father through direct working experience, such as the "children of the tomb" we see documented at Deir el Medina (Valbelle 1985: 123; McDowell 1992a: 201). Fathers were desperate to have their sons assume their positions, if profitable, and often bribed the necessary officials to ensure success in this regard. From the generations of scribes and draftsmen at Deir el Medina a pattern of common job continuity emerges. These boys were trained as scribes— literate artists who could attain wealth and status through their skill and entrepreneurship. Apprenticeship could occur in many jobs: craftsman, builder, fisherman, and so on.

Children certainly enjoyed activities such as ball games, music, dancing, and swimming, and had various types of toys—tops, rattles, animals, and dolls, some with movable parts. However, many Egyptologists have conflated female figurines and bed models with toys when their archaeological association has been with adult females, rather than attributing them to the sphere of sexuality and fertility, in this world and the next (See Figure 3.7). Luckier children, specifically boys, had schooling. Andrea McDowell (1999: 4) has suggested that at the highly literate village of Deir el Medina some 40 percent were schooled and literate, although this is exceptional. Scribal schools must have existed, although no location is identified in the texts and they have not been detected archaeologically. Others propose that schools were located in the Ramesseum and at the temple of Mut (Janssen and Janssen 1990: 76), both on the Theban West Bank. More often we are simply left with the school exercises the boys wrote. Student exercises, mostly extracts from Egyptian literary texts of the Middle Kingdom, have in the past been used as one of the chief sources of information about teaching methods. From those surviving it appears that a male relative was usually the tutor. The scribe Piay speaks to the scribe Amenmose as follows: *A third (chapter) is ready for you,* to which Amenmose replies *I will do it! See, I will do it, I will do it!* and Piay answers *Bring your chapter and come!*[15] Some fifteen texts have been signed by their student copyists, who identify themselves as assistants or apprentices working under the direction of an established member of the Deir el Medina workforce. On workdays they no doubt helped their mentors with the work in the Valley of the Kings, mastering the trade, and at other times pursued their education, which granted them access to the official class. Despite the hard work, theirs was a privileged position dependent on their sex, status, and opportunity, something that young girls could only observe.

What can be said about training for girls? Their immediate experiences of being female probably centered around the family and all its entailments, specifically tending household animals and the parallel experience of raising children themselves. Theban tomb scenes depict small girls involved in simple domestic tasks. One could argue that such scenes operate on a purely symbolic level, although it is likely that there is some real world referent. Others are shown serving food and drink, and while this is a likely activity, the degree to which "banqueting" scenes reflect reality is always questionable. Young girls are also depicted assisting older women with their personal adornment and hairdressing. It is unlikely that those from ordinary towns and communities were taught to write, but they may have grown to recognize various signs or names. In exceptional cases we may have evidence of female literacy, such as the depiction of Qenamun's wife (TT 162), who is shown with a scribal palette beneath her chair. However, this is a suggestive iconographic motif rather than hard evidence. Girls from wealthier households may have learned to sing, dance, and play musical instruments as may have servants who were hired out as entertainers. Poorer children probably only learned the arts of spinning, weaving, and cooking. All these activities contributed to household production and should not be seen as "doing nothing" or not working per se.

Much of the data used to glean information on the world of children is iconographic, and with that comes all the limitations of *representation* versus *reality*. Many of these scenes are idealized depictions from mortuary contexts. Apart from the artistic conventions, which cannot be taken at face value, many interpretations have to be viewed through the lens of the afterlife. For instance, children are canonically depicted as naked, whereas both Egypt's climate and the discovery of children's clothes in domestic contexts challenge that representation. Various tombs from Deir el Medina also show clothed children, so that different schemas existed concomitantly. Naked children lack the differentiation in dress witnessed in adults, and this gender ambivalence is only resolved with the transition to adulthood (Robins 1999: 57). In some scenes boys wear earrings and circlets that are otherwise depicted as worn only by adult women. Young girls are shown with the same signifiers of female adulthood: earrings, circlets, girdles, and light skin color. Girdles are an interesting case in point. While adult women were sometimes buried with girdles, they were not depicted wearing them in wall paintings. Thus in visual evidence the girdle might signify individuals who had not yet achieved adulthood.[16]

Children are naturally depicted as smaller in size than their adult parents, but not proportionally and certainly not in keeping with anatomical accuracy.

The viewer's best clue to identifying children is the artistic convention of portraying their heads as shaven, with a sidelock of hair (Aldred 1980: 17). The burial data at Deir el Medina supports this as an actual practice, rather than simply a visual motif. This "small adult" presentation fits with what we know of children's lives, at least of the nonroyal classes. It is important to note that when pharaoh Ramesses III has himself depicted as a child in a royal tomb he is shown as large as the gods that surround him, and while he adheres to the convention of nudity for children, his pose conveniently hides

FIGURE 3.11. Infants with Sidelocks from the Tomb of Inherkau, TT 359, Deir el Medina. (Photo courtesy of the IFAO, Cairo. Photograph by J. Morthelot)

all (Meskell 1998a). And we have to separate portrayals of children as youngsters and the representation of offspring in a familial relationship. The depiction of Ramesses III is clearly an example of the latter.

Informal ostraca from settlement contexts, papyri, and tomb paintings show children engaged in the variety of activities previously mentioned, as well as in some seemingly unorthodox ones. In the Theban tomb of Neferhotep (TT 49) a small vignette shows a woman drinking beer, holding a Hathoric sistrum and *menat* necklace, and leading two children (see Hodel-Hoenes 2000: 188). The young girl with her holds part of a convolvulus plant, known for its erotic associations. The drinking of beer and the woman's accoutrements all illustrate an overtly sexual connection that is unhampered by the presence of the children. The ostraca sometimes depict children in the midst of adult sexual encounters, occasionally assisting in a kind of public display. In one example a small girl and boy are positioned to either side of a copulating couple, while another adult looks on.[17] This is reminiscent of a scene in the Turin erotic papyrus (see Chapter 5) where two girls, whose youth is indicated by their shaved heads and sidelocks, help with a chariot on which a sexual encounter takes place. Apart from the obvious sexual surroundings and the panoply of erotic signifiers, the girls appear to be approached by a small boy or man with an enormous penis. Despite the fact that the young girls are assisting, rather than being penetrated themselves, their age does not seem a barrier to these activities. In another scene a young girl helps carry off an unwell or exhausted male who has been involved in sexual activities. Whether the contents of the papyrus had any basis in reality or was imaginary or satirical, this general association of young girls and sexuality is common in Egyptian iconography and might have been socially acceptable.

Adolescents

Little is known of the ceremonies that marked the passing from adolescence to adulthood—if such events were part of Egyptian experience. In adolescence, the shaving of children's heads appears to have ceased. Scholars have long debated the practice of male and female circumcision in Egyptian society, using textual, iconographic, and physical data. The writings of Herodotus and Strabo on male and female circumcision are often cited as historical sources, yet this is problematic, since they wrote about Egyptian life in a genre of the-world-turned-upside-down. It is worth briefly examining the evidence for the practice in the New Kingdom, beginning with male circumcision (e.g., de Wit 1972; Janssen and Janssen 1990; Feucht 1995; Bailey 1996). Scenes of adolescent circumcision, like those in the Old Kingdom tomb of Ankhmahor, are restricted to a much earlier date and may relate to the initiation of priests rather than ordinary people (Roth 1991: 72). Roth argues cogently that such scenes may relate to the shaving of the pubic region for ritual purity, rather than circumcision, and that what we see depicted are razors rather than knives. There is a much later scene depicting the circumcision of royal children found in the precinct of Mut at Karnak (Bailey 1996: 20–21; Nunn 1996: 169). There is also a stela at Naga ed Deir, that mentions a man being circumcised with his peer group. Nude men in Old and Middle Kingdom iconography, such as field workers, are usually shown as circumcised. This pattern does not occur in the New Kingdom, since men are generally shown clothed as indicators of their status. There are, of course, exceptions, such as the nude marsh workers netting birds in the tomb of Nakht (TT 52), although genitalia are not depicted. Nothing relevant occurs in the medical texts, and the operation may have been performed by priests rather than doctors—again pointing to a specifically religious ritual. The recently examined bodies of Nakht, a weaver of the Twentieth Dynasty (Millet et al. 1998: 98), and a young boy showed no sign of the operation (Reyman and Peck 1998: 113). Similarly, the bodies examined earlier by Bruyère (1937) and by Strouhal and Vyhnánek (1980: 25–67) suggest that neither male nor female inhabitants of Deir el Medina were circumcised. Bodies from other Egyptian sites bear out this finding. It is possible that circumcision may have been performed in ritual contexts, for people of elite status (e.g., Amenhotep II, Thutmose IV, Ramesses IV and V), for certain ethnic or regional groups, and so on. But it is doubtful that it existed as a pervasive practice in the New Kingdom.

There is no evidence, visual or textual, for female circumcision at this date. Texts dating to the Graeco-Roman period mention the practice, yet they also refer to Greeks rather than Egyptians. There is no physical evidence for such practices in the Deir el Medina Necropoleis, and in one instance the excavator specifically noted that in tomb 1382 the perfectly preserved body of a woman called Nubiyity showed her genitalia to be intact (Bruyère 1937: 188). A number of other (elite) female mummies from the period confirm that circumcision was not widespread, nor was it directly linked to status. The old idea of "pharaonic circumcision" may have had little relation to the practices of ancient Egyptians, and it is our own preoccupations with rites de passage that have colored our interpretations. In a society that had no known public marriage ceremony, it might also be possible that the transition to adulthood may have been a gradual progression that started much earlier than puberty itself.

Anthony Giddens (1991: 33) has suggested that "transitions in individual's lives have always demanded psychic reorganization, something which was often ritualized in traditional cultures in the shape of rites de passage. But in such cultures, where things stayed more or less the same from generation to generation on the level of collectivity, the changed identity was clearly staked out—as when an individual moved from adolescence into adulthood. In the settings of modernity, by contrast, the altered self has to be explored and constructed as part of a reflexive process of connecting personal and social change." Such a premodern/modern dichotomy, permeated with ethnocentric claims, fails to accord with Egyptian evidence of the life cycle. Similarly, we have attributed to our own culture an emotional complexity and depth of feeling that is somehow distinctive, whereas the ancient data challenge our temporal chauvinism, forcefully highlighting the sensitive and manifold nature of ancient relationships.

We might adduce that for young women, the progression of life might not have been as distinct as it was for their male counterparts. I have argued that girls were depicted in both iconography and material culture as sexual beings from an early age onwards. There is a whole corpus of artifacts representing adolescent girls, some still having the shaved head of childhood, in a nude or seminude state replete with the erotic signifiers of lotus flowers, hip girdles, ducks (Derchain 1975: 62; see Figure 3.12), and musical instruments. Very young women were sexualized, and images of them appeared on toiletry objects, such as spoons, mirrors, bowls, and combs (Robins 1996; see Chapters 5 and 6). All such imagery was loaded with obvious sexual overtones to an Egyptian viewer. The discursive creation of "childhood" as a sanctified category or desexualized sphere, separate from the overtones of adult life, is relatively recent (Foucault 1978: 47). I would

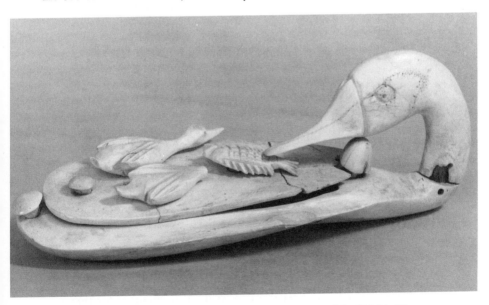

Figure 3.12. Duck Cosmetic Container. (Photo courtesy of the British Museum, EA 5946)

therefore suggest that the female life cycle was less marked than one might expect and that their sexual and social roles began quite early in life. Young men may have experienced more marked transitions, moving from the domestic sphere of their mothers to the world of work. It also seems likely that girls were much younger at the point of "marriage" than boys, creating different social expectations of the sexes and their life trajectories. The instructional texts of Ani and Ankhshoshenq (Lichtheim 1980: 168) tell us something about social maturity and marriageable ages—for girls it was around twelve or thirteen whereas it was approximately twenty for boys— yet provide little information concerning puberty.

Another aspect of women's life cycles, linking sociality and temporality, is obviously the menstrual cycle: the ancient term was *ḥsmn*. The word has the same root as for *natron*, associated with purification, suggesting *ḥsmn* was a euphemism. Drawing on the work of Wilfong (1999) we might suggest possible social practices that drew women to certain spaces and at regulated times. *Year 9, fourth month of the season of Inundation, day 13: The day when the eight women came out [to the] place of women when they were menstruating. They got as far as the rear of the house which [...] the three guard posts.*[18] Wilfong gives detailed reasons why menstrual synchrony would have been operative at Deir el Medina and cites texts detailing the names of women menstruating at the same time over most of the year. He also cites texts, such as the day books of work in the Valley of the Kings, that document how various men took days off work at such times. Given the recorded frequency, this was probably permitted only when there was serious disruption to the household. Wilfong suggests that the "place of women" was a menstrual hut outside of the village, the exact location of which is unknown. *Ḥsmn* could also take place in parts of the house in later times, and I have suggested (Meskell 1998b: 235–37) that we might have early evidence for this practice in several larger houses at Deir el Medina. However, if these groups of women left the village, it obviously had a marked social impact on household relations and functioning. Linkage between time, space, and social custom forms a fundamental nexus throughout the life cycle.

MATURATION

Maturation in our own culture most often refers to the joint processes of passing through adolescence and sexual maturation. In Egyptian society it was perhaps the latter, rather than the former, that was the true demarcator. Egyptologists derive much of their information for this stage of life from the so-called "love songs," penned by men, and the pictorial evidence, also crafted by men. There was no room for nonconformists in representations of Egyptian life. In both contexts we are presented with an idealized view of life, free from the constraints of society or individual circumstance. Each body of material presented women and spoke for them, so female conceptions of self or life experience are entirely absent. Both provided a kind of template for life, one directed at this world and the other aiming for the next.

Perpetuating the cycle and perpetuating the family were central concerns of Egyptian adult life. The person was perceived as being linked to family members in an extended network of connections. The individual came from the body of the parent, and this was often expressed as such in literal terms (Pinch 1993: 126). This concept obviously impacts upon themes of relatedness and kinship. The pressures to create a family were real and tangible. As we have seen, those who were infertile consulted village seers for help, visited shrines to the goddess Hathor, adopted other children, or purchased magical intervention or objects of material culture which possessed an efficacious agency of their own. Many of these objects took the form of female statuettes, nude and sexualized, with all the associations of erotic iconography. They often accompanied the deceased into the next life, attested in the tombs of Setau (1352) and Sennefer (1159A) at Deir el Medina (Meskell 1998c: 367–8).

In the later years of the life cycle it was customary for children to look after their parents. Again, Deir el Medina provides the best evidence. Older workmen at the site might have been provisioned by the state, but they still needed support from their families. One text suggests that older workmen left their job so that their sons could assume their positions (McDowell 1999: 37). In return the son had to provide rations for his father regularly in his retirement; Weskhetnemtet gave his father over half his own monthly salary. Moving into old age, many people felt financially insecure, in particular widows and unmarried individuals. It was the duty of family members to provide for them, but that duty could easily be neglected. Recalcitrant children could not be forced to repay the debt to their parents, but legal action could prevent them from inheriting at the point of death. The woman Naunakhte had eight children, but those who failed to support her in life were punished in her will: *This day, the lady Naunakhte made a record of her property before the following court: the chief workman Nakhtemmut, the chief workman Inherkhau . . . She said: As for me, I am a free woman of the land of Pharaoh. I raised these eight servants of yours, and I outfitted them with everything that is usual for people of their character. Now look, I have become old, and look, they do not care for me. As for those who put their hands in my hand, to them I will give my property; (but) as for those who gave me nothing, to them I will not give of my property.* [19] Naunakhte did not have a great deal to leave her children, but her statement served to give symbolic weight to the cultural importance of familial responsibility.

We often assume that in ancient societies people lived fairly short lives, never reaching what we would consider old age. However, burial data from the Eastern Necropolis reveal several elderly men and women found in tombs 1370, 1379, and 1389. Recent analysis has shown that one woman named Iyneferti, buried in the Western Necropolis, lived to an age exceeding seventy-five years (Mahmoud 1999). The more informal tomb iconography found at Deir el Medina also illustrates elderly individuals with gray and white hair. These specific representations of the elderly break with the traditional portrayals of the human body as youthful, beautiful, and perfect. In old age, men could be shown stooping, with rolls of fat around the stomach and with white hair. But what was acceptable for men did not ipso facto extend to women, and it was not customary for women to be portrayed as old and unattractive. In the tomb of Pashedu

FIGURE 3.13. Painting from the Tomb of Pashedu, TT 3, Deir el Medina. (Photo courtesy of the IFAO, Cairo. Photograph by J-F Gout)

(TT 3) in the Western Necropolis at Deir el Medina, there are various depictions of his aged relatives: his father is shown with completely white hair, his mother with gray, his father-in-law with black hair streaked with gray, and his mother-in-law completely gray (Janssen and Janssen 1996: 23). Despite these indications, the faces and bodies of these individuals are depicted as youthful. In the Nineteenth Dynasty tomb of Ipy (TT 217) the owner is repeatedly shown with dark hair, except for the scene where he is deceased and pouring libations before the gods. In that vignette he is depicted with gray hair, at the point of leaving this world to go to the next.

Throughout this book I argue that the template of the life cycle coheres more closely with the Egyptian evidence than the traditional categorizations outlined in the first chapter. Textual, pictorial, and archeological evidence makes clear that the cycle itself was open to gendered differences. The experiences of adolescence and aging were significantly different for males and females, with consequent effects in social relations, whether it be earlier sexualization of girls, more marked male maturation, or the surplus of women who were divorced or widowed. Clearly men could also be widowed or divorced, although their life chances were greater as a result of their capabilities for work, wealth, and tomb provisioning. Marital experience in the *domus* forms the subject of the next chapter.

CHAPTER FOUR

Founding a House

I̶N EGYPT the household was the social and material bedrock of private relations. For the archaeologist and historian the house itself provides the critical framework from which to analyze everything from the material residues of the household to the social spaces and domains of inequality enacted in those spaces, along with specific individual experiences as expressed in letters and documents. The house was not necessarily a "home" in the Western sense, hence my choice of the term *household*. Much of the settlement data available suggests that extended family members, friends, and servants or slaves all resided under the same roof. The strict nuclear family does not mesh adequately with the Egyptian evidence: we might look critically toward anthropological studies of village life today to find alternative ways of envisioning private life in the New Kingdom.

HORIZONS OF MARRIAGE

Writings in the form of letters, verse, and legal documents allow insight into personal relations and social networks in the New Kingdom. Scholars have been drawn to the evidence for marriage, divorce, and the status of women, since they are interrelated topics that sustain great contemporary interest. It is perhaps for this reason, coupled with their seemingly familiar modes of expression, that these writings seem so evocative to a modern reader. In addition, there are no sources of comparable complexity in the ancient world dating to the second millennium; they are matched only by the later classical sources.

Idealized vignettes of romantic love and emotional maturity are derived predominantly from the "love songs" of the New Kingdom, discussed at length in Chapter 5. These evocative writings demonstrate that love between partners was supposed to be passionate, emotional, and sexual. Yet these texts were authored by a male elite and present a unitary picture of harmonious life that tends to flatten out diversity and difference. In many societies poetry occupies a liminal space where individuals can escape the narrow confines and rigid expectations of social order. This discrepancy between poetic and nonpoetic discourses seems also to have existed in pharaonic Egypt, where love poetry often seems at odds with legal and economic texts. This prompts the question: which is the more authentic expression of personal experience, and can various aspects exist simultaneously? Many unions may have been based upon real feelings and choice, rather than merely upon social or economic prerogatives. For example, scholars have suggested a closely knit pattern of organized marriage between higher-status families at Deir el Medina (Robins 1993a). Given the frequency of serial marriages, separations, and divorces in the texts from Deir el Medina, I would question the notion of arranged marriages that implies a rather more serious, socially sanctioned undertaking. Parents might have orchestrated some marriages; however, most documentary evidence points to consensual arrangements between men and women. Since there was no formal marriage ceremony, this suggests that "marriage" was a private rather than public event invested with the weight of religious and state pressure. The didactic texts of the period such as the *Instruction of Ani* recommend a man marry while young. The Middle Kingdom *Teachings of Ptahhotep* advises a husband to *love your wife with proper ardour*, and to *fill her belly, clothe her back*. He contends a man should not divorce his wife, because she is like *a fertile field*. Such texts also instruct a man how to construct his house and gardens, since these tasks were his responsibility. More pointedly Ptahhotep warns against women: *Remove her from power, suppress her!... Restraining her is how to make her remain in your house; a female who is under her own control is rainwater.*[1]

Marriage is generally considered a formative ritual, changing life status with concomitant social reorganization. Some Egyptian phrases have been interpreted as analogous to this arrangement: *bringing a bundle, to live with, to found a house*. A young man relays a story of deception by his new "wife" by saying *I brought the bundle to the house of Payom, and I made his daughter (my) wife.*[2] *Bringing a bundle* might refer to the provision of a dowry. These acts of reciprocity also had significant import when things went wrong. A marriage could be dissolved in a manner similar to its instigation. And there are numerous instances of marital problems, adultery, and divorce. Obviously there must have been an entire spectrum of sociosexual relations that existed outside the confines of that specific relationship. In New Kingdom Egypt, one could argue, women had a certain amount of social freedom, yet this did not add up to equality of social standing or to economic independence.

When looking at the sources, we confront the familiar problem, that the towns of Amarna, Gurob, or Deir el Ballas have yielded virtually nothing in terms of textual data. The vast majority of information stems from Deir el Medina, and it is the experience of those villagers in the Ramesside Period that has shaped interpretations. For an unusually literate village with thousands of personal texts, it is surprising that there is no documentation about the reasons behind partner choice, the dates of these events, or related celebrations. Such processes are also invisible in the archaeological record. Young couples may have founded a house through the bonds of love, but this did not mean that they could always live separately without the attachments of family. At Deir el Medina it is likely that the new couple would have to live in a parent's house, for rea-

FIGURE 4.1. Deir el Medina House, NE3. (Photo courtesy of the author)

sons of tradition, expense, or housing limitations. Evidence from Roman Egypt also suggests that married children resided with their parents, and the conjugal family was often the result of attrition or death (Bagnall and Frier 1994: 61). Adult life was fraught with the tensions that these domestic scenarios presented in the course of everyday life. The accommodation and provisioning of extended family members no doubt exacerbated strained situations: *From Takhentyshepse to her sister Iye ... I shall send you barley, and you shall have it ground for me and add emmer to it. And you shall make me bread with it, for I have been quarrelling with Merymaat (my husband). "I will divorce you," he keeps saying when he quarrels with me on account of my mother in questioning the amount of barley required for bread. "Now your mother does nothing for you," he keeps telling me and says, "Although you have brothers and sisters, they don't take care of you," he keeps telling me in arguing with me daily.*[3]

House data from Deir el Medina suggest another alternative to living with one's parents, that of having neighboring residences. In some cases it is possible to determine the names of specific house owners from surviving inscribed lintels on the outer doorways of village houses. Without fail the house was ascribed to the male head of the household, followed by his title and then the "woman of the house." This term was mainly used in the contexts of monuments, whereas the term *ḥmt* was more generally used to denote both a woman and a wife in documents. The word for husband in such texts was *ḫЗy* (Toivari 2000: 23). A look at the small number of known names and patterns of relatedness shows that sons often resided in houses adjacent or close to their fathers. One example is Sennedjem in house SW6, whose son Khabekhenet lived next door in SW7; the mechanisms by which Khabekhenet obtained the property, however, are unknown. Nevertheless, the small number of surviving named lintels limits the possibility for establishing a conclusive pattern.

LIFE CHOICES

The textual data suggest there was little restriction (other than opportunity) on marrying outside one's own social stratum. There are well documented royal cases such as Amenhotep III and queen Tiye, who was nonroyal but who came from a local elite family. At Deir el Medina it seems to have been possible for a prominent man, in this case a sculptor named Neferenpet, to make pregnant and thus raise the status of a household slave (O. Nelson 13 in Toivari 2000: 160). He writes home to the rest of his family urging them to provide adequately for her. Whether she then lived as his wife or as a dependent woman is another matter and is unclear from the letter.

In another case, a man named Nebnefer and his wife, Rennefer, together bought a slave girl who subsequently gave birth to three children. Rennefer raised these children, since she was childless. One of the children was then married to Rennefer's younger brother, Padiu, and all three were granted their freedom (Eyre 1992: 208). In this case a slave was brought into a household to provide progeny, which may have been a common and acceptable solution for childless couples. Adoption may have been another strategy that ensured provision for old age and similarly facilitated generational succession. Instances such as these attest to some of the major social changes experienced in the lives of ordinary people, relating to freedom, choice, and, to some degree, personal relationships.

In this village there are numerous examples of local men marrying foreigners, a practice which seems to have occurred frequently and apparently without censure. Ramesside times were marked by multiculturalism, including the presence of foreign individuals and the use of foreign names by Egyptians. William Ward (1994) proposed that foreigners, from Mycenaeans to Persians, were present at Deir el Medina. He concluded that the majority of these individuals lived in the village, that their recent ancestors were foreign, and that many of the women were "housewives" to ordinary workmen. The latter did not reach the position of scribe or chief workman, suggesting a possible link between ancestry, ethnicity, and status. Ward suggested that local custom or prejudice may have restricted their social mobility. An interesting case is Iyneferty, who was married to the prominent scribe Sennedjem and whose parentage seems to have been foreign—her father having the Hurrian name Zilli, her mother Ati. Although Iyneferty has an Egyptian name, her son Bunakhtef was also known as "the Canaanite," and a niece was named Ataya after her maternal grandmother (Ward 1994: 71–72). Irrespective of her possible roots, Iyneferty went on to marry one of the wealthiest and most powerful men of the village.

At Tell ed Daba in the Delta, the Hyksos capital of Avaris, there is evidence from the Second Intermediate Period onward for foreign men living in the town and marrying local women. Biological anthropologists have determined this from the physical remains, and archaeologists have confirmed the finding by analyzing the Canaanite weaponry and objects placed with the deceased. Even tomb styles reflected the waxing and waning of Syro-Palestinian influence in the city (Bietak 1995). Given the wealth of these tombs, we might adduce that such relations were acceptable, perhaps even encouraged.

Another issue is that of brother-sister marriages among ordinary people. Jaroslav Černý analyzed some 490 marriages from the First Intermediate

Period to the beginning of the Eighteenth Dynasty and found two possible cases of brother-sister marriage. According to later analysis by Robins (1979), even these two instances fail to provide evidence for a marriage between siblings. It is likely though that marriage between cousins, stepsiblings, and uncles and nieces was fairly common. Using the Stato Civile, Černý claimed that there was no conclusive evidence that married couples in the village were directly related. These results were largely corroborated in a study of familial relations in tomb paintings of the Eighteenth Dynasty, where brother-sister marriages were not attested (Whale 1989: 251–52). Kinship terms used in the tombs, such as *snt*, *nbt pr*, and *ḥmt*, have a range of meanings that changed in nuance and referent during the Dynasty. Finally, love poetry that refers to lovers as brother and sister seems to have wrongly induced scholars to take this metaphor of closeness literally. Černý demonstrated (1954: 5) that such terms for lovers were not employed prior to the Eighteenth Dynasty.

But what of those people who could not or chose not to marry, for whatever reason? One text tells of a woman who repeatedly threw a man out of her house despite him bringing all his *property in order to live with them*[4] with the intention of becoming her husband. The didactic texts as well as personal letters and ritual representations give the impression that the optimum social scenario entailed a heterosexual relationship with many offspring. Magical spells and votive offerings record the trauma for women and men who were without children as well as their public shame, as in the case of scribe Nekhemmut (see page 65). Egyptian society largely revolved around the family and its cycles of reciprocity, both in this world and the next. However, it is probable that unmarried individuals might have been resident in many households, just as those who were widowed or divorced were taken in. Unsurprisingly, those who failed to conform to the heterosexual norm were not mentioned in the official sources and thus were hidden from history (see Chapter 5). And while we know same-sex relationships existed and even mythical texts accept their possibility, we are unable to reconstruct those unnamed aspects of private life.

ADULTERY, DOMESTIC VIOLENCE, AND DIVORCE

Where texts are abundant, it is clear that marriage, divorce, and remarriage were prevalent states of being. Remarriage occurred irrespective of age, number of marriages, or negative experience—common also to Euro-American culture. Both men and women could instigate a divorce, but at Deir el Medina the ratio exhibits a marked disparity—12:3 in favor of men divorcing or threatening to divorce women (Toivari 1998: 1162). Adultery was not necessarily a punishable offence, and wrongdoing was attributed to the husband of a guilty wife, since it was he who was ostensibly compromised. An affair involving a married man and a single woman caused little disruption. Didactic texts such as those of Ptahhotep or Ani all hint that adultery was construed as an abuse of a man's property, not a criminal act per se. Instructional texts, and the stereotypes they reflect, exemplify the contempt in which women were held in terms of their honesty, discretion, and fidelity (Eyre 1984: 98). It was not always necessary to go before a court to instigate a separation, but it was advisable when money, wrongdoing, or violence were involved, as the text cited below illustrates. As Eyre has argued, the texts present a picture in which sexual behavior in the New Kingdom was not governed by a rigid moral code.

> *If you want to make a friendship last*
> *inside a house you enter—*
> *whether as lord, or brother, or friend,*
> *wherever you enter—*
> *beware of approaching the women!*
> *There is nothing good about the place where this is done.*[5]

Different levels of social freedom were exercised by individual couples, probably depending on status, economic expectation, or village politics, as well as personality. In a close-knit village such as Deir el Medina many marriage arrangements, and disintegrations, were publicly known. An acrimonious event is documented in Papyrus BM 10416, which narrates how a group of men and women went to find and punish a woman whom they accused of having an eight-month affair with one of their relatives (Janssen 1988: 137): *we are going to beat her, together with her people.* The writer appears to be related to the woman, possibly her son. He suggests that the man, Nesamenemope, go to court with his own wife and settle the matter formally: *If the heart of that man is after you, let [him] enter the court together with his wife and let [him] swear an oath and return to your house.* Such practices must have been crucial as mechanisms regulating behavior within local communities. In situations like this, with the possibilities of excessive violence, approaching the court may have been the final recourse. Presumably other, less volatile, separations were even more common.

One text from Deir el Medina documents the date of formal separation between Hesysunebef and his wife Hel, possibly due to an infidelity on her side: *Year 2, third month of summer, day 24, of pharaoh Sethnakhte, life, prosperity, health: (day) Hesysunebef divorced the lady Hel. I spent 3 years giving to her an oipe of emmer every single month, making 9 sacks. And she gave me a sash, saying, "Offer it at the riverbank (the marketplace); it will be bought from me for an oipe of emmer." I offered it, but people rejected it, saying, "It is bad!" And I told her exactly that, saying, "It has been rejected."*...[6] We know something of the lives of these two individuals, as we do for many for the Deir el Medina villagers. Hesysunebef started his life as a slave and was later adopted by his master to become a member of the team of workmen. He rose to the important rank of deputy. Devoted to his adoptive parents, he named his children after them and dedicated a stela to his father (McDowell 1999: 43). His wife Hel formerly lived with the workman Pendua, but was unfaithful to both these men with the same man, the notorious chief workman Paneb. As Andrea McDowell suggests, this infidelity may have prompted the divorce, especially since Paneb had threatened to kill Hesysunebef's father. Intense social relationships and ruptures seem to have been enacted rather publicly in the village and were subsequently recorded. Yet, private life is often correlated with the preserve of the house. Individual houses at Deir el Medina have many stories to tell. Furthermore, they encompass a series of social spaces which offer substantive information about sex, relationships, and status (Meskell 1998b).

The frequency of marriage breakdown might be conjectured from a single text, in the form of an oath between a concerned father and his prospective son-in-law that was sworn and witnessed in front of four men including a chief workman and a prominent scribe. The proposed punishment for transgression was severe, and one wonders how such a threat could be put into practice. But it serves to highlight that the possibility of a woman being abandoned was a real concern and that its ramifications for the family as well as the husband were worrisome matters: *Make Nakhtemut take an oath of the lord, life, prosperity, and health, saying, "I will not abandon my daughter." Oath of the lord, life, prosperity, and health, that he swore: "As Amen endures, as the ruler endures, if I go back on my word and abandon the daughter of Tenermonthu in the future, I will receive one hundred blows and be deprived of all the property that I will acquire with her."*[7] The terms for divorce attested in the texts are *to repudiate, to throw out,* and *to go away,* the latter being reserved for use by the wife (Toivari 2000: 86).

Numerous texts recording the breakdown of marital relations demonstrate that these ruptures were chiefly to the detriment of women. If a woman had not been found guilty of adultery, she could ideally expect one-third of the conjugal property (Janssen and Pestman 1968: 165). Economically and socially, the exclusion of women from their familial home meant a life of insecurity and poverty. Divorce sealed their fate, and, unless their own children provided for them or they remarried, the rest of their lives was guaranteed to be difficult. What happened to children with respect to separation or divorce is unknown to us. Women were frequently ejected from their marital home, and presumably their own parents had to provide for them once again. Sometime in the Nineteenth Dynasty the workman Horemwia promised his daughter Tanetdjesere that if her husband Baki threw her out he would give her a room in his storehouse. Horemwia's own house was provided by the state, but he built and owned the storehouse outright and thus could offer it as a refuge to his daughter.[8] It is unlikely that the state actually monitored house occupants, although the Stato Civile may reflect such a process. As previously noted, the document gives the impression of smaller households than other documentary and genealogical data (Bierbrier 1975) might support.

The hardships posed by unmarried life were even more evident in a woman's burial. For the most part, women were included in the Eighteenth Dynasty tombs of their husbands, examples being Kha and Merit or Sennefer and Nefertiry (Meskell 1998c). But in the Eastern Necropolis there were examples of women buried on their own, or with other women, who may have been single or divorced. These burials were located toward the peak of the necropolis in the region assigned to adults. If fortunate, these women may have been able to prepare their own funerary arrangements or, alternatively, relied on their children, mainly sons, for such preparations. In tomb 1371 the poorly preserved body of the woman Nub is buried in an anthropoid coffin, surrounded by worldly possessions: bed, furniture, mirror, toiletries, ceramics, and food (Bruyère 1937: 158–61). Another woman was buried alone in tomb 1380 and on her anthropoid coffin was inscribed the formulaic *ḥmt n* . . . (wife of) . . . but no male name is inscribed. Bruyère incorrectly interpreted this as a mark of her status as a "concubine." His conclusion is not founded on particularly firm evidence, but rather his early impression that the Eastern Necropolis was the burial place of female musicians and dancers. Lastly, there was the unorthodox interment of two women buried together in tomb 1388. These women appear to have been of similar age and had approximately the same type of burial equipment with corresponding cost (Meskell 1999a: 155–56). Contrary to the excavator's suggestion, there was no male interred with them, and the tomb was found largely intact. Individual women, buried alone and perhaps living outside the parameters of family life, probably represent a larger sector of the community than previously recognized. Such circumstances were part of many women's lives, and the fluidity of the marriage union meant that its dissolution was prevalent, producing a number of individuals, at various life stages, who found themselves outside the usual network of social support. Older women probably found themselves replaced in later life by younger women (see Chapter 5). The male habit of serial marriage ensured a surfeit of divorcees in antiquity, just as it does in modern rural Egypt.

From the workman Khnummose to his colleague Ruty:
My son spent two years carrying his water. A wall fell down in his storehouse, and I built it up; and I used 5 donkey-loads of water for it, too. I plastered 3 places on top of his house, and also the stairs of his tomb. His wife spent 40 days dwelling with me in my house, and I provided for her, giving her 1 sack of emmer and 10 loaves. And he threw

FIGURE 4.2. Tomb Assemblage, TT 1388, Eastern Necropolis. (Photo courtesy of the IFAO, Cairo)

her out again, and she spent 20 days in the house of Menna, while I supplied 3 oipe of emmer, 1 inet-garment (?), 1 khet-measure of sety-fruit.[9]

SOCIAL AND ANTISOCIAL SPACE

Through the processes of excavation, recording, and presentation of settlements, archaeologists inevitably leave us with the impression of static villages and normative life. House plans and room assemblages do little to animate our interpretations of daily occurrences. By using the textual data dialectically we may be able to apprehend those sensuous biographies, at least for some of the people at Deir el Medina. When we overlay their experiences onto the framework of the houses, we see that private life was neither static nor even "social" for much of the time, and that many incidents in it might make us recoil, as they do in any society.

The most notorious man in Deir el Medina's history was Paneb, who was both violent and sexually abusive (Janssen 1997: 106). He was accused of various crimes such as murder, rape, bribery, theft, and physical abuse, yet through his position and influence he always managed to escape retribution. He and his son Aapahty were accused of either raping or having intercourse with married women such as Tuy, Hunero, and Hunero's daughter (Černý 1929: 245; Eyre 1984: 94). In all likelihood these incidents took place in or around village houses: one rape is charged as occurring at the *top of the wall*. Similarly, he forced women to weave for him, exploiting their only means of production. At the height of the feuding he went to the house of his adoptive father and *took a stone and broke his doors,* shouting, *"I will kill him in the night."*[10] His presence must have been a potential source of fear to both men and women alike. In the end a case was brought to the vizier, and a copy of the letter written by the scribe Amennakht survives to this day: Černý thought it unlikely that the vizier ever received it.

As previously highlighted, domestic problems and violence seem to have been commonplace. This need not surprise in a village such as Deir el Medina where the population was circumscribed, several generations lived together, and families intermarried over the years. The Amarna workman's village might have been a short-lived parallel. At Deir el Medina there were jealousies and rivalries over prestigious positions in the workforce and presumably over rights to the limited housing available. The men left their households for days at a time, and many people lived with servants or slaves, presenting their own sets of problems. We have seen evidence for prominent men having sexual relationships with servants, some of whom bore children. There is no consensus on the issue of "concubinage," but polygyny seems unlikely for many among the nonelite. A late Twentieth Dynasty marriage settlement, witnessed by necropolis workmen, refers to one woman as both *ḥmt* and *ḥbswt* (Černý and Peet 1927), the latter sometimes translated as "concubine." Given the interchangeable or synonymous nature of the terms it is unlikely that *ḥbswt* signified a specific, incontrovertible status. In fact, the meaning of the word *ḥbswt* has been discussed by Egyptologists for over a century. The Middle Kingdom letter of Heqanakhte to his household warns them not to mistreat or have intercourse with his *ḥbswt* (Eyre 1984: 98), but this does not prove the term's meaning (see also Robins 1993b: 61). William Ward suggested (1986: 66) that it refers to a legal second (or third, etc.) wife, and in the context of the squabbles of the Heqanakhte household, this makes good sense. Ward's view may be supported by a passage in the tomb robbery papyri where the woman Mutemheb is referred to as both *ḥmt* and *ḥbswt* of the goldsmith Ramose. She states: *I am the fourth wife, two are dead and the other is (still) alive.*[11] Similarly, other texts from Deir el Medina present a picture of serial marriages rather than contemporaneous ones. Again this pattern is replicated in the depictions of relationships in tomb painting of the period (Whale 1989: 273). This still leaves us with questions about the acceptance of women who were not wives: female servants or slaves were an obvious avenue for sexual activity and producing offspring. How did other women of the household respond? Some may have divorced over it, others may have turned a blind eye, and still others may have felt relieved of certain responsibilities. Multiple scenarios must be envisioned.

Whether the Egyptians had "slaves" as well as "servants" is a long-standing point of contention. Relying on translations of terms such as $b3k$ or hm can be misleading since we inevitably miss the cultural nuances they provide. There was a host of other terms used in royal decrees and administrative texts we might translate as "dependent," "personnel," "forced laborers," "workers," "servants," "royal servants," and "prisoners of war" that might also denote slave status (Loprieno 1997; 185). It seems certain, however, that people could be bought and sold, as in the case of Tentuendjede and her son Gemiamun, both described as slaves.[12] Both were owned by a builder named Wenenamun, who entrusted them to the merchant Amenkhau. The latter had passed them on, and their ownership had been thrown into question. Wenenamun was understandably upset that his property had been taken, and it is clear that this sort of situation was common: *it is just like those many others who were carried off*. Later in the same text Tentuendjede is referred to as a *conscriptable servant*, which further complicates her status for the modern interpreter. Given the ambiguity of these terms we might do better to view people like Tentuendjede and Gemiamun as those whose services were bought and sold for indefinite periods. Their servitude may also have been temporally circumscribed, since people may have expected to be released after repaying their debts— or even generational, whereby an unfree person's children would have been free. As noted previously, this was the case with workman Nebnefer's children (Eyre 1992: 208), born to a slave but later freed.

Loprieno (1997: 186) sensibly argues that, from a hermeneutic perspective, interpreting the social structures of one civilization by means of the paradigms of reference of another is always a spurious activity. In Egypt, it is best to view slavery as a sliding scale, ranging from those slaves captured in military campaigns, such as Libyans or Hyksos, to native Egyptians who may have been forced to sell themselves because of economic hardship. In his autobiography, Ahmose, son of Ibana, talks of the destruction of Avaris and the spoils of war: *one man, three women; total four persons. His majesty gave them to me as slaves*.[13] From the various campaigns in Nubia and the Delta he was given twenty slaves in reward for his good service. During the height of the empire, military and commercial exploitation brought many Asiatics into Egypt either as booty or as slaves bought from slave markets (Loprieno 1997: 202). Analysis by Loprieno suggests that foreign slaves, in contrast to Egyptian servants, were treated as objects to be traded rather than as individuals employed for a specific service.

There were also cases where private slaves were conscripted for state service, as in the reign of Akhenaten, in this case for the purposes of gathering saffron (Murnane 1995: 237). Misuse of a slave or servant of the state by an individual could be met with legal prosecution and severe punishment: an example is the workman Baki from Deir el Medina who unlawfully employed a woman called Paanmahu (Davies and Toivari 1997). Despite the ambiguities, we can say that there was ownership of people in Egypt, whether by the state or by individuals, and that there existed a wide range of levels of subjection within the world of work. People could be disposed of in bequests and their services sold by their owners. In later periods these procedures were marked by written agreements, as was self-sale (Bakir 1952: 81). However, the model of chattel slavery connotes a picture heavily influenced by the Classical example and colored by the Western imaginary and is inappropriate to these complex and fluid variations in status.

Some of the best evidence for the employment of a servile group comes from Deir el Medina. Jaroslav Černý demonstrated that the state provided female slaves for individual households. Both workmen and slaves were paid in grain rations.[14] Although these women were servants employed and administered by the state, they probably lived in the village and formed attachments to families. One theory is that the villagers privately owned numerous slaves whom they used to farm the nearby fields (McDowell 1992a: 201), providing an additional source of income. The female servants provided by the state may have occupied a servile status but might not have been bought in the same way as the woman Irynefer "bought" her own slaves from a trader (Eyre 1998: 179, see also the following section, "Personal Freedoms"). Some householders must have had to carry out the work themselves when they exchanged the duties of their servants for commodities. Texts demonstrate that people could trade their servants' labor for other goods or services.[15] The workman Kasa sells *his day of servant*, only receiving a basket and sieve in return.[16] Other slaves were "rented" for small sums to help with mundane tasks such as cloth production, as in the case of a woman called Harit purchased by the shepherd Mesi.[17] Our views on Egyptian households must thus include the presence of related and nonkin individuals and concomitant patterns of social organization.

As the above suggests, the *house* should not necessarily be conflated with a *home*. The texts give an impression that the house was a private domain and that there was a certain sanctity to this space. The idea that a woman might depart the house leaving the door open suggests a symbolic link between the specific act and the opening up of the household to public view (Borghouts 1981: 18). Some sixty-eight houses were crowded into the enclosed compound at Deir el Medina, arranged in house blocks sharing communal walls and narrow laneways. The close proximity of villagers and the interrelatedness of so many families inevitably led to many trysts and tensions. Life in the village was peppered by social and antisocial events: festivals, adoptions, infidelities, strikes, robberies, assaults, and

FIGURE 4.3. Deir el Medina Laneways. (Photo courtesy of the author)

homicide. *Really, it was not in order that you might become blind to your wife that I took you aside and said, "You should see the things that you've done [on behalf of (?)] your wife." You rebuffed me only to become deaf to this crime...I will make you aware of those adulterous acts that your [wife] has committed at your expense. (Response to the preceding): But she isn't my wife! Were she my wife, she would cease uttering her words (charges?) and get out leaving the door open.*[18]

PERSONAL FREEDOMS

Before discussing many of the issues surrounding domestic life and social relations, it is necessary to reconsider the position of women in the New Kingdom. Previous studies have tended to overplay the personal freedoms of elite women, treating women as a homogeneous group without considering the entire social spectrum. The work of Gay Robins has done much to adjust this picture (1993b, 1994–95, 1996); however, the illusion of equality persists. Some of the most common misconceptions about women's lives are summed up neatly in the following unsubstantiated generalizations: "All in all, women could not complain of their lot in comparison with the lives of women in other countries, or indeed those of women in many an Eastern country now. In day-to-day matters she was in numerous respects an equal partner, subject of course to her social background. We have plenty of evidence of this from prehistoric times onwards. The wife was always entitled to her own grave and funerary gifts, statues, steles, false-doors, etc. Even in the range of offerings laid in her grave a woman's burial was no different from a man's of the same background" (Strouhal 1992: 58).

First, there is a tendency to compare the favorable lot of Egyptian women with cultures we barely understand, and the experience of very different social categories of women is conflated. As Eyre (1998: 173) has argued, this is neither accurate nor helpful. Second, it is assumed that we can make a coherent statement about women's social position as if a single sphere defined it—primarily the legal and economic. In Western culture what looks equitable on paper does not always translate into the social realm or into individual experience. Moreover, a closer examination of even these spheres in the New Kingdom suggests that the opportunities for equality were indeed rare, and the exceptions might have needed recording, precisely because they were exceptional. Third, it was rare that women received their own tombs. Nonroyal women rarely owned funerary stelae or had statues, stelae and inscribed goods in their own right: they were normally an adjunct on their husbands' monuments. Strouhal's statement betrays a common scholarly sentiment, mainly derived from the aesthetic images of women and male-constructed love poems, that she was unconstrained and equal to any male. I suggest that a more complex picture be developed, one that looks at as many spheres of life as possible—economic, legal, social, domestic, religious, funerary, and so on—and takes into account disjuncture between those spheres, much as this is recognized in contemporary private life.

Christopher Eyre (1998) has shown that economic freedom, such as the well-attested practice of women trading, was an extension of women's role in domestic production. Scenes depicting women trading are known from tomb scenes from Old Kingdom times onwards. Women could also accumulate wealth if they belonged to the right socioeconomic group. A text regarding a lawsuit involving the woman Irynefer and her slaves documents this financial independence while simultaneously outlining the very different positions of the individual women. Irynefer states: *I am the wife of the Overseer of the District Samut, and I came to live in his house, and I worked on spinning and I wove my cloth. Now in year 15, in the 7th year since I entered the house of Samut, the trader Ria came to me with a Syrian slavegirl—she being a child—and he said to me, "Buy yourself this child, give me her price."*[19]

In a time before currency, bartering in goods with ascribed values was the mechanism of trade. So Irynefer paid for the young girl with several pieces of costly linen, objects of copper/bronze, and produce that had taken seven years to accumulate as a surplus (Eyre 1998: 179). This demonstrates that women of her rank could accumulate such capital independently and dispose of it freely. Indirectly it shows the marked discrepancies of women's experience and their complicity in the oppression of others, irrespective of sex or age. The cloth women wove was a valuable market commodity worth more than many metal items, as seen in the relative costs of tomb goods in burials such as those of Kha and Merit (Meskell 1998c). Cloth production was an important household activity. It was not industrialized but operated through a network of households and was a valuable source of income for women both married and divorced. The latter is an important point, since women without the traditional family networks must have required some skill to support themselves. And they could work from home without the possibilities of social stigma attached to "outside" work. Weaving was no doubt preferable to working in the fields. Numerous texts, as well as archaeological finds from Deir el Medina, attest to the importance of producing, buying, and selling cloth and clothing that were independent of state provisioning (Valbelle 1985: 249–50; Eyre 1998: 182). Other texts suggest women could keep poultry or small animals, maintain small vegetable gardens (Eyre 1998: 186), or trade dairy products.[20] The entrepreneurial spirit was high among women, whereas at Deir el Medina men were heavily occupied with royal tomb construction.

The evidence for cloth production may relate to the dowry or "bundle" that women brought to the marriage agreement. As her primary source of capital, she was in principle free to administer it. Yet it is easy to envisage situations where women's husbands curbed their economic activities: it was an ideal, perhaps not always the norm. Texts also show that women could be legal holders of agricultural land, although they needed male relatives or lessees to administer their holdings. But as Eyre notes (1998: 184), their activity and influence in decision making is completely invisible. In pharaonic times the profile of women as landholders is restricted to tax registers, which may suggest that their names were used for financial reasons and not because they controlled their holdings. Only in Graeco-Roman times do we see women mobilizing their landholdings. Here it may be better to see many women operating as adjuncts to their husbands, whether in supplementing the household economy through textile production or in administering their property.

Andrea McDowell (1999: 40) has argued that the legal position of women with regard to their own property was equivalent to that of men. Both inherited equally from their parents, and any property that a woman brought into a marriage remained her own. If the marriage was dissolved by divorce or the death of her husband, she would keep this property and also one third of the wealth the couple had acquired together, unless it was her adultery that brought on the dissolution of the marriage. However, these ideal scenarios must have been moderated by serious forms of exploitation. In theory, women could buy and sell, and use the courts or be prosecuted in them, just like men. Yet by a significant ratio they were more often the defendants than the claimants. As previously cited, men divorced women four times as often as women did men (see page 5). Both facts suggest that while the possibilities existed, the realities for women were much harsher and more circumscribed. In legal terms women may have been directly or indirectly cast as equals, but the delivery of justice was another matter and those silences do not go unnoted.

DOMESTIC SCENARIOS: RITUAL SPACE AND DOMESTIC CULT

The sites that have yielded the greatest evidence for domestic cults are the two well-excavated workers' villages of Amarna and Deir el Medina. From the former we have only archaeological materials, while at the latter we also have a vast documentary record of cultic duties, local festivals, and personal rituals. The *qnbt*, or local court, also met in the chapel area at Deir el Medina (McDowell 1990). Sixteen seats, some inscribed with workmen's names, were excavated from these chapels, possibly relating to the court or other secular activities. At both sites there were zones in close proximity to the village for private chapels, where personal worship took place (see Figure 4.5). At Deir el Medina, chapels and courtyards of private tombs adjacent to the settlement provided an additional forum. Individual Ramesside tombs incorporated chapels for the most part, as opposed to the simpler Eighteenth Dynasty tombs, which did not. Unlike mortuary chapels, votive chapels were dedicated to deities such as Ptah, Meretseger, Taweret, and Sobek, or to deified royalty such as Amenhotep I and Ahmose Nefertari (Bruyère 1930: 4). Men in the village performed priestly functions, some having titles relating to Hathor and her cult. They may have made sacred objects that were offered at various shrines (Pinch 1993: 300). There were other options for cultic practice: people could leave votive offerings at the nearby temples and worship in their own houses. Additionally there were people who offered assistance as "seers" or as oracles and those who prepared spells or amulets for the purposes of magic. Sometimes these questions were short and direct, requiring a yes or no response: *My good lord! Shall we be given rations? As to the cattle that the woman is claiming, does she have a share in them? As to the dreams which one sees, are they good?*[21] Much of this activity may have taken place in the community chapels. Ancestor busts may have been paraded around the chapel area on specific occasions, since some examples have been found outside the domestic context: six were discovered north of the Hathor temple (Friedman 1985; Bomann 1991: 69). On a strictly household level, evidence comes from wall paintings, ritual fixtures, votive stelae, and ancestor busts (Figure 4.4) as well as an array of ritual objects. Favored deities included Bes, Taweret, Hathor, and Meretseger, each of whom had a direct connection with people residing in these communities.

The Deir el Medina houses offer substantive evidence for ritual life and were recorded in some detail in the 1930s by Bernard Bruyère (1939). The majority of wall paintings and fixtures were located in the first and second rooms. This first room was notionally female-oriented, centered around elite, married, sexually potent, fertile females of the household. It was laden with what we would describe as sexual and ritual images. Yet this space may also have been used for sleeping, eating, and general domestic duties for many hours of the day. I have previously suggested (Meskell 1998b) that the significance of the second room, or divan room, which had the highest frequency of ritual finds, revolved around the socioritual lives of the elite men of the household.

The first room is usually designated the room of the enclosed bed, or *lit clos*. The majority of the houses have conclusive evidence of this bedlike structure. Its dimensions were roughly 1.7 m long, 80 cm wide, and 75 cm above floor level (Friedman 1994: 97). In house SE5 the *lit clos* was plastered, with molded and painted figures of Bes, the male deity associated with women, sexuality, fertility, music, and magic (Pinch 1994: 43, 116). Bes predominates in this room throughout the site. House C5 has a *lit clos*

FIGURE 4.4. Painted Ancestor Bust. (Photo courtesy of the British Museum, EA 61083)

Figure 4.5. Chapels at Deir el Medina. (Photo courtesy of the author)

with an associated Bes painting, and in the house of the woman Iyneferty, SW6, there are also Bes decorations. The enclosed bed was associated with a constellation of features: white walls, paintings, moldings, niches, Bes decorations, cultic cupboards, shrines, etc. (Meskell 1998b). Bruyère introduced the term *lit clos*, and the concept of the bed, primarily the birthing bed, has been a pervasive interpretation (Friedman 1994: 97). The *lit clos* meant something very specific in his own French culture, a type of day bed, which is undoubtedly inappropriate in this context. But there are additional difficulties with this theory. For instance, there is ample evidence, in the form of figured ostraca from the site (Vandier d'Abbadie 1937), for the traditional birthing apparatus being a stool (or bricks), rather than a bed. As proposed in Chapter 3, birth arbors may have been specially constructed outdoor buildings. Most enclosed beds are of a size and form that preclude sleeping or other activities.

Archaeological evidence linking cultic practices with the *lit clos* can be found in individual houses at Deir el Medina and Amarna (Robins 1996: 29–30). At Amarna there is evidence of something like a *lit clos* structure in the wealthy house of Panehesy (Frankfort 1927: 11–13). On closer examination however, the structure is more akin to a small shrine, constructed from limestone, depicting Akhenaten and the royal family in this case, rather than the

FIGURE 4.6. A *Lit Clos* from House NE13, Deir el Medina. (Photo courtesy of the author)

traditional deities such as Bes who were later so prevalent at Deir el Medina. This structure could represent an early form of the *lit clos* or a more elite, expensive version than we witness at Deir el Medina. In house NE11 at Deir el Medina, Bruyère excavated a *lit clos* containing several items: a limestone headrest, part of a statue, and a fragment of a female statuette in limestone. In front of the *lit clos* was an offering table. In C7 the finds were similar. In NE15 and in Iyneferty's house, SW6, the structure is built with an associated cultic cupboard. These shrinelike constructions may have contained a stela, statue, or ancestor bust. This suggests a more generalized cultic function and one which may not exclude men, since a number of finds name men of the house: associated limestone offering tables or stelae often bear a male name, rather than a female one. Room 1 assemblages consist of primarily ritual artifacts: stelae, shrine busts, offering tables, and statues. This evidence warrants the general conclsion that a household cult, centered around mature females, was focused in the front rooms of Deir el Medina houses. In addition, this space could have been utilized on a daily basis for domestic activities, since troughs and mortars were found there in houses NE14 and SW1.

It is important to contextualize the wall paintings located in the first room. The front rooms were heavily decorated, having whitewashed walls with female-oriented paintings, scenes of nursing or grooming, and deities pertaining to women's lives. In SE1 there was a wall painting showing a

Figure 4.7. Painting of a Woman with Convovulus, House NE8, Deir el Medina. (Redrawn by the author)

woman breast-feeding, in C7 a scene of a female grooming with her attendant, and in NW12 a person on a papyrus skiff, probably female. The iconography of these wall paintings also appeared on items of everyday material culture. In SE8 workman Nebamun must have commissioned, either for himself or his family, the painting of a nude female musician with a tattoo on her upper thigh (Figure 4.7). She plays a double flute and is surrounded by convovulus leaves, which had an erotic symbolism (Pinch 1993: 220). This representation would have been immediately obvious to anyone entering the house. How did the Egyptians view these ritual and sexual images? My sense is that they were not considered separate spheres. Their messages of religiosity and sexuality exist side by side. This imagery should not be viewed as sexual in a pornographic sense, since ours is a highly articulated category (Hunt 1993) with a well-developed attendant discourse. In refiguring Egyptian experience, we might look to anthropology. For example, the contradictory character of sexual perceptions and attitudes can be seen in many cultures, especially in the Middle East today (Atiya 1984; Attir 1985: 122; Abu-Lughod 1986).

In the workman's village at Amarna only a couple of wall paintings have been preserved. These too were found in the first rooms of houses (Kemp 1979). In Main Street house 3 the scene consisted of a group of dancing

Bes figures, possibly adopting different postures with their heads and arms. At the right end of the painting was a depiction of the goddess Taweret holding a protective symbol. She was an important deity for woman and the household, primarily in regard to pregnancy and childbirth and was invoked to ensure protection at this dangerous and liminal time. Another wall painting was found in Long Wall Street house 10. The design was executed in thick white paint outlined over a plain gray plaster surface and, although it is badly damaged, we can discern a line of human figures advancing to the right. These represent three women wearing long, fringed gowns and separated by two girls, one of whom is naked, as was common for young girls. One of the women appears to have her foot raised as in a dancing position that is most commonly associated with dancers and musicians. Similar scenes of women celebrating have been found in the rock-cut tombs at Amarna, and there is a much published example in the tomb of Neferhotep on the Theban West Bank (Hodel-Hoenes 2000: 189). An associated find of a bin or fixture in front of this painting is suggested by Kemp to have been an altar of some sort, used in domestic ritual. The Amarna village provides a window on the persistence of ritual. Despite Akhenaten's instigation of a new religious program, there is scant evidence for ritual worship of the Aten in the village. Instead of depictions of the pharaoh and the sun disk we see the traditional deities that were a pervasive part of ritual and practical magic.

Also worth considering is Kemp's (1979: 52–3) early interpretation of wall paintings from domestic contexts at both Amarna and Deir el Medina. He suggests that the imagery could be read not merely as the celebration of childbirth, but also as reflecting the cessation of a dangerous, liminal time for women with its associated state of pollution, including taboos with serious effects on mature males in the household. Since the men would have constructed the *lits clos* and painted the murals in these rooms at Deir el Medina, they too probably had a vested interest in the experiences of women at this time. Given the elaborate decoration, ritual fixtures/objects, and generous use of red paint as potent protectors, male intervention cannot be underestimated. Underscoring this may have been fear, concepts of pollution or protection, or an amalgam of these. However, as Mary Douglas (1966: 3–4) famously cautioned, despite the prominence of such sexed patterns in so many societies, it is implausible that they say anything about actual relations between the sexes.

Moving further into the house, I propose that the second room, or divan room, had a predominantly elite male focus. This room, which is often the largest, has more intense use of ritual colors, fixtures, and objects, and its floor level is generally higher, indicating the approach to an enhanced ritual space, with a higher ceiling. Evidence from wealthy Amarna houses indicates that this main room had symbols that would impress the visitor,

FIGURE 4.8. Divan from Deir el Medina at the Time of Bruyère's Excavations. (Photo courtesy of the IFAO, Cairo)

notably the use of columns and decorated lintels. Columns are status symbols in themselves, often made from exotic imported wood. In addition, they could be plastered and painted with the names and titles of the house owner (Crocker 1985: 58). There are ethnohistoric parallels for such a space, with accompanying emplacements, reserved for men and their entertaining of other men for example, in early nineteenth century Islamic Egypt, as recorded and illustrated by E. W. Lane ([1836] 1989: 23–28). However, the segregation of the sexes here could be specifically Islamic.

The central focus in the elite male sphere would be the divan itself, which has a long history in the Middle East as a symbol of male activity, status, power relations, and hospitality among other elite males. Divans are also amply paralleled in the larger houses at Amarna. Many examples were noted by Peet and Woolley in East Street (nos. 1, 10, 11, 12, for example), Gate Street (no. 11), and Main Street (nos. 3, 5), though these represent only a selection of the overall sample (Peet and Woolley 1923: 70–76). Generally, their construction and decoration and their location in

FIGURE 4.9. Cultic Cupboard, House NE7, Deir el Medina. (Photo courtesy of the author)

the second room of the house were consistent with those found in the Ramesside houses at Deir el Medina.

In examining the divan room in NE13 (Bruyère 1939: 259), once belonging to the sculptor Ipy, the full impact of the room and its decoration becomes clear. One would enter the room after passing out of Room 1 with its decorated *lit clos*, through a limestone-framed door painted red. The walls of the divan room were brick and rough stone and decorated with white skirting to a height of 90 cm—an Egyptian practice that continues to this day. In the north wall above the skirting, a rectangular niche was inset, 25 cm by 35 cm, and 28 cm deep. The ground was stuccoed, and a column rose in front of the divan. The divan itself was constructed of brick and painted white. It had flaring armrests reminiscent of a column capital, the flaring part in yellow, the inside being white with a red band. There was also a small hearth with a brick curb, filled with ash and potsherds. The stone curb was a few centimeters above floor level with an attachment to the divan, so that Ipy could stand food containers there without direct contact with the fire. The overall effect of the painted divan in this columned room with a niche that probably contained a bust or stela was no doubt quite impressive.

These divans tend to be constructed in brick, are sometimes stone-lined, and always abut a major wall. Just as Room 1 with the *lit clos* has a constellation of associated features signifying its ritual focus, the divan room has its own specific markers. In NE12 it is a cultic cupboard (Figure 4.9), in SE6 an altar; more frequently we see false doors painted red and yellow. Nebamentet in SE7 had a false door and a wall painting; Nebamun next door in SE8 had a divan bordered by stone with two pilasters against the western wall, plus red false doors with a central yellow band (Bruyère 1930: 275). In mainstream mortuary practice, false doors were niched structures through which one's spirit could move back and forth freely, between this world and the other, to receive offerings. Such structures were common throughout Egyptian history, dating back to the beginning of the Dynastic period, though they are not generally considered part of the domestic repertoire. They may have facilitated contact with the spirits of ancestors, especially in view of the frequency of ancestor-related artifacts in this room (see Figure 4.4).

The divan room in Sennedjem's house, SW6 (Bruyère 1939: 332–34), produced additional finds of ritual objects, coupled with the standard ritual fixtures and decoration (although I speak of Sennedjem, it is possible that a later occupant completed the extant decoration). Sennedjem entered this room by walking through a limestone threshold, with jambs and lintels painted red. The brick frame of the door was also red, ensuring protection and ritual potency. Once inside, the divan room had a painted white skirting on the walls. The floor was stuccoed and painted red. His divan was situated against the east wall, having a limestone flagstone and also painted white. Though there was no false door, Sennedjem had a niche cut above the skirting line and possibly an altar along the west wall between the two doors. In this niche he may have kept an ancestral bust or stela. Archaeological finds indicate that Sennedjem kept an array of cultic items in this room, statues and shrines featuring Sobek, Maat, and one which he personally dedicated to Meretseger. Among the many shrine fragments, one was

FIGURE 4.10. Divan Room of Sennedjem, House SW6, Deir el Medina. (Photo courtesy of the author)

dedicated by his son Khabekhenet. Additionally, there was a limestone offering table, an amulet, an enigmatic sculpture of a pierced donkey, possibly used in magical practices, and some administrative papyri. The overall picture gleaned from Sennedjem's divan room is that of a space centered on the high-status man of the house, in both ritual and social spheres.

The villagers also called upon the deceased members of their own families, now in the realm of effective spirits and known as the *3ḫ iqr n R'*, "effective spirits of Re." We know this from the stelae they inscribed and erected in their houses and chapels. Examples have been found in houses C6 (Baki, Mose), SW5 (Khamuy and Pennub), and SW2 (Khonsu, Sherire). They are small round-topped limestone stelae, generally less than 25 cm high. They were dedicated to one, two, or three individuals, usually without mention of their relations: in only a few cases do wives or children occur as offerants or dedicators (Demarée 1983: 174). Another form of cult focus was the ancestor bust, which operated in much the same manner as the stelae. Of these approximately seventy-five examples are from Deir el Medina, while some one hundred and fifty exist in total from all sites (Friedman 1994: 114; see Figure 4.4). These busts represented the potent dead, who were capable of interceding benevolently or malevolently in human affairs. They were human beings who had been admitted to the afterworld, but, more immediately, they were deceased relatives who could be called upon in times of need. Their effectiveness was sustained by the ongoing practices of their descendants in the family cult. These practices probably occurred in the second room, or divan room, since most ritual finds emanate from there, as do the ritual fixtures and niches into which the stelae were placed. The materiality of the stela acted as a conduit for transactions between this world and the next, establishing contact with family members past and present. The fact that more men are named as dedicants and deified ancestors sits well with the location of these objects in the divan room, the area of greatest male potency.

HOUSEHOLD ARCHAEOLOGY

Archaeology at the household level can only be conducted at a few sites, including Amarna, Deir el Ballas, Deir el Medina, Gurob, Memphis, and Tell ed Daba. To date, the only sites to have produced an adequate amount of available and analyzable household data are Amarna and Deir el Medina.

Although there was marked individual variation in New Kingdom houses, a number of attributes are common to most examples. Archaeologists refer to a single New Kingdom house type, often tripartite in general structure. Kemp notes that at Amarna, where there is a wide range of housing across the city, the plans of households are remarkably uniform irrespective of size. Although it is rare to find two identical houses, the same elements are repeated in slightly different combinations. The main feature at Amarna is a square central living room. At one end stood a low brick dais. This was the divan room, discussed above. One or more wooden columns supported the roof; because this main room was at a higher level, windows would have been cut near the top of the wall to allow light and ventilation. In large houses windows took the form of stone grilles set into the wall.

Around the central room were grouped others: an outer reception room, storage rooms, and the more personal domestic quarters. Kemp (1989: 296) maintains that there was such a thing as a main bedroom, but there are problems with such Western segregations (see Wegner 1998). Kemp has identified an alcove where he believes the "master bed" stood. However, all the beds we have from domestic sites are single: wealthy individuals such as Kha and Merit had a single bed each. Beds were probably marks of wealth and status, and clearly most people did not own or sleep in one. Kemp says that ideally next to the bedroom was a bathroom and toilet, yet the architectural evidence for such features at this site or any other in the New Kingdom is absent. Much has been made of an oddly shaped single stone seat with a narrow opening found in North Suburb house at Amarna

(Freed et al. 1999: 253); yet its function remains elusive. As Kemp himself points out, there was no drainage facility or plumbing of any kind at the site. Amarna was not Knossos, and lacked both plumbing facilities and "bathrooms." We must treat such interpretations with some skepticism.

The houses in the main city at Amarna do not appear to have had much interior decoration. Outside and inside walls were simply plastered with gypsum and painted white. The richer houses had wall paintings of some sort, mostly geometric patterns. Houses of the rich and poor were distinguished in terms of size rather than design, although larger houses or villas had extra features such as an entrance porch, which denoted high status. Examples of elite villas are found at Amarna, Deir el Ballas (Lacovara 1993, 1994) and Tell ed Daba, with a number of desirable features: a garden, a shrine, separate kitchens, granaries, animal pens, sheds and enclosures for craft activities, and additional accommodation including a lodge at the gate (Kemp 1989: 296–98). This specific vision of an ideal estate is further reinforced in textual sources such as Papyrus Lansing, which contains practice texts written by a student scribe: *Raia has built a beautiful mansion: it lies opposite Edjo. He has built it on the border. It is constructed like a work of eternity. It is planted with trees on all sides. A channel was dug in front of it. The lapping of waves sounds in one's sleep. One does not tire of looking at it. One is gay at its door and drunk in its halls. Handsome doorposts of limestone, carved and chiselled. Beautiful doors, freshly carved. Walls inlaid with lapis lazuli.*[22]

These are markers of elite status, whereas the bulk of our evidence comes from the workers' villages and their modest dwellings. At the workman's village of Deir el Medina houses within the enclosure walls were organized into residence blocks, each house forming a horizontal strip across the block. At Amarna there is less variety, since the short duration of the community precluded substantial building modification or generational expansion. Moreover, we should not think of these houses as excessively small, given that in many ancient and modern cultures people have lived in houses of similar or smaller size (see Chapter 2).

As outlined, the first room was constructed around the experience of mature, elite females and their sexual and procreative lives. The second room, or divan room, was very much a male preserve with very different iconography, fixtures, and archaeological finds (Meskell 1998b: 229–33). What of other rooms and those who dwelled in them? Rooms toward the rear of the house were relatively small and undecorated, reserved for the storage and preparation of food. This domain was probably reserved for the female slaves or servants who were provided by the state to perform domestic duties such as grinding grain and preparing bread and beer (see Černý 1973: 175–81; Meskell 1997: 233). In attempting to trace domestic activities such as bread preparation, Delwyn Samuel's work (1994, 1999) at Deir el Medina and

FIGURE 4.11. Ovens in the Back Room of House NE2, Deir el Medina. (Photo courtesy of the author)

Amarna is particularly instructive. She notes that mortar and quern emplacements tend to be associated within the houses, linking these associated activities to specific spaces. She argues that winnowing and sieving probably occurred near the quern emplacements, since cereal-processing installations tended to be grouped together (Samuel 1994: 175). Animals that were presumably housed at Deir el Medina, as they were at Amarna, may have been fed from the chaffy by-products of cereal processing. At Deir el Medina it is unlikely that these back rooms were roofed with anything other than permeable material, rushes or straw, especially in view of the proximity of ovens and cooking activities. Samuel looks specifically at the spatial arrangement of NE5, where all the elements of cereal processing were present in the rearmost room. A mortar was set roughly in the center, and there was a quern emplacement in the southeast corner. A stairway rose just outside the door, providing convenient access to the rooftop. There was a cylindrical oven in the northwest corner and the entrance to a cellar in the northeast. She suggests that all the daily processing and baking could have taken place in this one self-contained room, possibly with cereal drying and grain cleaning being undertaken upstairs. Alternatively at Amarna, cooking was done in the front rooms, although the excavators claim that in a well-ordered house it would have been undertaken in the back areas, a clear example being house 10 East Street. Troughs that were used for grinding showed evidence of burning, a practice that continues today to kill vermin. Stone mortars that were set into the floor were worn smooth at the bottom from grinding. Associated finds included ordinary cooking pots, shallow bowls, and baskets of all types.

Since Samuel's evidence generally supports the notion that food preparation took place in the back of the house, what might we infer from this about social interactions within the domestic context? Some households may have produced their own bread and beer, while others show no evidence of such processing, and their occupants might have had arrangements with other households. Here we are forced to examine Deir el Medina alone, given the lack of textual evidence from Amarna, and since that village was relatively poor, servants may not have been an option. Samuel points out that there are problems with reconstructing the activities of female household servants or slaves in various households at Deir el Medina. The number assigned by the state varied from one to sixteen, though these may have been shared among households (Černý 1973: 176; Janssen 1997:23). It is impossible to tell whether these women were attached to individual houses or were shared on a rotating basis (Černý 1973: 177–81). On a social level, people who were regularly assigned to a specific household, and were thus their members, would become enmeshed in the social fabric of that family, whether that was desired or not. In a sense they might become extended members of the family; an adoption text shows servants becoming upwardly mobile in this way (Eyre 1992: 211–18). A servant who gave birth to a male child, fathered by the sculptor Neferenpet at Deir el Medina, also raised her status through childbirth (p. 97).

If servants represented an ever-changing stream of individuals, rotating on a daily or weekly basis, then social and kinlike bonds would have been significantly harder to form. Their separate placement in the rear rooms would serve to reinforce their low status and the hierarchical relationships of the household. This is not to say that higher-status women of the house did not participate at any level in these tasks, and they certainly would not have been isolated from such spaces. General patterns of domestic space at Deir el Medina are shown in Table 4.1.

We can situate these back rooms within a pattern of decreasing elaboration and ritual importance, beginning in the front two rooms and declining toward the process areas bordering the village wall. For the most part, these rooms were never whitewashed or decorated with paintings. Their only surface treatment consisted of a layer of gray paint on the walls. Similarly, they lack ritual fixtures and objects, having only processing equipment and emplacements.

Overlapping spheres of domesticity, sexuality, and ritual life coexisted in New Kingdom Egypt. These experiences were interlaced with other

TABLE 4.1
General Patterns of Domestic Space at Deir el Medina

Room 1	⇒	Room 2	⇒	Other Rooms
Ritual fixtures		Ritual fixtures		Ovens, cooking area
Cultic objects		Cultic objects		No cultic objects
Female imagery	⇒	Male imagery	⇒	No imagery
Birthing imagery		Ancestor busts		Undecorated
Lit clos		Divan		Processing implements
Female space	⇒	Male space	⇒	Servile space

crucial variables such as an individual's sex, life experience, status, rank, or position in the household. For too long archaeologists have been concerned with single-issue approaches and strands of research. The recent preoccupation with finding women in the archaeological record is a salient example. In archaeological contexts we can never be clear where one cultural domain ends and another begins. We also have to interrogate what we have constructed as the facts of life, calling into question the constructions of motherhood, the domain of kinship, the spheres of sexuality and religiosity, and so on. Anthropologists, and by extension archaeologists, have read across other people's cultural domains (Yanagisako and Delaney 1995b). Indeed anthropology has shown us the inherent pitfalls of that approach, suggesting to those who study the past that they too have projected "natural" boundaries and categorizations onto unsuitable, very different cultural contexts (Meskell 2001). We cannot assume that in other societies cultural domains are structured like ours; nor can we expect the same analytic constellations and results. The archaeological and iconographic data shows that in Egypt what we term "sexuality" was truly embedded, pervading many aspects of social and ritual life and free of many of the moralistic connotations that we are familiar with. It has proved unproductive to hold to Euro-American categories when Egyptian ones were so culturally different. The latter are also fundamental to a more contextual understanding of social dynamics. Judeo-Christian sentiments may erase connections between family and sexuality, the sexualization of children, or the possibilities of sexuality in the next life—but the Egyptians did not share this framework. The interstices of all these networks of identity and experience provide the truly interesting terrain of ancient life, which forms the basis of the next chapter.

CHAPTER FIVE

Love, Eroticism, and the Sexual Self

Aɴ ᴀʀᴄʜᴀᴇᴏʟᴏɢʏ of emotion is a highly desirable but usually elusive endeavor for many scholars. The most extreme example within that repertoire of emotions might indeed be love, or what we know as love. Erotics is a closely linked and entangled topic: neither category is fully comprehensible, much less monolithic in our own culture. This raises the question of how we might conduct a study of love in antiquity? First, New Kingdom Egypt possessed a genre of lyric poetry reflecting emotional attachment, love, and erotic symbolism. Additionally, male artists created vernacular art that was replete with erotic signifiers, exclusively revolving around the sexualization of the female body, with no corresponding set of signifiers for the male body. Yet in terms of social equality women appear to have played a subordinate role, under the patriarchal control of husbands and fathers. Most researchers interested in questions about women or gender in Egypt have tended to favor unilinear equations of women's status: it was either incomparably high or invariably less than males. The ability to reconcile contradictory modes of being has not been addressed. Following Lila Abu-Lughod's work on the Egyptian bedouin (1986), I suggest we revisit both lyric and nonlyric modes of expression in Egypt, comparing them with the other sources of information about emotional life to produce a more complex and multivocal picture of the past. What is key here is the relationship between poetic and nonpoetic discourses, rather than the setting of contemporary Egypt: we should not interpolate any notions of cultural stasis or pharaonic lineage that might diminish the contextual specificities. Despite the cultural valences and vast temporal separation between ancient and modern contexts, there may be threads of connectivity that help illuminate the performative aspects of New Kingdom poetic discourse.

As we have seen, there is much New Kingdom writing in the form of letters, verse, and legal documents that gives insight into personal relations and social networks. Most scholars have been drawn to the evidence for marriage, divorce, and the status of women, since they are interrelated topics that sustain great contemporary interest. It is perhaps for this reason, coupled with the rather familiar modes of expression, that these writings seem so evocative to a modern reader. However, the interrelated spheres of love, eroticism, and sexuality have received less attention, presumably because of their sensitive subject matter. Lise

Manniche's *Sexual Life in Ancient Egypt* (1987) remains the only volume specifically devoted to this topic, although it is largely descriptive and tends to seamlessly include materials from diverse time periods. Egyptian data provide extremely rich sources for the study of ancient *érotisme* and are useful for a variety of approaches, from the archaeological to the purely literary. Ancient materials might offer culturally specific ways of accessing a particular, discursive production of sexual life with all its attendant discourses, such as love, eroticism, and embodiment. Jeffrey Weeks (1999: 35) describes the erotic as "a contingent, culturally specific, often unstable linkage of related, but separable, elements: bodily potentials, desires, practices, concepts and beliefs, identities, and institutional forms. It is highly gendered, but notoriously malleable. It may have hegemonic patterns, but these patterns in turn are usually defined by excluded others, and marked by variations shaped by culturally and materially defined differences: age, class, ethnicity, nationality, geography." This formulation offers much to the study of Egyptian culture where the mind:body split is not applicable. Additionally, the pervasive sphere of the sexual impacted upon specific groups in distinct ways, whether in terms of legal, domestic, or representational domains. An individual's age, social standing, sex, ethnicity, life stage, and occupation all determined how their erotic lives would be portrayed, performed, and scrutinized by society at large.

Bypassing the ancient data, social theorists have tended to locate romantic love within the development of Western European civilization, linking it to modernization and rationality. To paraphrase Lindholm (1999: 257–58), Western expectations and beliefs about romantic love have developed from a unique historical trajectory and cultural background. And yet this obvious truth should not blind us to deeper correspondences between our emotional lives and those of people in cultures different from our own, both past and present. Cultures such as New Kingdom Egypt recount the same sort of intense idealizations of the beloved, the same feelings of exaltation in their presence and intense despair in their absence. To counter this temporal chauvinism, ancient data indicate that romantic love is not necessarily the prerogative of a leisured class, nor does it require a complex society. It is not solely heterosexual, nor does it always lead to marriage. Romantic attachment is not intrinsically linked to capitalism, small families, sexual oppression, the cult of motherhood, or a quest for identity. Rather, romantic attraction is an attempt to escape from certain types of social contradictions and structural tensions through the transcendental love of another person. The contours of romantic love evidenced in Egypt are just as nuanced and complex as those documented for Western Europe many centuries later. Sentiments expressed in love poetry suggest that feelings of intensity were visceral; that love, longing, and desire were inextricable; that separation meant physical pain and melancholy; but also that love might be a realizable goal in an individual's life. In sum, we can focus on the intimate connections between the three domains—sex, eroticism, and love—that have been termed "amatory feeling" (Paz 1995: viii).

POETIC LOVE

The great innovation of the Ramesside age was the textualization of some aspects of the oral tradition pertaining to pleasure and entertainment. Love songs certainly belong to this category, connected with the popular Egyptian sentiment expressed as *to make the heart forget*. Assmann argues (1999a: 7, 12) that they were part of a cultural sphere, or an aspect of embodied knowledge that similarly included all kinds of ceremonies, rituals, dances, customs, images, and symbols. Yet one could also argue for a general broadening of literary decorum in the New Kingdom, which until that time viewed this genre simply as performative literature. A parallel situation was the stronger articulation and material expression of personal piety in the Ramesside age.[1] It is perhaps not that love songs were invented at this time, but rather that they could be more fully and publicly expressed.

Egyptian love songs were evocative writings demonstrating that ideal love between partners was supposed to be passionate, emotional, and sexual: *I kiss her, her lips are parted, I am exhilarated without beer. Oh, how the gap has been bridged.*[2] One set of love poems was owned by a certain carpenter and then passed onto a village scribe, the well-known Qenherkhopishef. These poems, if indeed that is a suitable description, were called *sweet sayings* in Egyptian (McDowell 1999: 152); they are best defined as inner discourses and were probably meant to be sung or read aloud. The listener would thus be privy to the inner thoughts and intentions of the lovers, at the deepest and most intimate level. Bedouin poetry differs from that of the New Kingdom in that the former is a spontaneous genre, not necessarily written down, dealing with specific incidents and emotional moments in a person's life. Abu-Lughod (1986: 239) also points to the ambiguous and formulaic nature of poetry that protects the anonymity of the poet, the addressee, and the subject—names are never included. Lyric genres allowed people to frame their personal sentiments as though operating as universals, so that the true significance of the poem is often masked. Moreover, personal feelings expressed in everyday situations often ran contrary to poetic statements, and if the latter were uttered in mundane contexts they would threaten the moral and social order. In ancient and modern contexts various cultural discourses can operate simultaneously, are constantly in relationship, and thereby challenge the relationship between ideology and human experience.

The ancient Egyptians did not keep diaries, and it is unlikely that people read letters or documents silently as we do. Letters were found in abundance at the site of Deir el Medina, representing personal correspondence between friends and family, both male and female. Literacy can be seen as a sliding scale, with many individuals falling somewhere between literate and illiterate. Given that female literacy was negligible (Sweeney 1993: 525), it is likely that women had to dictate letters to the men of the village, as well as rely on them to read various communications. Performance of the spoken word was significant in Egyptian culture. For example, the spoken name had ritualistic potency and efficacy in both living and mortuary contexts. While the love poetry did not have specific ritual or religious substrata, as demonstrated by Fox (1985: 234–35) it may have been performed at festivals that had overt religious meaning. The imagery portrayed in the poems parallels the depictions of feasts and festivals seen on New Kingdom tomb walls. While we do not know the mechanisms by which the poetry came to be recorded, perhaps people recorded some highly favored oral poetry performed by men and women at these events or at special occasions. They may have been written down for posterity and thus became popular as a tradition. While men were responsible for writing, we cannot discount that women may have spoken their parts in these poems. For example a female passage goes: *Your love has joined to [me . . . like a seal-ring] to the finger [of a maiden; like ointment] to the limbs of princes; like garments to the limbs of the gods.* This is followed by a male response: *My sister has come! My heart thrills, my arms stretch out to embrace her. My heart is carefree in its place, like a red-fish in its fish-pond. Oh night, you are mine forever, since (my) mistress has come to me.*[3] There are various cycles in the Chester Beatty Love Song with parts indicated as spoken by girl and boy, or individuals assuming their gendered roles.

All extant examples of love poetry, with one exception, come from the village of Deir el Medina. It appears that they were not copied repeatedly like some of the didactic texts, but one manuscript bears a date that is typical of scribal exercises. So while we lack evidence for a canon of such poetry, we can argue that it might have formed a significant genre for scribal training (McDowell 1999: 152). Given the ages of those undergoing instruction, we might also deduce that the content of the love poems was deemed suitable for adolescents. This might reinforce the suggestion already made (Meskell 2000b) that sexuality was not considered a separate sphere in ancient Egypt, rather that it was a quality that pervaded many aspects of life, including what we would now term "sacred" and "profane" domains.

In Bedouin society today, the efficacy of poetry has to do with its idiom. Poetry is associated with weakness, vulnerability, helpless dependency, and intimacy. These states are clearly associated with childhood and the amoral place of children, unsocialized and free to express themselves (Abu-Lughod 1986: 243). Children are not subject to self-mastery and as such can escape many of the rigid confines established for adults. So too in pharaonic times, poetry expressed sexual intimacy, vulnerability, reckless abandon, and emotional dependency through phenomenological imagery. If we look at intimacy first, an immediate physical closeness between lovers is depicted as the wearing of bodily adornments. In the Cairo Love Songs, love is the conjoining of a ring to the finger, or garments to the limbs for the female speaker and the fetishization of her clothing for the male: *I would be strengthened by grasping the clothes that touch her body, for it would be I who washed out the moringa oils that were in her kerchief. Then I would rub my body with her cast-off garments.*[4] The realization that physical closeness may be restricted provides desperation: the boy admits his stomach turns at the thought, and his love is compared to an illness that only she can exorcise. Love is both the source of pain and the drug that remedies it. Indeed it is the male speaker who has more to say about his own vulnerability, as opposed to the female. He relinquishes any claims to status or control over her, saying *would that I were her Nubian slavegirl*—although the acknowledgement here is that female servants could presumably enter private quarters and help with grooming and dressing. Such activities are often depicted in New Kingdom domestic iconography. For similar reasons he wants to be her washerman, a particularly low-status job, so that he might look upon and touch her personal garments. But as Fox (1985: 42) has demonstrated, the girl performs as an artefact of male fantasies that ultimately constitute the world of the poem. She is remote and undelineated, and the contours of her personality are never drawn. Devoid of agency, the girl's thoughts and desires are never interpolated into the fantasy. Even the young man's overtures to serve her render him passive, and he takes no action to achieve his goal of attainment. He may envy her servants, yet what he envisions is limited to his own erotic rewards: viewing her naked body, having intimate physical contact, and fetishizing her clothing.

Sensual experience is foregrounded in the New Kingdom poems. Sight, smell, taste, touch, and the aesthetic qualities of bodies, flowers, fruits, luxury items, and intoxicants are all recurrent motifs (see Chapter 6). In the Turin Love Songs the body of the desired woman is figured as a bountiful sycamore tree, ripe and laden with fruit, *redder than red jasper*. In this poem, as in most, love is portrayed as an intoxicant, something the

Egyptians endeavored to show in wall paintings through the representation of incense and perfume. These were particularly important items for ritual and festive performances and were subsequently deposited in tombs, while flowers and ointments were placed on the body of the deceased. Similarly the girl will say: *"your voice rejuvenates my limbs . . . like fat mixed with honey . . . Your love has joined to me . . . like incense to the nose of [?] . . . It is like a mandragora in the hand of a man; it is like the dates he mixes with beer.*[5] Sweetness, breath, and aromatic items such as cinnamon oil are linked to the sensuousness of the beloved. He too responds with sense-filled declarations of desire: I kiss her, her lips are parted. *I am exhilarated without beer. . . . Her limbs are found to be like something drenched in cinnamon oil.*[6] The desire for togetherness is likened to abundant greenness and blossoming flowers, something that was considered beautiful and "ideal" in Egyptian thought. Surrounded by the desert, often described as a red, hostile land, the presence of trees and gardens spoke of luxury and perfection on earth. Various plants were further associated with hallucinogenic or intoxicating qualities: *the safflower blooms, the merbeb-plants are fresh, the blue plants and the mandragoras have come forth.*[7] It is not surprising that these are mentioned in conjunction with festivals, another site of intoxication, celebration, and possible sexual activity. At these moments it may have been more appropriate to "assume another lived experience, where one's lost love is remembered, where one may have chosen another life course, and so on, and can lament the loss of those other possibilities in a semi-public space" (Abu-Lughod 1986: 243). Performing nostalgia in this manner could iterate tales of lost love, misfortune, or death. Just as festivals proffer a very different space for sociosexual activity, recitations and singing advance additional reflective and creative opportunities, offering another mode of being. Love, then, should not just be seen as a practice or a physical relationship; the history of love could also be described as the history of a literary (and artistic) genre (Featherstone 1999: 2). Literary motifs described in the poetry directly parallel the artistic renderings of sensual delights and female bodies depicted in tomb paintings, domestic imagery and objects of material culture. The cohesive delineation of sensual and erotic life again reinforces the notion that sexuality pervaded numerous spheres of life and death: the signifiers of the erotic were coherent across domains.

It has been said that the relationship of poetry to language resembles that of eroticism to sexuality (Paz 1995). This interlacing of domains is also clear in the ancient texts—although even the most explicit references to sexuality and bodily intimacy in Egyptian poetry are couched in metaphorical language. There is much mention of revealing the limbs, usually associated with bathing or the presence of water. The girl states, *I desire to go down to wash myself before you. I shall let you see my beauty in a tunic of the finest royal linen, soaked with cinnamon oil.* Later her lover responds by taking her to the bed, placing fine linen between her limbs, that are similarly drenched in cinnamon oil. He desires to see *the complexion of her whole body,* which needs little explication. More metaphorical are the several references to *carrying a red fish, excellent on my fingers*[8] and placed before the beloved. On one level the heart is likened to a red fish swimming in its pond, the color red having symbolic resonances of power and magic. Red paint was also added to female statuettes that promoted sexuality and fertility in domestic and mortuary spheres. Moreover, various fish were known to have erotic overtones, such as the fish that swallowed the penis of Osiris in later mythological accounts. Moreover, the *Tilapia Nilotica* notably takes its offspring into its mouth in times of danger and then regurgitates them in a manner resembling ejaculation. Fish would then seem to have direct associations with genitalia in Egyptian thinking, and since it is the female who presents the fish to her lover, this might also be read as the intimate revealing of her body. In the Chester Beatty Love Songs, the young woman also gazes inadvertently on her lover's body: *My brother is at the watercourse, his foot planted on the riverbank. He prepares a festival altar for spending the day, with the choicest of the beers. He grants me the hue of his loins. It is longer than broad.*[9] According to Fox, this sexual gaze provides a rare instance where the woman remarks on male genitalia as a site of desire, even if through a male authorial voice. While sexuality makes eroticism possible, eroticism transcends reproduction through its capacity to elaborate sexual experience and invent a separate realm of associated pleasures. Egyptian love poetry is one such genre of pleasure, blending desire, love, and eroticism within the specifics of an Egyptian semiotic system.

Bernard Mathieu has conducted a contextual study of the love songs, along with their settings, locales, and motifs. His research has shown that some 70 percent of the amorous encounters center around the girl's house (1996: 152), suggesting that it occupies a central role in the space of protocol and social custom. Her house, and more specifically her door or door bolt, are used as metaphorical symbols for her person. Entry to the house is equivalent to the lover's possession of the young woman: *Bolt, I will open (you)! Door, you are my fate! You are my very spirit.*[10] The specific sequence of courting alluded to in the love poetry is as follows. First, the young man makes his request to the girl's mother, and if the request is accepted, he is given access to her house. The girl is then given to him as a spouse, and the "new wife" stays for a time in her own family home. After that time she enters the house of her husband's mother, confirming the expression *to found a house,* which traditionally designates the marriage. Given the spatial frame implied by these social conventions, the house of the man is the point of materialization for the relationship, bringing the courtship to fruition (Mathieu 1996: 153–55). However, the fantasy setting presented in the love poetry must be contrasted with the social reality that houses were occupied by numerous family members and servants, both male and female (see Chapter 4). The negotiation of romantic relationships within this dynamic is not articulated, and we cannot ascribe literal meaning from these texts.

Unsurprisingly the romantic trysts are traditionally set at night. Time spent away from each other is described as intolerable solitude and silence, juxtaposed against the exaltation of reunion. Such tension and rhythm mirrors the amorousness of the lovers. It is clear that the space and time of love had specific resonances to the ancient Egyptians. Yet at the core was an intense emotional experience that relativized an individual's identity and sense of self. There were extreme situations in a person's lifetime where the unifying and centralizing control that the self exerts upon its multiple constituents was threatened, as was mentioned in Chapter 3. The malady of love is one such example primarily because it is described as a dissociation of heart and self and the possible disintegration of personal identity (Assmann 1999b: 384). Here the heart is capable of acting on its own, as would not be acceptable in other social contexts: *My heart quickly scurries away, when I think of your love. It does not let me act like a (normal) person, it has leapt <out> of its place.*[11]

One clear difference between the content of ancient and modern poetry, however, is the way in which sexuality was perceived by each group. New Kingdom poetry exhibits no rigid sanctions on sexual behavior; sexual liaisons are not depicted as forbidden, and amorous passions do not threaten the moral order. Yet the picture presented by such a genre must be recognized as an ideal that might be contrasted strongly with lived experience. Representations of Egyptian sexuality, in all its manifestations and domains of reference, can only be described as polymorphous. Sexuality operated differently in specific spheres and was represented coherently according to each context—yet contradictory modes existed. Such a conflictual situation should not be surprising given the numerous cross-cultural studies that parallel this heterogeneity. Sherry Ortner's (1981) analysis of Polynesian ethnographies demonstrates that complex and contradictory formulations of sexuality can coexist without disrupting cultural coherence. In these societies virginity is prized, yet young women are actively beautified and overtly displayed as sexual objects for the male gaze, and marriage by capture or rape is almost institutionalized. Eroticism may have been pervasive and cultivated across a wide range of domains in Polynesian societies, although it cannot be detached from other politicized arenas, be they social power, economics, or reproduction. In previous sections I have suggested a more nuanced examination of women's lives, taking into account the multiplicity of roles and representations, drawing interpretative force from the contestation of these

domains. Studies of ancient sexual life can only benefit from the same inter-
rogation of the diverse evidence at hand, and the multivalent pictures produced by these very different representations of life.

REPRESENTING EROTICS

Erotic life in Egypt is powerfully figured in the visual arts, including
motifs on material culture, domestic wall paintings, sketches on ostraca
and papyri, and funerary paintings on tomb walls. Often the representations of young women in revealing garments—surrounded by either musical instruments and festivities or sensuous Nilotic scenes—have been read
seamlessly as images of uncomplicated beauty. Their aesthetic qualities are
resonant for a contemporary Western gaze: they are youthful, slim yet
voluptuous, sexually appealing, and glitteringly adorned. In a wider cross-
cultural study of eroticism, Bataille (1993: 141) identified a range of signifiers that is pertinent to the New Kingdom: "That sparkling finery and
that make-up, those jewels and those perfumes, those faces and those bodies dripping with wealth, becoming the *objects*, the focal points of luxury

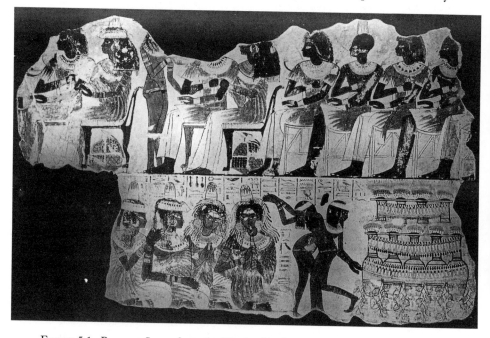

FIGURE 5.1. Banquet Scene from the Tomb of Nebamun, Western Thebes, Now
Lost. (Image courtesy of the Media Center for Art History, Archaeology, and Historic Preservation, Columbia University)

and lust, though they present themselves as goods and as values, dissipate a part of human labor in a *useless* splendor."

The vast majority of these well-known Egyptian images stem from a funerary setting. These wall paintings were not simply part of a decorative schema but were simultaneously symbolic and functional images loaded with specific meanings about order and harmony in this life and the maintenance of a parallel unity and perfection in the next life (Figure 5.1). As part of that idealizing vision, social and sexual inequalities were encoded into the scenes. Men were more important, powerful, and visible, and their need for sexual revivification was paramount. The bodily specificities of male sexuality were absent from the tomb walls, although there were visual motifs and puns that metaphorized the processes of ejaculating or begetting, such as spearing fish or brandishing a throwstick, which any literate male or cultured female could decode (see Chapter 6). Cryptic cues signifying male desire and bodily pleasures were juxtaposed with explicit depictions of the female body layered with sensual and sensory imagery. As a result, woman becomes the passive spectacle and primary site of male desire and can occupy the contradictory positions of good woman and bad. Women were contrasted as either under male control or out of control, as those who nurture versus those who are aggressive destroyers. Both formulations were articulated in didactic literary texts, such as the *Instructions of Ptahhotep* (Troy 1984). Female sexuality lies at the heart of these constructions: it is both desired and feared—a common pattern attested cross-culturally.

The female body may have provided the sexual focus for the male viewer, yet a woman's own sexual life and afterlife were not elaborated upon. Women were secondary and subservient and formed a necessary commodity for men to take with them into the afterlife. Very little of women's lives or experiences can be read from the tomb walls, and it is always difficult to extrapolate from imagery to living contexts. The situation is similar for children, who are secondary individuals in the representative schemas and are there to complete a sense of family and fecundity. This is not to say that elite men did not care for either wives or children, rather that there is a politics of representation encoded in these paintings (Meskell 1998a). Tomb imagery provides only one source of information about women's social status, yet it was a system that deprivileged women in their representation and also in their chances of attaining an afterlife commensurate with men. While they may be iconographically present, this does not entail a notion of equality on the part of the artists or tomb owners. As has frequently been noted, the tomb was very much a male preserve and was constituted around the owner's life, accomplishments, and afterlife potentials. There are striking examples where images of women were erased from the tomb walls, possibly when they were divorced or died early: examples are Renni at el Kab, and Amenemhet (TT 82), Mentiywi (TT 172), and Menw (TT 109) at Thebes (Whale 1989: 246).

Representational data from tombs present one vision of life that is in contradiction with that of the love songs. However, there are other images of women that are even more telling in their rendering, namely the hundreds of figured ostraca from Deir el Medina. These informal sketches on limestone were presumably done by the workmen themselves, and many of them are satirical or ironic pictures of everyday life, or conversely, the world-turned-upside-down. Some show men in older age, fat, bald, and very much at variance with the canonical renderings of the human body in elite Egyptian art. However, the depictions of women are generally consonant with the ideal: they are shown as young, slim, beautiful, and sexually charged, replete with erotic signifiers such as the lotus, the hip girdle, large wigs, and Hathoric motifs (Derchain 1975; Pinch 1993; Robins 1993b; 1996). Several ostraca show scenes of sexual intercourse where the woman typically adopts the passive role. A number of less well known examples show penetrative scenes and men with inordinately long penises (Keimer 1941: Plate 5). Less explicit imagery, still redolent of sexuality, such as gazelles and monkeys, was also popular in these representations. Others show women reclining on beds with elaborate drapery and surrounded again with erotic signifiers: these images often parallel the sorts of tropes we hear portrayed in love poetry. Another group shows a specific genre of women, those associated with music and dancing and possibly extracurricular sexual activities (Manniche 1987). These young women are typically depicted wearing only a hip girdle, doing acrobatics or playing musical instruments. From a male perspective these were inherently sexualized activities and mirror the paintings in tombs of elite men such as Nebamun (see Miller and Parkinson 2001).

There is no iconography of women shown at anything less than their physical peak. All of the female imagery is basically commensurate and can be compared to that of the Turin Papyrus. This unique papyrus depicts a series of sexual encounters between short, aged men and young, hypersexualized females. We cannot say whether it is simply a pair of individuals represented in a series of vignettes or a number of people. Some scholars have suggested these scenes represent a brothel, although there is no physical evidence for such establishments. It is not known what such a place would look like archaeologically. These are problematic, Western assertions influenced heavily by presentations of prostitution and brothels in the classical world, such as at Pompeii. Leaving aside the issue of prostitution, both in formal or informal settings, we might question what are the stereotypes of women set forth in the vernacular imagery of these ostraca and papyri. First, they are at

FIGURE 5.2. Ostracon Showing Sexual Intercourse. (Photo courtesy of the British Museum, EA 50714)

odds with the mutuality and expressions of love in some love poems. There is no equivalent female voice or gaze to reflect back or give the semblance of equivalence. Second, these images sexualize and commodify women through their construction as visual subjects. This situation is analogous with contemporary culture, as de Lauretis (1984: 37) brought to the fore: "The representation of woman as image (spectacle, object to be looked at, vision of beauty—and the concurrent representation of the female body as the *locus* of sexuality, site of visual pleasure, or lure of the gaze) is so pervasive in our culture . . . that it necessarily constitutes a starting point for any understanding of sexual difference and its ideological effects in the construction of social subjects, its presence in all forms of subjectivity."

The Turin Papyrus is a striking example of a culturally specific erotic canon. One might deduce its other function was as a satirical piece, given that other associated images on the papyrus consist of monkeys, lions, and donkeys playing musical instruments. Assmann argues (1993: 35) that it satirizes a fundamental Egyptian myth, the nightly travels of the sun before

FIGURE 5.3. Three Scenes from the Turin Papyrus. (Redrawn by the author)

the dawning of a new day and its attendant discourses of rebirth and resurrection. Additionally, we see the world-turned-upside-down motif so popular with the Egyptians: mice attacking cats, birds attacking cats, mice in chariots led by lions and dogs, and so on. These scenes are featured alongside the human scenes of sexual intercourse. In the latter, several motifs are repeatedly shown. First, men are shown with inordinately long penises—to the point where they are comical. Sometimes these penises have added red detail signifying potency, ultramasculinity, and the deity Seth. Irrespective of the male's stature, short or tall, the penis remains out of proportion. Second, the women adopt acrobatic poses in the throes of sexual intercourse, whereas the men do not. Women are shown bent over, standing on one leg with the other in the air, upside down, over a chariot, and posed against a sloping wall or ladder. Beside one scene is a fragmentary text that says: *Behold, come behind me with your love.* Another states . . . *because of the movements. I make the work pleasant.* Next to a woman we read, *your phallus is in me, see, you don't bring me a good reputation.*[12] Third, these women bear all the visual cues signifying sexuality or even Hathor herself: lotuses, hip girdles, makeup, kohl jars, musical instruments, convovulus leaves, sistra, *menat* necklaces, and mirrors (see Figure 5.3). In one scene an exhausted man with a flacid penis is carried away by a woman and some young helpers. One could hardly view these as scenes of mutuality or reciprocity in any way. Clearly the papyrus was drawn and written by a man for other men's viewing pleasure, perhaps by one of the scribes at Deir el Medina. It fits well within the schema set forward by Bakhtin (1984) to analyze humor and parody in the Renaissance and Middle Ages. His study converges upon the symbolic iconography of the grotesque body and its sexual functions, which finds its ultimate display in fornication. He argued that such representations were in flagrant contradiction to formal literary and artistic canons: in these the body was a finished product where all apertures were closed. Conception, pregnancy, childbirth, and intercourse were not displayed (see also Friedl 1994), as was true of elite Egyptian iconography. In both contexts then, one could argue that parody and humor defied the status quo and were linked to other cultural practices, such as festivals, which challenged the constraints of everyday existence.

How did men and women perceive these gendered inequalities in the representational schema of the New Kingdom? This same question has frequently been posed in contemporary society with reference to the reception of sexualized and commodified female images. Egyptian material culture, wall paintings in houses and chapels, and monuments with female imagery would have been visible to ordinary citizens, including women. Conversely, depictions within the tomb chambers may not have been commonly viewed. The owners of the elite tombs on the West Bank of Thebes must have commissioned artisans who lived on the East Bank. The

FIGURE 5.4. Toiletry Equipment and Mirror. (Photo courtesy of the British Museum, EA 38188, EA 2674, EA 5897, EA 22830, EA 32150)

individual combinations of scenes may suggest elements of personal preference, yet that does not necessarily entail the patron or his family's repeated presence during decoration. The situation may have been different in communities like Deir el Medina, where settlement and cemetery were in close proximity. The male residents of the village, being trained scribes and artists, must have worked continually on their own tombs and those of their colleagues, within view of the community. There were also rituals and festive activities that took place within the space of the tomb. One can only posit a range of possible reactions by female viewers. Given the general coherence in female representation across media, it is likely that the style of depiction struck them as inherently familiar. Yet this is not to say that viewers passively and unquestioningly observed their constructed position in the hierarchy. This particularly applied to women who were painted at a small scale in relation to their husbands, as in the tombs of Sennefer (TT 92), Menna (TT 69), or Nebamun. Wives and daughters were often indistinguishable. How women viewed their explicit sexualization, along with their female offspring, is incalculable. While there is no basis for positing some form of incipient women's emancipatory movement, it is nonetheless possible that female viewers were aware of, and even dissatisfied with, their unequal treatment.

QUESTIONS OF SEXUALITY AND FERTILITY

The marked sexualization of women in Egyptian iconography has traditionally been perceived as an index of fertility and the central place it occupied within the Egyptian psyche. It has often been argued that the sexual images prevalent in Egyptian tombs or on items of material culture have at their core a desire to perpetuate fertility and one's lineage. While these two spheres, sexuality and fertility, are often inseparable and impermeable, we should not simply conflate them at every opportunity. The Egyptians certainly had notions of recreational sex that precluded pregnancy and went to some lengths to prevent conception. Additionally, there were contraceptive formulae and prescriptions to induce abortion.

The earliest preserved medical texts from the Middle Kingdom (c. 1850) include prescriptions for preventing pregnancy. Many involve the use of dung, especially that of the crocodile, which was associated with Seth, inserted into the vagina. Feces may have tended to inhibit conception by effectively blocking the seminal fluid at the base of the cervix or altering the pH level. Seth often appears on uterine amulets to either open or close the womb. Images of Taweret, who protected throughout pregnancy, on the contrary appear rarely (Riddle 1992: 67). Prescriptions in the Ebers Medical Papyrus (c. 1500) use colocynth, dates, honey, and the unripe fruit of the acacia. Modern studies of the fermented mixture show that it produces lactic acid anhydride, which is used today in contraceptive jellies. Even without fermentation the plants had contraceptive attributes. Honey may have spermicidal properties through its osmotic effect (Nunn 1996: 196). Colocynth is well attested as an abortifacient. The Ebers Medical Papyrus also contains a number of prescriptions for abortion, described as "loosening" or "stripping off." Ingredients used were terebinth resin, beer, bird dung, wine, juniper fruit, beetle, turtle, and some unknown plant types (Riddle 1992: 71). Some potions were rubbed into the abdomen, others were drunk, and others were inserted: *Beginning of the prescriptions prepared for women to allow a woman to cease conceiving for one year, two years, or three years: qaa part of acacia, carob, dates; grind with one henu of honey, lint is moistened with it and placed in her flesh.*[13]

The earliest attestation of an oral contraceptive is the Nineteenth Dynasty Berlin Medical Papyrus: *emissions of semen [...] a woman without becoming pregnant. You should fumigate her vagina with emmer seeds to prevent her receiving semen. Then you should [make] for her a prescription to loosen [or release] semen: oil five parts, celery five parts, sweet beer five, heat and drink for four mornings.*[14] Assuming that the other ingredients are carriers, attention turns to celery, which is not otherwise known as an abortifacient before the eleventh century C.E. No modern analyses attest its efficacy, which remains inconclusive.

Related to this notion of sexual freedom was the anxiety over the male's ability to perform. *This incantation is to be recited [...] with beer. To be drunk by the patient (?) I am Re, who comes to you [...] with his erect phallus*[15] This Text is similar to other aphrodisiac incantations: *Be stiff not soft. Be strong not weak.*[16] There are no parallel incantations for females concerned with their capabilities. Such desires, however, are ambiguous and may relate to anxieties over performance or fertility or perhaps both. While erotics, sexuality, and concerns over fertility in the earthly realm and beyond were often deeply enmeshed, we cannot rule out the desire for recreational sex in ancient societies. What is insightful for the modern scholar is the particular cultural articulations of those domains and perhaps their different definitional settings.

Whatever the historical context, the particular construction and understanding of sex cannot be isolated from its discursive milieu (see Foucault 1972: 52, 157). Moreover, we should recognize that sex is itself troubled terrain—sex also has a history (Butler 1993: 5). Clifford Geertz (1966) famously described sexuality in the image of an onion. In sexuality, as in culture, we peel off each layer (economies, politics, families, etc.) and imagine we are approaching the kernel, but it soon becomes clear that the whole is the only "essence" there is. Sexuality cannot be abstracted from its surrounding social layers, since it is so firmly intertwined within social relations and power relations. As discussed in previous chapters, the social embeddedness of sexuality should also incorporate kinship and family systems, sexual regulations, and definitions of communities (Ross and Rapp 1997: 155).

SEXUAL SPECIFICITY

Egyptian sexuality was neither unitary nor monolithic. In Euro-American culture, there is on one level the social construction of biological sex, with all its variable manifestations. Then there is the social and cultural interpretation and performance of those categories, referred to as gender, negotiated at both societal and individual levels. *Sex*, as far as we understand the term within Western discourse, is something that differentiates bodies, while *gender* has been defined as the set of variable social constructions placed upon those differentiated bodies. Yet even this binary formulation has been forcefully challenged (Butler 1993; Gatens 1996; Nicholson 1997). The Egyptians had no such schema. Throughout this work I have used the word *sex* when discussing Egyptian contexts, given their own lack of dichotomous thinking about biology (sex) and culture (gender). However, the Old and Middle Kingdom execration texts give three designations for sex. They hierarchically list as categories all people, all elites, all subjects, all males, all intersexed, and all females. Intersexed may not be the right rendering; Osing translates *castrati*, which is culturally inappropriate (1976: 153). This classification may be intended to cover all human beings, even those who do not appear as male or female, though what we can read into these scant references is minimal. More concrete textual and representational evidence for what we would describe as other genders and hermaphroditism comes from Ptolemaic, Roman, and Late Antique Egypt (Wilfong 1997: 87; 2001).

Sexuality and sex are a complex constellation of interrelated expressions and experiences influenced by a host of social and biological factors. It is also important, for instance, to consider the influence of time. Individual sexual identity is fluid and may change not only over the course of a lifetime, but also, for example in accordance with the rhythms of the festival calendar. Sexual experience or expression was not considered a separate or clandestine sphere. At certain times of year, such as sensually charged festivals, sex might have quite different manifestations from other times (see Chapter 6). Moreover, sexuality did not have the same associations with guilt and shame that it has acquired in Judeo-Christian traditions. It could resonate with ecstatic religious experience, allow one to commune with the gods, or even parallel mythological encounters.

Apart from the more explicit renderings of female sexuality already discussed, it is important to recognize that sexuality was pervasive in Egyptian society (Meskell 2000b, 2001). As in many cultures, sexuality did not exist as a separate sphere, and there was no word for "sexuality" in the Egyptian language. One was not designated heterosexual or homosexual; there were names for practices rather than people (Parkinson 1995). From the archaeological and iconographic data it appeared that what we term "sexuality" pervaded so many aspects of Egyptian social and ritual life that it was a truly embedded concept, free of many of the moralistic connotations we are familiar with. Various scholars within Egyptology have interpolated fertility, rather than sexuality, into discussions surrounding images of the female body in Egyptian art. In some contexts the two domains are clearly inseparable, such as tomb paintings of specific female kin. Yet they could also operate as exclusive domains of desire, as evidenced in the Turin Papyrus where sexual pleasure is the primary objective.

Thus far I have focused on heterosexual relations as the vehicle through which we might approach the relationship between the sexes. A growing body of scholarship addresses the position of same-sex relations in ancient sociosexual life. Yet as Foucault warned (1985: 187), the entire "notion of homosexuality is plainly inadequate as a means of referring to an experience, forms of valuation, and a system of categorization so different from ours." Homosexuality was an invention of the 1860s in Foucault's view (Weeks 1997: 33), whereas Halperin (1990) dates it to the

1890s. Despite these vagaries, a new understanding of sexuality emerged in the Nineteenth century whereby sexual acts and desires became the markers of identity. Homosexuality as the condition, and thus identity, of specific bodies was inextricably linked to that particular historical moment (Somerville 1997: 37). So terms and categorizations such as gay, lesbian, homosexual, or queer are modern products with contextually specific designations and developments and as such cannot simply be projected through time and space to overlay onto other cultures. How then do we apprehend the possible range of sexual identities in antiquity? In modern society "sexual citizenship can be understood as an extension of this process in terms of control over one's own body, one's access to relationships, representations, public space and choice of identity and gender experiences" (Featherstone 1999: 13). Given the relative silence of the archaeological and iconographic record in regard to individuals outside the normative heterosexual regime, we might posit that representation of multiple sexual identities was implicitly circumscribed. There was an explicit ideological focus on the family and marriage, and the affairs of state and of pharaoh were generally defined in terms of kinship. The iconographic tradition reinforced a strictly binary gender division, with no rendering of an intermediate sex. Certain sexual relationships and pleasures could not be depicted publicly. And as stated at the outset, while individual cultures might marshal hegemonic patterns, these patterns in turn are usually defined by excluded others.

Drawing on the work of Richard Parkinson (1995), we can explore the evidence for same-sex relations from textual sources in pharaonic Egypt. While there was no term for sexuality, the verb *nk* refers to having penetrative sex and has no particular overtones, positive or negative. Its derivation *nkw* could be used as a term of abuse and implies a passive role. A *nkk(w)* is "a man on whom a sexual act is performed." Yet these words relate to practices, rather than to categories of individuals. They are attested primarily in the Negative Confession in the *Book of the Dead*, which might suggest that such sexual activity was an ethical concern rather than a source of introspection. Other sources such as some spells in the *Coffin Texts* infer that sodomy was a demonstration of power over someone rather than an outcome of sexual desire. Representational evidence is elusive and ambiguous, since official art rarely depicts sexual encounters of any nature. *Homosociality* is difficult to separate from the *homosexual* in pictorial representations, and this point must be taken into account when considering the material. There has also been a tendency to push the ancient data in the service of contemporary sexual politics, irrespective of the evidence (e.g., Reeder 2000).

We are on stronger ground with the more direct literary evidence. These texts were originally composed in the Middle Kingdom but were copied and well known in the New Kingdom. In the thirty-second maxim of the *Teachings of the Vizier Ptahhotep* it is warned that *you should not have sex with a woman-boy, for you know what is condemned will be water on his breast. There is no relief for what is in his belly.*[17] Parkinson (1999: 270) has argued that this section warns against sexual intercourse with a boy prostitute who adopts the female role, as this will not satiate his desire. The active partner is not condemned as such, but the boy's desire is regarded as perverse and unacceptable. The phrase *water on his breast* also resonates with the wordplay between water and semen. In the didactic context of this composition this section fits neatly with others warning against adultery and other antisocial activities. There is also evidence from other literary sources at this time. In the Twelfth Dynasty version of the literary *Tale of Horus and Seth*, Seth says to Horus: *How lovely is your backside! Broad are [your] thighs.*[18] This is a play or parody on the ritual greeting *How fair is your face.* Seth's attempts to have sex with Horus appear to be intended to humiliate Horus, but are a source of pleasure for Seth, which he describes as *sweet to his heart.* It is an act of desire for Seth, not simply an attempt to exert power over Horus. When Horus tells his mother Isis, she advises him if Seth makes any future overtures to say *it is too painful for me entirely, as you are heavier than me. My strength shall not support your strength.*[19] Thus Horus is advised to use his youthful weakness as an excuse. However, this does not preclude Seth's desire and sexual enjoyment of the act itself (Parkinson 1995: 71). Finally, the *Tale of King Neferkare and the Military Commander Sasenet* is a tale known from Nineteenth Dynasty and later fragments, but probably composed late in the Middle Kingdom. It tells of a nocturnal relationship between pharaoh and his commander, the latter being stated as unmarried. One night Neferkare spends four hours at Sasenet's house, *and after his person had done what he desired with him he returned to his place.*[20] Neferkare's desire is sexual and the euphemistic language employed implies that his role was that of penetrator. His behavior is clearly scandalous and is conducted surreptitiously at night, but is nonetheless spied upon. As Parkinson outlines, the relationship is portrayed as mutually desirous and ongoing, couched in the same language as that used in other family or social relationships.

In general we can tease out a few themes from the evidence, scant as it may be. First, while the visual record is unhelpful, the textual data suggest that same-sex relations between men were accorded a significant place in Middle Kingdom Egyptian literature (Parkinson 1995: 74). Same-sex desire was known to the Egyptians and could be articulated as such. Second, the terminology is used to delineate practices rather than individuals, a very different scenario than that of high modernity. Practices rather than taxonomies of people are named. Third, from these accounts the passive position of receiving appears to have been denigrated, whereas the act of penetration might have no stigma attached. Passivity was linked to weakness and was frequently used to denote the place of the enemy. Here we are talking about expressions of power rather than love and/or desire, as the choice of language reflects. Lastly, as the relationships presented in the *Tale of King Neferkare and the Military Commander Sasenet* suggest, same-sex unions could be based upon some form of desire and mutuality, even if they were clandestine because of regulatory norms. It is likely that such acts and desires occurred, despite official ideology. Richard Parkinson is correct to point out that records of same-sex practices are lacking in the rich Deir el Medina corpus, whereas we have many cases of adultery. The latter may have been more frequent and more socially disruptive, as attested by the acrimonious episodes, violence, and hardship we read about in the Deir el Medina letters.

It might also be instructive to look at other cultures where Euro-American taxonomies do not necessarily hold and where sexual identities are fashioned in ways different from our own. Men who engage in same-sex relations in Latin American contexts, for example, often do not consider themselves *homosexual*. And their tacit masculinity is not questioned on the basis of such practices. In terms of activity and passivity, those who penetrate are gendered male, and those who are penetrated are gendered female. In the Brazilian context the sex/gender system is inadequate, as is the heterosexual/homosexual classification. Kulick argues (1997: 575) that gender is grounded in sexuality and that the categories are constructed around men and nonmen (which includes women and all those who are penetrated). His own work on the *travestis* of Brazil suggests that this system offers a framework for people to understand and organize their own desires, bodies, relationships, and social roles. Many commentators might posit the existence of a third gender or intermediate sex (see Herdt 1993), popular categories that have received much attention and have been layered onto the ancient world. However, Kulick correctly argues that *travestis* only arise and are culturally intelligible within a strictly dichotomous gender system. Thus body, gender, and sexuality are each enacting different scenarios that are at odds with a Euro-American conception of their intrinsic relationships. This has further implications for general questions of identity inasmuch as identity is founded upon the stabilizing concepts of sex, gender, and sexuality.

The limited available evidence shows that ancient Egyptian notions of love, desire, erotics, and sexuality were as complex and multilayered as we would describe for our own society. Yet the tendency remains to privilege modern culture over ancient in terms of emotional sophistication. Weber and Habermas on the one hand and Parsons, Simmel, and Luhmann on the other, have presented romantic love either as an instrumental aid to the maintenance of an ever more rationalized society or as a functional resource for increasing social integration and communication in a social universe that is fragmented and atomistic. Yet to turn love and deep attachment into a reductive mechanism would seem demeaning in contemporary society and similarly curtails the human dimension we see so vividly in Egyptian writings and iconography. The poetry, literature, and images all draw on a similar fount of embodied knowledge with their culturally specific signs of desire; as I have argued, this desire pervaded many spheres of Egyptian life from birth to death and beyond. I would prefer to see those expressions articulated as Octavio Paz (1995: 142) would describe: "Eroticism is social and appears in all places and eras. There is no society without erotic rites and practices, from the most innocuous to the most bloody. Eroticism is the human dimension of sexuality, what imagination adds to nature."

CHAPTER SIX

Embodied Knowledge

IN THE PREVIOUS CHAPTER I introduced the concept of embodied knowledge in discussions of sexual selves. Embodied knowledge can be defined as a way of knowing through bodily experience and the groundedness of our own corporeality. In Egypt, people were socialized and incorporated into their age, sex, and status groups through various kinds of rituals, dances, customs, images, and symbols, prompting us to question: how was sensual life coded, represented, and practiced in New Kingdom society, and how were those canons formulated and replicated over hundreds of years? Anthropology has long seen the importance of learning through embodied means, what might be termed corporeal knowledge. Central here are phenomenology, or the sensuous understanding of the body in the world, and what some define as an anthropology of the senses. Merleau-Ponty (1962: 146, 148) put this eloquently when he proposed that "[t]he body is our general medium for having a world . . . to be a body, is to be tied to a certain world, as we have seen; our body is not primarily in space: it is of it." Given the rich iconographic and material world of the New Kingdom, we can go some way toward reconstructing the sensual life of the Egyptians: the material pleasures, intoxications, tastes, aromas, music, and dances that they embraced and that enhanced their bodily being.

SENSUOUS LIFE

One of the most famous and iconic representations of sensuous life must be the tomb painting of Nebamun, scribe of the granary, dating to around 1400 (Figure 6.1). It depicts Nebamun's wife wearing a rippled, linen dress that is rendered transparent. She is drenched in scent from her unguent cone, there are lotuses on her head, and she holds a large floral bouquet and a sistrum, each evocative of sensuous and sexual life. Both adults are wearing festive floral collars. The larger male, who is the focus of the scene, rests on an impossibly small boat, holding three birds as decoys. The accompanying text reads: *Enjoying oneself, seeing something good and the deeds of the god of the trap, the works of Sekhet, by the one praised by the mistress of hunting, by the scribe and counter of grain. . . . Nebamun and his beloved wife Hatshepsut.*[1] They are enjoying every good thing in the place of eternity. The scene should not be read as a standard

FIGURE 6.1. Wall Painting of Nebamun, Western Thebes, Tomb Now Lost. (Photo courtesy of the British Museum EA 37983)

narrative from life. Fowling scenes were often paired with spearing scenes like that in the tomb of Menna, which is equally redolent with complex symbolism (Figure 6.2). Lotuses are plentiful in this scene: on the boat, being worn, being held, in the river, and so on. These flowers have long been recognized as playing a role in the transformation of the deceased immediately prior to rebirth (Desroches-Noblecourt 1954). The *Tilapia Nilotica* was also highly symbolic, being used both in fishing and fowling scenes. And in capturing the fish, one takes control of destiny. To the Egyptians the tilapia appeared to have multiple lives. Last, with regard to the tomb painting of Nebamun, the young girl is another important motif, squatting between the legs of the father, who offers her protection. She assumes her place in the lineage and is clearly the result

FIGURE 6.2. Fowling Scene, Tomb of Menna, TT 69, Western Thebes. (Image courtesy of the Media Center for Art History, Archaeology, and Historic Preservation, Columbia University)

of a sexual union. The visual symbolism, cues, and multilayerings are abundant in this scene.

There are notable literary puns and associations. For example, the word *qm3* can mean "spear" or "throw," as in the throwstick Nebamun wields, but it can also mean "beget," "create," or "ejaculate." The root of the verb *sti* ranges in meaning through odor and scent as well as the action of pouring and other connections with water. The root *sti* could mean to "beget," "produce," or even "sow" and was written with the determinative of the phallus issuing fluid. Despite any possible ambiguity, we can say that from Middle Kingdom times onwards the verbs certainly sounded the same and must have been metonymic verbal puns.[2] There is a clear linkage between scent, fluids, sexuality, and procreation. It has even been suggested that New Kingdom libation tables reflect this sexual allusion (Figure 6.3).

FIGURE 6.3. Libation Table of Haroua from Deir El Medina. (Photo courtesy of IFAO, Cairo)

These tables have grooves that allow liquid to flow from the *ḥtp* motif at the top, which resembles the phallus, so that the action of pouring or libating also mimics ejaculation.[3] Such an interpretation is bolstered by the fact that the Egyptian words for pour, liquid, hand, mouth, and drink all had erotic associations.

The well-known banqueting scenes from the tomb of Nebamun are also redolent of Egyptian sensual life (see Figure 5.1). The visual codes underlying these scenes with their numerous guests emphasize once again how important it is to look at New Kingdom Egypt in terms of its own values, to restore the cultural intertext. Events like these feasts may never have taken place, and their representation might have been aspirational or idealized. Elite villas could have accommodated large numbers of people, whereas ordinary houses would have been too small. Tombs tend not to preserve the sort of furniture that appears in the paintings. The best-preserved New Kingdom burial of an elite nonroyal person, that of the architect Kha, contained only one high-quality chair. Many of the less affluent Eighteenth Dynasty tombs contained poorer examples of chairs and stools, although none resembling Kha's. In fact, banquets might have taken place out of doors rather than inside houses, as is usually assumed. A detailed examination of the tomb paintings remains inconclusive simply because the physical setting was not the focal point of the compositions.

Scenes from the tomb of Nebamun include numerous sensory images of incense, scented flowers and bouquets, and garlanded wine jars. As well as their visual beauty, scent, and range of symbolic associations, flowers and fruit had multivalent connotations, and some had narcotic properties. Mandrakes, *Mandragora officinarum*, are a good example, featuring heavily in New Kingdom iconography and love poetry: *She would bring her (a bowl) of mandragoras [...] and it would be in her hand while she was smelling it. In other words she would grant me the complexion of her whole body.*[4] They are known to have both soporific and analgesic qualities (Sherratt 1995: 32). These fruits may have been used at festival times to enhance an experience psychoactively or may have been used more regularly as a magico-medical ingredient. The blue lotus, *Nymphaea caerulea*, and other water lilies indigenous to Egypt have also been associated with narcotic qualities and alternative states. Many historians have cast these as purely symbolic flowers, but some have argued that ancient Egyptians used them to induce an ecstatic state, stimulation, and/or hallucinations (Emboden 1981, 1989; Harer 1985). Effects can be experienced by ingesting the flowers or roots and by drinking wine in which they have been soaked, as some depictions suggest. Lotuses and lilies feature prominently in tomb iconography, including the scene from Nebamun's tomb. The blue lotus opens with the sun's rays, closes and sinks into the water, and reappears the next morning. The white lotus, however, flowers at night. Both are palpably symbolic of resurrection and rebirth and are linked to the birth of the sun god Re.

Evidence for less symbolic, but perhaps more powerful, narcotic substances such as opium can be found in material residues in imported ceramics. The opium poppy was cultivated by the first Neolithic groups in central Europe, and by the second millennium it was widely known in the Near East. Andrew Sherratt (1995: 28–32) has argued that it was cultivated on a commercial basis in Cyprus, prepared in an olive-oil base, and shipped around the Mediterranean in characteristic flasks known as Cypriot Base Ring II juglets, which resembled the shape of the inverted poppy capsule (see also Nunn 1996: 153–56). These vessels have been found in abundance in New Kingdom Egyptian settlement sites, although the forms and consequences of the use of opium have received little attention from Egyptologists.

ANCIENT AROMAS

Smell is cultural: odors are invested with culturally coded values. They are often intimate, emotionally charged, and interiorized in a deeply personal way. In the eighteenth and nineteenth centuries A.D. smell was effectively devalued in the West, while sight was elevated as the sense of reason and civilization (Classen et al. 1994: 8–9). In attempting to recapture some semblance of Egyptian experience, the olfactory will have to be reinstated to a level to which we are unaccustomed. In Egyptian art we can apprehend reflections of sensory experience, and particularly in tomb depictions we can determine that the olfactory and the visual were interconnected spheres, denoting aesthetic and sensual pleasure. Iconic examples were hair scented with oil, lavish and pleated clothing, women bedecked with flowers, and exotic resins, ointments, and goods brought into Egypt from Punt, Arabia, and the Mediterranean. Egypt imported quantities of fragrant materials from abroad (Manniche 1999: 25), and significant amounts of scent went up in smoke. Resin was shipped from centers in Mesopotamia, the Levant, and the Red Sea. There were also numerous oils: perfumed moringa oil, almond oil, sesame, balanos, and castor oil. One extant recipe for *hekenu*, a fragrant preparation used in temple worship at Edfu, took one full year for complete preparation.

Unguents were particularly high-status and expensive commodities. Unguent was applied to cult statues (Manniche 1999: 45) but was probably even more desirable for the living body. Jars of unguent have been found in tombs at Deir el Medina, and certain prices can be given to them. For example, an alabaster jar of unguent from the tomb of Kha and Merit cost about 25 *deben*.[5] Spoons for dispensing the unguent were often designed in the shape of a swimming girl or semi-nude serving girl with their obvious sexual associations. To bolster that affinity such young women are further surrounded by ducks, lotus flowers, floral settings, and musical instruments (Bosse-Griffiths 1980: 74). Unguent is usually depicted in tomb iconography in the form of cones, worn on the heads of young women. There has been considerable discussion over whether wearing a tall lump of greasy perfume, melting over the top of one's wig was practicable or desirable. Cherpion (1994) suggests that depictions of unguent cones were unlikely to relate to real objects worn as they are illustrated, yet she does not rule out the possibility altogether. It is more likely that they represent the concept of aroma and all that it entailed symbolically. Specifically the use of perfumed unguents ensured a good life, and in their representation with the deceased such exotica suggested a luxurious life in the afterworld. Bruyère was one of the first scholars to question the use of real unguent cones, claiming it was a metaphysical symbol (1926: 69–72) signifying that the

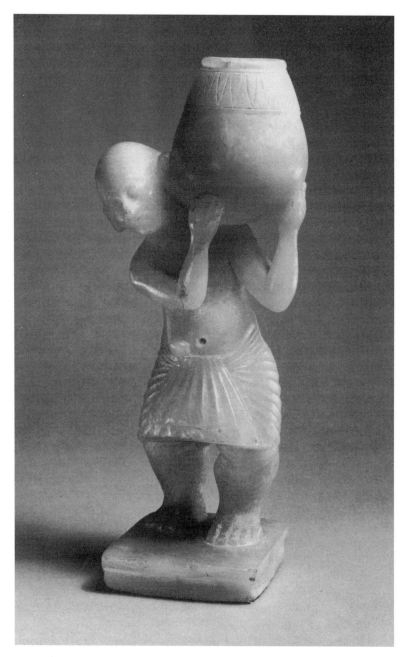

FIGURE 6.4. Cosmetic Jar in the Form of a Dwarf, Eighteenth Dynasty. (Photo courtesy of the Metropolitan Museum of Art, gift of J. Pierpont Morgan, 1917, 17.190.1963)

FIGURE 6.5. Two Women with Unguent Cones, Tomb of Userhet, TT 51, Western Thebes. (Image courtesy of the Media Center for Art History, Archaeology, and Historic Preservation, Columbia University)

FIGURE 6.6. Ostracon of Girl with Monkey. (Photo courtesy of the Petrie Museum, UC 15946)

deceased was blessed and justified, and enhancing the possibilities of resurrection (see Figure 6.5).

For the Egyptians certain smells had explicit erotic overtones, especially when coupled with other signifiers such as hair, skin, makeup, breath, and so on (see Figure 6.6). Aroma was linked to drunkenness, festivities, and sensual life. Gods such as Amun supposedly gave off a divine fragrance, evidenced in the tale of Queen Hatshepsut's divine conception. In the love poetry, the male lover is described as *my lovely myrrh-anointed one,* and the beloved describes herself as having a *bosom full of persea, my hair laden with balm.*[6] Another poem likens the closeness of one's lover to the heavens that *descend in a breeze* and that bring *you her fragrance: an inundating aroma that intoxicates those who are present.*[7] Scent became a coded message for sexuality: those viewers of images who did not understand all the allusions would perceive them as simply attractive (Manniche 1999: 97). Perfumed oils, like modern fragrances, were stored in small decorative glass bottles made to imitate precious stones such as turquoise or lapis lazuli, reinforcing their precious and aesthetic qualities. Scent was also redolent of rebirth, being both symbolic and deeply religious, and formed an integral element in the Egyptian funerary belief system. Specific smells were indissociably linked to the sphere of death and may have heralded its coming: *like the smell of myrrh, like sitting under a sail on a windy day. Death is today like the smell of flowers, like sitting on the shore of Drunkenness.*[8]

Bad smells were strongly negative signs or qualities. One text describes *a woman who is hated like a putrid fisherman, as she stinks.*[9] In the Middle Kingdom text the *Satire on the Trades*, widely copied at Deir el Medina, several occupations are explicitly decried through their exposure to filth, excreta, and vile smells. For instance, the field laborer's work is pitiable because his hands are covered with all manner of *excessive stinks*, the metalworker's fingers are like the crocodile *stinking more than fish roe*, and the stoker reeks of the smell of corpses. Perhaps the most famous text for olfactory representation is the *Dialogue of a Man and his Ba*, where the reek of one's own name is in direct contrast with his earlier hope that the soul's name would live in the West (Parkinson 1999: 163).

Look my name reeks,
look, more than the smell of bird-droppings
on summer days when the sky is hot.
Look my name reeks,
look, more (than the smell) of a haul of spiny fish
on a day of catching when the sky is hot.
Look my name reeks,
look, more than the smell of birds,
more than a clump of reeds full of waterfowl.
Look my name reeks,
look, more than the smell of fishermen,
than the creeks and pools they have fished.
Look my name reeks,
look, more than the smell of crocodiles,
more than sitting under the river edges with a swarm of crocodiles.
Look my name reeks,
look, more than a woman about whom lies are told to her man.[10]

In the richly scented world of ancient Egypt, perfume was used for personal attractiveness, adorning bodies and hair alike, in food and drink, for general intoxication, and during festivals and funerals, and it accompanied the deceased into the next world. Food and perfume were probably inseparable. Juvenal talked of drinking from perfume flasks at Roman banquets and adding unguent to wine, resulting in dizzy inebriation. But perhaps Pliny said it best: "The pleasure of perfume is among the most elegant and also most honourable enjoyments in life" (Classen et al. 1994: 13, 24).

Symbolism of Hair and Beauty

Just as perfume was multivalent and value-coded, so too hair was an important visual cue inflected with meanings of status, gender, and age that also reinforced an elite vision of order. Hair was deeply enmeshed with the use of perfume and unguents. New Kingdom men and women made extensive use of wigs and hairpieces during life and in the mortuary realm. Women could supplement their natural hair or wear wigs over the top of it, whereas men tended to keep their hair short or their heads shaved (Robins 1999: 56). On the basis of iconography it is often assumed that all adult Egyptians had permanently shaved heads and wore wigs as part of daily routine. However, bodies recovered from the Eastern Necropolis at Deir el Medina show that both adolescent and adult individuals of both sexes had their own hair and, in the case of women at least, it was often long. Both elite and non-elite men were depicted with shaved heads when not wearing wigs. Those wigs were short, whereas women's wigs generally fell below the shoulders to breast level. Elite men and high-ranking male relatives are shown with the shoulder-length wig, whereas their younger kin are shown with shaved heads or wearing a short, round wig. Thus hair can denote status and filial relationships (Robins 1999: 59). Robins's analysis demonstrates that the shaving of heads and the wearing of wigs were important status signifiers for elite men. This was in direct contrast to the vernacular depictions of laborers on ostraca from Deir el Medina. The Turin Papyrus also shows balding heads or men with unkempt hair and scruffy beards (see Figure 5.3). For women, hairstyles define age or status rather than hierarchies that are context-dependent (Robins 1999: 65). The lack of physical evidence that women shaved their heads prompts Robins to suggest that this connoted their associations with nature rather than culture. In the New Kingdom two styles predominated: the tripartite wig (divided into three sections) in the earlier Eighteenth Dynasty, followed by an enveloping wig (in a single mass) later in the period.

Literary texts suggest that women's hair was predominantly considered sexual (hair played a central role in Egyptian constructions of the feminine and sexuality, while also obviously having a mundane aspect). On the other hand, there is no evidence to suggest that male hair was sexualized. This is in keeping with the observations of historians and anthropologists working in other cultures on the connection and symbolism of hair with the female (e.g., Eilberg-Schwartz and Doniger 1995). In the Chester Beatty Love Song the girl's hair is likened to *true lapis lazuli*. It is also an alluring weapon: *with her hair she lassos me, with her eye she pulls me in, with her thighs she binds.*[11] In the *Tale of the Herdsman*, a man is confronted by a goddess: *My hair stood on end when I saw her tresses, and the smoothness of her skin.*[12] In the *Tale of Two Brothers*, the erotic overtones of the wig and voluminous hair are explicit. Elaborate hair made a woman sexually attractive and was another signifier alongside the imagery of flowers, birds, monkeys, hip girdles, and the like. However, only one tomb among several hundred at Deir el Medina, that of Kha and Merit, contained a complete wig. There was also an accompanying wig box inscribed with Merit's name. In other tombs at the site, such as 1375 and 1388, there were offerings or inclusions of hair in small quantities, sometimes braided. It is likely that elaborate wigs such as Merit's were beyond the financial reach of most people and were probably worn only on festive and special occasions. By adding to the individual's own hair, wigs enhanced the feminine and sexual characteristics of the wearer. For children and adolescents, amulets could be added to the hair. Texts suggest that these fish amulets may have had protective and erotic significance. Certain hairstyles were worn for occasions such as childbirth and nursing, and others for festivals and feasts. A clear example of the former can be seen in pictorial ostraca from Deir el Medina (see Chapter 4). The dressing and scenting of hair with perfumes and oils, the preparation of elaborate styles such as braiding, and the iconography of grooming with female attendants, as well as the actual implements themselves, all suggest a kind of ritualized behavior that went beyond mere care of the self.

Myriad toiletry articles have been found in cemeteries such as those at Deir el Medina. Combs, pins, tweezers, and razors were common. Interestingly, the bodies found in the Eastern Necropolis were described as hairless by Bruyère. The topic is little studied, but some scholars claimed that the pubic area was probably shaved, along with much of the body (see Brovarski et al. 1982: 189). Shaving may have been partly for aesthetic reasons, but more importantly it implied purity and seems to have been done for males in ritual contexts (Roth 1991). This may go some way to explaining why razors have been found with both male and female bodies. Building on a study of Derchain's (1975), Manniche suggests that the shaven female body can be linked to the "smooth skin" mentioned in love poetry—which is sometimes likened to the qualities of faience. Derchain (1975: 74) suggests that bodies were made smooth or hairless in order to enhance sexual attractiveness. This suggestion, however, runs contrary to the many images of

Figure 6.7. Razor, Comb, Unguent Spoons, and Toilet Items. (Photo courtesy of the British Museum, EA 5945, EA 23056, EA 26357, EA 2623, EA 51050, EA 27730, EA 2597, EA 37924, EA 2674)

Figure 6.8. Duck Container and Toiletry Items. (Photo courtesy of the British Museum, EA 2662, EA 37187, EA 21895, EA 12753, EA 37234, EA 2598, EA 5946, EA 5965)

naked women in paintings, figurines, and statuary that clearly show a darkened pubic triangle, and thus the evidence remains inconclusive.

Iconographic images present physical perfection, while reality will have been very different. Skin would be imperfect, aging would become apparent, and hair would turn gray or fall out. Such concerns affected men and women equally. Texts show that black hair was desired, and various potions were concocted to maintain it. Metonymic ingredients such as ox blood, blood from a black calf, and fat of a black snake featured prominently. Baldness also had its treatments, most of them including fat as an ingredient (Manniche 1999: 133). Treatments for skin included oil of various types, gum, powders, resins, honey, and milk. Kohl was also important for men, women, and children, having both symbolic and practical qualities. Green and black kohl as well as raw materials such as galena have been found in tombs at Deir el Medina. Slate palettes for the grinding and preparation of eyepaint have been found from Predynastic times onwards. Production of this eyepaint has recently been shown to be a laborious process of "wet chemistry" (Manniche 1999). The application and wearing of makeup was an erotically charged activity, as demonstrated in the Turin Papyrus, where we see a girl with a stibium applicator and mirror. Tattoos were another erotic signifier, apparently restricted to women. Goddesses and elite women were not shown with tattoos (Meskell 1998a), which are depicted on seminude singers, musicians, dancers, and women of similar status shown on wall paintings, bowls, statues, figurines, and items of material culture (Derchain 1975) that were common in settlement sites (see Figure 4.7). These tattoos may have been permanent or may have been applied like other makeup upon the body. Often they represented the deity Bes, again signifying a connection to music, dancing, and female sexuality. The presence or absence of a tattoo might have indicated to the viewer the status, profession, and sexuality of the subject. In many cultures, including modern Egypt, singers and dancers occupy an ambivalent status, despite the widespread popularity of such performances (van Nieuwkerk 1995).

Maintaining a perfect outward appearance must have been such an exacting task that only the elite would have had both the time and the wealth to afford the extensive bodily regimes involved. As Assmann (1996: 70–71) has summarized: "Cosmetics as practiced in ancient Egypt was an art in itself, applied to the body and giving the uniformity of perfection. Epilation, hair dressing, the wearing of wigs, eye makeup, dress and other demanding operations collaborated in transforming the individual appearance of a person into something super-individual and uniform to a degree where people closely resembled each other, and even the sexes may have been hard to distinguish. Cosmetics, to use Kent Weeks' term, is a device of 'personification.'"

CLOTHING

As in many cultures, the ancient Egyptians regarded cloth and garments as an important element in a person's life and a signifier of wealth and status. Cloth could operate as a form of currency, function as security for a loan, and be sold, given away as a gift, or handed on from generation to generation (Vogelsang-Eastwood 1993: 2). A woman named Isis at Deir el Medina sent a message to her sister Nebemnu begging that she *weave for me that shawl very promptly before Amenophis, life, health, prosperity, comes (in procession) because I am really naked. Make one [for] my backside(?) because I am naked.*[13] Clothes were clearly recycled because of their inherent value: *And you shall be attentive to this rag of a kilt and this rag of a loincloth in order to rework the kilt into a red sash and the loincloth into an apron.*[14] Cloth and clothing feature prominently in tomb depictions, were included in tomb assemblages like that of Kha and Merit, figured heavily in economic transactions, and were fetishized in love poetry. One cannot simply read tomb iconography for information about clothing in daily life (Janssen 1975: 249–50), but it is still a viable indicator of the variability of clothing according to social position and activity. Furthermore, tomb iconography reflects the cultural importance of clothing and dress, such as its sensual, erotic, and gendered characteristics. Wraparound garments such as kilts, skirts, cloaks, shawls, and some dresses consisted simply of a length of cloth. In archaeological contexts it may be possible to identify larger linens used in female clothing as opposed to shorter male garments such as kilts. A second category included cut-to-shape garments such as loincloths, bag-tunics, and dresses. The basic shape was a triangle or rectangle, sewn at some of the edges and fastened with cords. These items do not show signs of being tailored to fit, and there are no darts to indicate shaping (Vogelsang-Eastwood 1993: 6). This has obvious implications for the sort of gendered iconography in New Kingdom tombs where women are often shown in revealing and tight-fitting dresses. The purpose there is to highlight the body, and this is privileged over the accurate depiction of the garments. Such images are reflections of a desired, somewhat canonical world constructed by the male artisan.

The preservation offered by some tombs and the detailed economic evidence from the Ramesside Period (Janssen 1975) make it possible to assign a relative value to the linens of individual people. Our best intact example is again Kha and Merit from Deir el Medina. As Table 6.1 demonstrates, a significant proportion of the overall tomb costings (approximately 5,700 *deben*) consisted of linen garments and cloth for the couple. Kha's linens are more numerous and expensive than those of his wife. Some of his clothing showed signs of tapestry and compound-weave

TABLE 6.1
Linen from Tomb 8, Kha and Merit

Kha's linen pall over coffin	50
clothes of Kha: 17 tunics, 26 skirts and loincloths, 56 loincloths, 1 heavy tunic	1,395
bed linen of Merit	100
Merit's linen/clothing	65
TOTAL	1,610 *deben*

bands, while others had sleeves (Schiaparelli 1927: 67–69). Many have the insignia of Kha on them, suggesting that they belonged to him rather than to Merit. However, it is possible that some of his linens were used by her. In tomb 1379 a new tunic was found in a large basket (Bruyère 1937: 59–60), suggesting that garments could be included simply for the tomb, rather than being cast-off clothes worn in life.

Certain garments were worn by both men and women, including loincloths and tunics, with little variation over the dynasties. However, leather loincloths were traditionally worn by men, while various types of dresses were worn only by women. Evidence for children's clothing is more limited (Vogelsang-Eastwood 1993: 7). The quality of cloth and decoration was the great demarcator. Color was probably key here: whereas elite individuals could have purchased dyed cloth, the extreme case being the garments found in the tomb of Tutankhamun (Vogelsang-Eastwood 1999), others made do with colored threads interwoven into linen fabric.

THE SOCIAL LIFE OF THINGS

Specific objects, sets of commodities, and pleasurable activities played an important part in representations of sensory experience. Particular care and craftsmanship were lavished on items connected with cosmetics and grooming, as can be seen in the myriad kohl jars, kohl applicators, cosmetic scoops, combs, mirrors, and unguent jars from the period. These activities went beyond the level of adorning or embellishing an individual body to become one of the most distinctive aspects of Egyptian culture. Adornment, clothing, appearance, and bodily *hexis*—comportment, gesture, taste, and the use of implements—are culturally particular and charged with a host of social meanings and values (Bourdieu 1977: 87).

Alphonso Lingis (1994: vii) claims that every "great culture is not only an elaboration of specific kinds of ritual, costume and raiment, technology, science, and metaphysico-religious speculation—a specific kind of mind, but also an elaboration of a specific body-ideal." In Egypt one can apprehend this regime of bodily *hexis* through textual references, iconography, and a wide range of material culture. The layerings of symbols and meanings around items pertaining to bodily adornment and decoration are different from those of other categories of artifacts such as household goods, work tools, and funerary equipment, demarcating them as specific cultural products.

There has been an outpouring of publications dealing with cultural constructions of the body throughout history (e.g., Turner 1984; Feher et al. 1989; Richlin 1992; Dean-Jones 1994; Meskell 1996, 1999a; Montserrat 1998; Wyke 1998). In archaeology we have witnessed a shift from more Foucauldian notions of a socially mapped and inscribed body to one that is more phenomenologically experienced. Part of the project of this book is to reinstate the lived quality of bodily life in New Kingdom Egypt and to discuss how aspects of material culture were potent symbols, encoded with multivalent meanings about sex, class, status, age, and so on. Among those of greater wealth, burial evidence shows significant expenditure on gold jewelry, in particular for men. This is clearly demonstrated by an analysis of tomb 8 at Deir el Medina. An X-ray analysis has shown that Kha's mummy has a gold collar around his neck under the many layers of wrappings. This type of ornament was bestowed upon individuals by pharaoh himself, and Kha was a royal architect. He also wears a collar made from a string of gold rings; a long necklace of plaited gold supporting a heart scarab; a *tyt* amulet probably in carnelian; an amulet in the form of a snake's head, probably also in carnelian, on the forehead; a pair of gold earrings; and a bracelet on each arm made of a strip of gold (Curto and Mancini 1968: 78–79). This is also of interest since men are generally not represented wearing earrings in tomb iconography, with the notable exception of Sennefer (TT 92). X-ray analysis of Merit's body revealed a broad collar made up of eight strings of hard-stone plaques; two pairs of gold earrings; and a girdle hanging low on the pelvis consisting of eleven gold plaques linked by five strings of glass or faience beads. These plaques are in the form of bivalve shells, which were symbolic of female sexuality (see Chapter 4). Such analysis also demonstrates that Merit has considerably less jewelry than her husband and that it is made from less expensive materials.

The material culture of bodily adornment is extensive. Wooden combs, razors, pins, and mirrors have been found in abundance at sites including Amarna, Deir el Medina, and Gurob. This was not necessarily confined to elite culture but was diffused throughout socioeconomic groups. Some

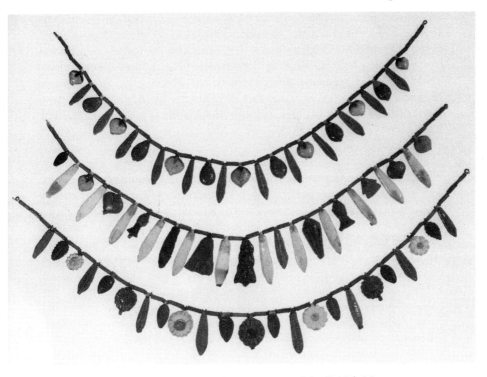

FIGURE 6.9. Jewelry from Amarna. (Photo courtesy of the British Museum, EA 57884, EA 57885, EA 57886)

recent small-scale excavations at Kom Rabiʿa, an artisan's settlement at Memphis, illustrate this clearly in the sheer number and variety of personal ornamentations and other items of material culture (see Chapter 2). The quantity of pendants, plaques, earrings, ear studs, bracelets, rings, and beads uncovered in the small excavated area (Giddy 1999) highlights the importance and ubiquity of personal adornment at various socioeconomic levels. Earrings became popular in the Eighteenth Dynasty for men, women, and children of both sexes. At the Deir el Medina Eastern Necropolis, the Eighteenth Dynasty burials demonstrate that both men and women possessed such jewelry during life and took them to the grave. Hairpins were made from various materials and zoomorphic boxes were used for jewelry or unguents, while spoons with decorative handles and dishes (Brovarski et al. 1982: 207) were common items in both daily and funerary repertoires. Bodily adornment, the application of makeup, and the attention to grooming were not specific to women and thus were not gendered in ways that archaeologists commonly assume. These items reflect much about the owner's status, wealth, and age. While women like Merit had the most expensive toilet items, crafted from metal and alabaster, poorer women such as Madja in tomb 1370 and Satre in 1388 made do with pieces of lesser value. Throughout dynastic times, luxurious objects made of turquoise, lapis lazuli, jasper, serpentine, and other prized hard stones were emulated in less expensive materials such as colored faience and glass. The desire to possess and copy prestige items further supports the argument that there was a commodity culture, and we see different styles of evidence of this culture, from poorer communities such as Memphis to wealthier villages such as Deir el Medina.

Living experience in the New Kingdom was highly commodified through hundreds of categories of material culture. Possessions, or commodity culture, and "the good life" were inextricably linked. As we have seen from the iconography and artifacts, such items were worn, carried, given and received as gifts, inscribed, mended when they broke, and ultimately deposited in tombs or passed on to heirs. Texts from Deir el Medina document all these aspects of the social life of things (see Appadurai 1986), and the archaeological record from the site provides the material corroboration. The Eighteenth Dynasty tombs at Deir el Medina and elsewhere in the Theban Necropolis were constellated around life experience as mediated through material possessions. Since almost all these tombs have been plundered, the only hints at the possessions they once contained are the wall paintings, and the occasional text.

Figure 6.10. Pottery and Imitation Stone Vessels from Deir el Medina. (Photo courtesy of IFAO, Cairo)

Year 25, first month of summer, day 9. List of the inspection of everything found in the ruined tomb across from the burial place of the scribe Amennakhte (son of) Ipuy:

> 1 coffin of god's stone
> 1 sarcophagus with a linen (?) pall
> 1 coffin with a linen (?) pall
> 1 ebony folding stool with ducks' heads, mended
> 2 couches
> 1 box of papyrus
> 3 headrests
> 1 irqes-basket filled with rags [...]
> 2 pairs of sandals
> 1 scribal palette
> 1 bronze bowl
> 1 water bag
> 1 box (contents: 1 knife, 1 pin, 1 metal dish, 1 juglet, 1 razor case, 1 razor,
>   1 scraping razor)
> granite vessels: 5 menet-jars
> 1 metal dish
> 1 pot
> 1 staff
> food basket (with) bread
> 1 wooden qeren (unknown object)
> 1 alabaster kebu-jar
> 2 wooden neshi-containers of medicine
> 1 box (contents: 1 faience amulet, 1 alabaster kebu-jar, 1 pot of ointment, 10 [...])
> 1 box (contents: 1 alabaster kebu-jar, 1 comb, 1 tweezer)
> 1 alabaster nemset-vessel
> a khar (unknown)
> 2 pieces of scenting material.[15]

An exception is the intact burial of the wealthy architect Kha, who probably died in the reign of Amenhotep III. As we have seen, it is not difficult to construct a picture of Kha as an individual. His elevated social position is demonstrated through items left in the tomb that were specific to his profession: a whole array of specialized scribal equipment, and most prestigious of all, a gold necklace of valor and a gold cubit-measure that had been presented by Amenhotep II. Other objects, such as his clothes, jewelry, furniture, toiletries, and gaming board, give glimpses into his personal life (Meskell 1998c: 372). The sexual inequality reflected in these intact tomb assemblages is borne out by cost analysis of the intact burials of Kha and his wife Merit. Kha had some 196 goods bearing his name or directly associated with him, costing a total of about 4,000 *deben*, whereas Merit appears to have had only thirty-nine objects, with a total cost of just under 800 *deben*. Their jointly owned goods, bearing the names of both spouses, came to only 129 *deben* (Meskell 1998c: 375). Figures like these illustrate how social inequalities within marriage could be played out on the material level.

Other finds of artifacts serve to highlight Egypt's commodity culture and the ways in which elite Egyptians negotiated their own identities, keeping and discarding specific items within the ritual of gift giving. A refuse dump excavated near the building in the center of Amarna known as the King's House is revealing in this connection. This was where Akhenaten distributed luxury goods to officials of similar rank to Kha, as a reward for good service. The goods were also a form of movable wealth that was handed out at appropriate times: there are representations of these occasions in the tombs of Akhenaten's officials at Amarna (see Figure 6.11). What is perhaps surprising about this dump is that it soon accumulated a mass of materials discarded from these ritual distribution ceremonies. Among the objects dumped were glazed finger rings with bezels of Akhenaten's cartouche, colored glass bottles, and pottery oil-containers imported from the Mediterranean. Apparently the recipients took away the more desirable or valuable things given at the ceremony and threw away the rest, even though these items of refuse would be quite desirable in other contexts (Kemp 1989: 292; Shortland 2000: 72).

In a nonmonetary system like that of New Kingdom Egypt, it is perhaps hardly surprising that commodities attained such a central cultural importance. Yet the sheer volume of Egyptian material culture, and the endless repetition of its canonical forms across various media, are still a phenomenon unique to Bronze Age Egypt. Consider the Mesopotamian city-states—Ur, Babylon, Assur—that were contemporary with the New Kingdom and that attained a comparable level of technological sophistication. In these cultures there does not seem to have been the same emphasis on status expressed through a standardized suite of luxury commodities, and certainly not on the representational forms that are so important in Eighteenth Dynasty funerary art. Objects of fine craftsmanship, elaborate clothing, jewelry, adornments, and things of natural beauty such as flowers were central to Egyptian life experience, to ritual enactments, and to the realm of the tomb. One context that consolidates these domains is the festival, articulating as it does many of these experiences and sensory pleasures and drawing together the major topics discussed in this chapter.

FESTIVALS AND FEASTING

In the New Kingdom people had various avenues through which to access religious experience, primarily through a notable suite of ritual practices.

Figure 6.11. Akhenaten Distributing Gifts from the Tomb of Meryra, Amarna. (Photo courtesy of the Egypt Exploration Society)

The Ramesside Period was a great age of personal piety, where individuals could access the gods through their perpetual submission (Baines 1987, 1991). Yet temple life remained the sphere of priests and pharaoh, whereas ordinary people were excluded from the inner spaces. A hierarchy of relationships had to be negotiated and maintained (Shafer 1997: 1). Yet the ritual life of the non-elite was hardly impoverished: they had access to oracles and magical intervention and could make offerings to a host of deities and deceased relatives. Baines (2001) refers to such practices as forming a type of religious microenvironment. Scores of votive stelae and statues were found at Deir el Medina deposited in houses, chapels, shrines, or tomb markers, rather than being donated at state temples. But there were other opportunities for ritual participation, such as visiting shrines and presenting votive offerings, partaking in festivals, or employing intercessors to take one's case to the temple. An example of the latter is contained in a text written by a man on the Theban West Bank, who sought the help of someone who did have access to the cult statue in the temple.

> *When I was looking for you (the god) to tell you some affairs of mine, you happened to be concealed in your holy of holies, and there was nobody having access to it to send it to you. Now as I was waiting to encounter Hori . . . and he said to me, "I have access." So I am sending him to you. See you must discard seclusion today and come out in procession in order that you may decide upon the issues involving seven kilts belonging to the temple of Horemheb and also those two kilts belonging to the necropolis scribe. . . . Now as for one who is in the same position as you, being in the place of seclusion and concealed, he sends forth pronouncements, but you haven't communicated anything at all to me.*[16]

Festivals provided occasions for a variety of pursuits: ritual, religious, social, sexual, sensory, visceral, and so on. All these domains coexisted as overlapping spheres integrating both the living and the dead. Jan Assmann has offered one interpretation, influenced by Bakhtin's (1984) writing on European carnivals and the social functionalism of Luhmann.[17] He describes Egyptian festivals as highly stylized events, where everyday life is transformed into art (1989: 7; 1993). From this perspective activities such as dancing, music, and erotic signifiers that are central to festivals are read as *representation* rather than *reality* (1989: 11). Assmann sees this as a process of aestheticizing pleasure as Foucault (1978) would construct, an *ars erotica* like that of Japan, so that festivals did not revolve around sexual activity but rather deployed those codes and symbols for effect. Shock may have formed a substantial part of the drama, marking disjunctures between contexts. Following diverse scholarship on *carnivale*, he argues that festivals forged social links, as one can imagine for any community. Assmann posits that society was less divided in antiquity, and spheres of life—between households, between work and leisure, between public and private—were less distinct than in modern contexts. As such, festivals acted to produce difference. They had their own codes, moral values, and norms, significantly different from those of actions in other situations: they represented a break with formal decorum. In festival time one could legitimately *follow your heart*, whereas social decorum would traditionally promote keeping the heart under control.

During festival times people are freed from the tedium of daily life. There is a cessation of labor and an unrestrained consumption of the products of labor (Bataille 1993: 90). People escape into a sensual, intoxicating realm and are transported into a state of elation. Ecstatic experience is foregrounded: Bataille even suggests that the pursuit of ruination features heavily in that experience. Festive events constitute the highlights and crises in the rhythm of the religious life of both community and individual (Bleeker 1967: 24). Festivals are also inflected with narratives of the life course: sowing and harvesting, seasonal festivals, calendrical dates, family festivals, religious events, festivals honoring divine figures, and the commemoration of events. The word for festival, *ḥb*, was written with the determinative for a hut and a dish or bowl. The former was a primitive "tabernacle" or simple temple, the latter was used in purification or libation ceremonies (Bleeker 1967: 27). In the various depictions of festivals, such as the Opet festival shown in the Luxor temple, small, temporary huts are shown sometimes covered in leaves and are often associated with jars, presumably containing beer or wine. Both this festival and the "Beautiful Festival of the Wadi" were held in honor of Amun. The latter event was particularly important to the villagers at Deir el Medina.

Religious festivals actualized belief; they were not simply social celebrations. They acted in a multiplicity of related spheres. There were festivals of the gods, of the king, and of the dead. We have already seen the potency and popularity of the cult of the dead, such as ancestor veneration (Chapter 4) and the interconnected fear of the dangerous dead and affection for the deceased. Dead individuals are mourned and their benevolence desired. Bleeker argued that the Beautiful Festival of the Wadi was a key example of a festival of the dead, which took place between the harvest and the Nile flood. In it, the divine boat of Amun traveled from the Karnak temple to the necropolis of Western Thebes. A large procession followed, and living and dead were thought to commune near the graves, which became *houses of the joy of the heart* on that occasion. Supposedly the images of deceased individuals were taken along in the procession and then returned to the grave. On a smaller scale, a family festival also took place in which the deceased again took part (Bleeker 1967: 137). In this way a link was forged between celebrating the gods and the dead in a single all-encompassing event.

The connection between religiosity, ritual experience, and sexuality is most fully articulated in this festival. We should not envisage these as separate or mutually exclusive spheres. Festivals appear to have been free of moralistic overtones or acts of contrition. They provided a site for a multi-tude of delights, desires, memories, adorations, and experiences. Some of those were intensely personal, sensual, and even sexual. For example, we might posit that votive offerings such as phalli were made at festival time, perhaps at the Festival of the Wadi when the image of Amun-Re in ithy-phallic form visited and "slept" with Hathor at Deir el Bahri (Pinch 1993: 244). Couples may have used this moment to invoke blessing on their sex-ual lives, possibly associating themselves with the divine couple and their union. As Pinch proposes, by the Twentieth Dynasty women or couples may have slept at the Hathor shrine on a festival night in the hope of a dream from the goddess. Personal names may give us further insight. Many individuals bear names connotative of the festival, such as Amenem-heb "Amun-is-in-festival" or Mutemwiya "Mut-is-in-the-carrying-bark," which may refer to their being born or conceived at this time. Mutemwiya is a very common name at Deir el Medina, where the Festival of the Wadi was a major event in the ritual calendar.[18] The increase in Ramesside phalli at these shrines, as opposed to the numbers in the Eighteenth Dynasty, suggests that this mass presentation was a later development per-haps parallel to the Wadi Festival. Inscriptional evidence demonstrates that a great variety of people visited Hathor's shrines: high-ranking and minor officials, artisans, soldiers, priests, and obviously women.

The best-attested festivals of the New Kingdom are those in the Theban area, in particular the Beautiful Festival of the Wadi, though the adjective often translated as good or beautiful, *nfrt*, also has connotations of vitality, perfection, wholeness, and completeness. Ramesside Period prayers, inscribed in graffiti from Hathor's temple at Deir el Bahri, show that people went to the goddess's shrine at the time of the festival in order to pray for bodily integrity and physical vitality, sometimes enumerated on the level of individual body parts (Marciniak 1971: 59). The festival, whose name evoked completeness and perfection, was an obvious time to ask the gods to bestow bodily health: *They [i.e., the pilgrims to the shrine] are in the favour of Amun-Re, King of the Gods, Mut, Khonsu, and all the gods and goddesses of Thebes. May they (i.e., the gods) give bread to the heart of he who loves them. . . . may they grant favours, may they grant an existence in the favour of men and a body in the presence of the gods. May they grant them eyes to see and legs to walk. May they grant a long life and a vital old age.*[19]

At Hathor shrines such as the Eighteenth Dynasty site at Mirgissa in the Second Cataract, festivals may have been marked by offerings of jewelry, since numerous beads and votive necklaces were found during excavation (Pinch 1993: 338). One may envisage a priest or priestess coming and col-lecting the offerings and then replacing the baskets, some of which have been detected archaeologically. The fact that these items of jewelry were personal objects suggests a powerful and intimate link with the goddess.

Moreover, at the shrine site of Timna in the Sinai, votives were ritually smashed to signify the handing over from human to deity, attesting to the range of ritual practices occurring at the time. There was a high proportion of female donors in the New Kingdom, although generally tomb paintings tend not to show the religious practices of women but rather focus on male activities. Votive material in the archaeological record, some inscribed with women's names, is one of the only strands of evidence for personal piety. Personal texts written by men at Deir el Medina also reveal that the villagers were heavily involved in festivals celebrating Hathor (Valbelle 1985: 323–25; Pinch 1993: 344).

Elaborate preparations were made to celebrate the Festival of the Wadi by gathering together the garlands, incense, and other offerings required for various ceremonies (McDowell 1999: 96–97). One man requests: *Send me a skin and some paint and some incense; and send us greenery and flowers [on] day 18, because they will pour a libation on day 19.*[20] Textual evidence reinforces the idea that singing, playing tambourines and sistra, and dancing were all part of such festive occasions. The local festival of Amenhotep I was celebrated at least six days each year (Valbelle 1985: 332–35) and was a time for drinking: *the gang rejoiced before him for four solid days of drinking together with their children and their wives.*[21] Drinking was also directly associated with Hathor in her ritual aspect as Lady of Drunkenness. The journal of the necropolis similarly mentions the festival of Sokar-Osiris, which was deemed a free day for the workmen. It was especially celebrated at night. People went about garlanded with onions around their necks and brought offerings to Sokar-Osiris and the deceased. The festival was recorded in texts from the site, as well as by representations in tombs, such as those of Amenmose (TT 9), Khabekhenet (TT 2), and Inherkhau (TT 359) (Janssen 1997: 128). There were no theatrical performances as such in Egypt, but the calendar of festivals may have linked magic, ritual, intoxication, and a certain amount of personal experience. One text relates that a workman went to drink in the village during four days, over a weekend, suggesting a serious yet sanctioned degree of celebration (O. IFAO 1357 in Janssen 1997: 93).

Texts from Deir el Medina provide some insight into the preparations and foodstuffs brought by individuals to festivals or other feasts. One text records some thirty-one women, some identified by the name of their daughter or son, but only three men. Each brought bread loaves of various types, oil, and jars, undoubtedly containing beer.[22] Janssen argues that this represents a feast with people bringing presents, although no actual occasion is specified. A series of similar texts shows women bringing food. O. DeM 134 records ninety-three loaves being brought by thirteen women, whereas O. DeM 222 lists twenty-five men and three women bringing loaves, vegetables, meat, fish, wreaths, and jars. Janssen sees this

FIGURE 6.12. Musicians from the Tomb of Nakht, TT 52, Western Thebes. (Image courtesy of the Media Center for Art History, Archaeology, and Historic Preservation, Columbia University)

as gift giving (1997: 67); alternatively, these may be festival preparations involving numerous members of the community. In other related texts people bring mats and baskets, while others supply dates, persea fruits, cakes, wooden boxes, and other forms of equipment. Such texts are formulaic, with the name of a person listed and then his/her gift. Janssen suggests (1997: 85) that when a text lists more women, this implies that the celebration is for a woman, but this seems a rather reductive and simplistic reading. These could perhaps be private feasts that involved substantial numbers of people making preparations in a highly ordered and regulated fashion, supported by the act of recording itself. Another possibility is that some of these texts may relate to larger, more formal occasions such as festivals involving the entire community and requiring considerable organization.

Festivities were marked by troupes of female singers with sistra and *menat* necklaces, male singers clapping their hands, and the sound of musical instruments. Bouquets of flowers, which enhanced the visual and aromatic quality of the event, were also brought to the deceased, who could perhaps employ the scent to attain new life. This is reflected linguistically: the word

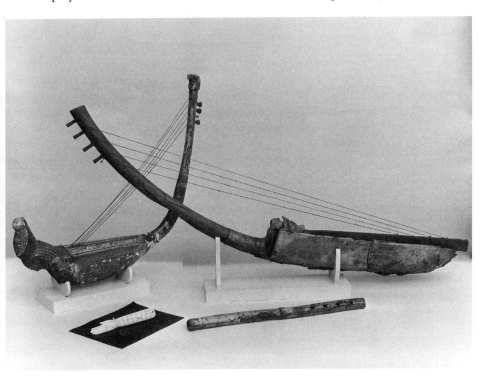

FIGURE 6.13. Musical Instruments. (Photo courtesy of the British Museum, EA 24564, EA 37302, EA 38170, EA 6385)

for bouquet or garland, *'nḫ*, was phonetically the same as the word for "life." Flowers such as the lotus were used to symbolize life for both the living and the deceased. Banquet scenes in the decorated elite tombs, like those of Nebamun, may relate to the Festival of the Wadi, showing feasting to excess and other sensory pleasures. Servants are depicted anointing guests, with women being more often decorated with flowers and funerary cones than their male counterparts. As previously discussed, unguent cones were probably metaphysical symbols rather than actual objects (Bruyère 1926: 69–72). In the banquet scene of Paheri a number of female relatives are shown with their nurses, smelling flowers and receiving bowls containing alcohol. Accompanying the image was written *For your ka, drink to drunkenness, make holiday.* A distant cousin named Nubmehy says to a servant, *Give me eighteen cups of wine, behold I should love (to drink) to drunkenness, my inside is dry as straw.* Tjupu, a female relative says *drink, do not spoil the entertainment, and let the cup come to me* (Tylor and Griffith 1894: 25). Tomb scenes such as these probably parallel the activities enjoyed at festivals. Indeed the iconography of festivals and of funerals has much in common, and the ritual practices of the two may have been comparable (see below). Bleeker described (1967: 138) that at festivals drinks were raised and participants exhorted *for your ka, drink the good intoxicating drink, celebrate a beautiful day.* The phrase "celebrate a beautiful day" probably links the presence of Hathor at the festival, bestowing great happiness upon the dead.

Later festivals at Edfu and Bubastis were feasts of drunkenness that were simultaneously associated with "roaming in the marshes" and the goddess Hathor.[23] Sexuality was euphemistically referred to as "a holiday," "to roam the marshes," and "to follow the heart," all of which were associated with Hathor and sexuality. Hathor was specifically associated with the pleasures of drunkenness, and the place of drunkenness could also refer to the temple itself. It resounded with positive qualities rather than negative or moralistic ones, being very different from the Western cultural milieu. For the Egyptians, such sensual states bridged the divide between the divine and human worlds. Smelling lotuses and flowers with mildly narcotic properties would have added to the experience of communing with the dead and the deified: *O my god! O my lotus!* is one line of adoration in the Cairo love poetry.

Cross-culturally, festivals take place in a supranormal time and space in which people experience themselves differently for the period of celebration, whether it be ecstatic experience or sensual/sexual activity. Reading Bakhtin (1984) more closely, and employing his insights to an Egyptian context, proves even more illuminating than Assmann has indicated. The feast is always related to time—cosmic, biological, or historic. Festivals were linked to moments of crisis, the breaking points in the natural cycle or in the life of human society. Death and revival constituted such moments, as did change and renewal, leading to a more festive perception of the world. Whether organized by the state or informal, such festivals created no other existential order but rather reinforced the existing one (1984: 9). During carnivalesque revelry, social hierarchy may have been suspended, and inferiors and superiors may have interacted together: each individual was an indissoluble part of the collectivity. They were each released from the mundane and utilitarian, providing a taste of utopian possibilities. Yet festivals cannot be separated from bodily life, the earth, nature, and the cosmos.

Festivals and funerals were both powerful episodes in the Egyptian life cycle, sharing many of the same symbols, practices, rituals, and paraphernalia. They were transitional moments that served many functions: emotional outpouring, feasting, social interaction, religious observance, and communing with the gods. The *Harper's Song* from the tomb of chief workman Inherkhau at Deir el Medina evinces how those worlds conjoined for the ancient Egyptians.

> *Put ointment and perfumed oils gathered beside you,*
> *and garlands of lotus and mandragora flowers to your breast.*
> *The one who sits beside you is the woman of your heart.*
> *Do not let your heart be angry on account of anything that has happened.*
> *Set song before you, do not recall evil,*
> *the abomination of god.*
> *Concentrate on delights.*
> *Oh righteous one, oh truly just man!*
> *tranquil, kindly, content and calm,*
> *who is joyful and speaks no evil,*
> *give drunkenness to your heart daily,*
> *until that day comes in which there is a landing.*[24]

CHAPTER SEVEN

Cycles of Death and Life

IN THIS BOOK I have taken as my template the cycle of human life and attempted to isolate its culturally specific manifestations in the Egyptian experience of the world. To bring the discussion full circle one should consider that other aspect of life, the ever-present spectre of death, about which the Egyptians had ambivalent feelings. The Egyptians conceived of death and rebirth as cyclical processes; even in the afterlife, the cycle continued. The *ka*, the individual's twin self or vital force, lived on, as did other components of the person's individual identity. The unity of life created a biography that accompanied the individual to the next world. The "autobiographies" surviving in a few New Kingdom nonroyal tombs give a sense of this. They combine personal information with narratives of life achievements that were a subject of pride to the deceased and accompanied him to the next world. Ahmose, son of Ibana, writes in his autobiography: *I grew up in the town of Nekheb, my father being a soldier of the King of Upper and Lower Egypt, Seqenenre, the justified. Baba son of Reonet was his name. I became a soldier in his stead on the ship "The Wild Bull" in the time of the Lord of the Two Lands, Nebpehtire, the justified. I was a youth who had not married. . . . Now when I established a household, I was taken to the ship "Northern," because I was brave.* [1]

ATTITUDES TO DEATH

Using elite autobiographies such as Ahmose's to examine Egyptian culture from the top down might lead to the assumption that death was seen as a state to be celebrated and accepted, not feared, since wealthy Egyptians prepared throughout their lives for death. Evidence from monuments, tombs, and many formal texts presents a rather optimistic scenario that must have been ingrained in numerous aspects of living experience. However, views from the ground up, from the more individual accounts of death and dying, suggest a radically different picture—one that showed death and decay in all their horror. Ordinary people knew that tombs were plundered, that mummies were despoiled, and that the offering cults were not maintained for ever. Fears were real and tangible, and despite all the religious and ritual hyperbole there was an acknowledgement of the uncertainties of the next world. This is illustrated by the literary text the *Dialogue of a Man and his Ba* (Parkinson 1997:151–65): *If you think of burial, it is agony, it is the bringing of tears through making a man miserable, it is taking a man from his house, being cast upon the high ground. You shall not come up again to see suns.*

Egyptian culture had no sense of gerontocracy, unlike societies that placed great importance on the wisdom and teachings of the elderly. Yet the *Instruction of Amenemope* underscores the respect that should be accorded to the old (Lichtheim 1976: 161). Not surprisingly, the end of the cycle brought with it great pains and fears that were duly recorded in the *Instruction of Ptahhotep: Old age descended; woe is come and weakness is renewing itself; the heart passes the night in pain, every day; the eyes are shrunk, the ears made deaf; strength now perishes.*[2] Egyptian culture stressed the preservation and revivification of the body at the point of death and thereafter, and it must have been frightening to witness and experience corporeal decay firsthand. It is a popular misconception that Egyptian society, with its belief system that posited everlasting bodies and the afterlife, was somehow comfortable with the process of aging and life's end. Elaborate remedies for baldness and gray hair reflect a familiar preoccupation with youthfulness. Death was depicted as an enemy, as were the physical signs that heralded its coming.

Embodying Death

In pharaonic times the body, or physical form, could be perceived in a variety of ways. I have discussed elsewhere how the various components of the living person covered a multiplicity of aspects and survived bodily death (Meskell 1999a: 111–13). Several essential components of the individual may survive after death: the name (*rn*), the shadow (*šwt*), and personal magic (*ḥk3*), along with the *ka* and *ba* discussed below (Pinch 1994: 147; Zandee 1960: 20). The corporeal body had a tangible trajectory after death, which was divisible or multifaceted. The self was comprised of several elements, none of which was exactly equivalent to *soul*. First, the *ka* has been described as a series of relations and representations. It was the memory of the deceased and physical representations that served to activate this memory—acting as a channel, reviving the image of the person (Bolshakov 1997: 145–52). The *ba* was linked closely to the body and was usually depicted as a human-headed bird that journeyed between the underworld and this world and was also at risk of dying a second and final death. After passing various obstacles the deceased might attain the status of *3ḥ*, or transfigured and effective spirit. According to the *Instruction of Ani*, one should *satisfy the akh; do what he desires, and abstain for him from abomination, that you may be safe from his harms.*[3] There were other troublesome spirits termed *m(w)t*, the dangerous dead. These entities retained the lifetime sex of the individual, and female spirits seem to have been more feared: the dead were not sexed differently from the living. So within this schema the various elements remained, and an individual could ultimately adopt specific trajectories through time, benevolent or otherwise. Each of these aspects of the self retained the character of the individual (Assmann 1996: 80). And it was because of one's earthly achievement that a person may aspire to an enduring place in the larger social memory. One could not simply rely on collective distinctions such as elite descent or group membership; only individual achievements were of consequence.

The Egyptians viewed death itself as a transitory state that did not prevent people from involving themselves in the world of the living. Although memories of the deceased did not appear to transcend the generations, the dead could intervene in daily affairs (Baines 1991). Requests, advice, and

Figure 7.1. Shabti Box of Ipu Showing Hathor, Goddess of the Sycamore and the Ba Bird. (Photo courtesy of the British Museum, EA 35648)

magical intervention could all be sought from the deceased. Texts from New Kingdom Deir el Medina provide vivid testimonies to the belief that the dead could be a powerful force in the world of the living, who could communicate and interact with the dead. Perhaps most vivid are the requests from individuals to their deceased relatives. These are conventionally known as *Letters to the Dead*; fewer than twenty have survived from all periods of Egyptian history. In the letter to Ikhtay, written by the scribe of the necropolis Butehamun to his dead wife, he asks Ikhtay to petition the Lords of Eternity on his behalf. We see clearly Butehamun's sense of the inevitability of death together with its unknowability, while his doubts that his words would reach his wife in the afterworld contrast strikingly with the hopefulness expressed by the very act of writing. The deceased holds a privileged position, being closer to the gods and acting as intercessor for human individuals in the living world. Texts like these were usually left at the tomb of the deceased, as is evidenced at Deir el Medina during this period. Some of the letters were written on the interiors of bowls, which may have been filled with foodstuffs to attract the *ba* of the deceased on its visits to the tomb. The *ba* would stop to consume the food and see the request at the same time. In magical terms such direct requests would appear to be the most promising point of contact with the other world.

> *If one can hear me*
> *(in) the place where you are,*
> *tell the Lords of Eternity,*
> *"Let (me) petition for my brother,"*
> *so that I may make [...] in [their] hearts,*
> *whether they are great or small.*
> *It is you who will speak with a good speech in the necropolis.*
> *Indeed, I did not commit an abomination against you*
> *while you were on earth,*
> *and I hold to my behaviour.*
> *Swear to god in every manner,*
> *saying "What I have said will be done!"*
> *I will not oppose your will in any utterance*
> *until I reach you.*
> *[May you act] for me (in) every good manner,*
> *if one can hear.*[4]

EGYPTIAN RITUALS OF DEATH

Perhaps the most recognizable images of New Kingdom death are the scenes of funerals in elite tombs. Though formulaic, these scenes are suffused with the experiential and sensory aspects of death: the scent of garlands and incense, the weeping of mourners, the pouring of water offerings, and the recitation of prayers. All these were powerful and emotive at the time, but they leave few archaeological traces. It is important to reinstate them into our discussions. When such emotions as grief at death and fear of ancestors correspond with the values of a living society, then these emotions will be enacted through material practice, principally ritual. Looking at Egyptian funerals gives some insight into the culture as a whole.

It is usual to divide Egyptian rituals of death into a mourning period, preparation of the corpse, interment, and regular cultic practices for the deceased intended to be maintained indefinitely (Lloyd 1989: 124–131). These practices were often preceded by the much earlier construction of the tomb for wealthier individuals. Such an emotional and material investment presumably affected the experience of death, if only in terms of preparation and determinacy. John Baines (1991) states that the Egyptians, like many groups, tended to dramatize their loss on a communal scale, thus making loss bearable through its public display. Loss creates loose ends in terms of orphans, widows, and the aged, who have no tangible source of support. Most scholars see a project of three stages: separation and bereavement, recovery and readjustment, and maintenance, where the dead are incorporated into the world of the living via continuing rituals. This tripartite framework is based on the influential model formulated by the Belgian anthropologist Arnold Van Gennep ([1909] 1960), who was very interested in Egyptian funerary rituals. Indeed, the tripartite model he suggested as applicable to all life stages may have been influenced by his friendship with the Swiss Egyptologist Gustave Jéquier (1868–1946) and his 1892 French translation of the *Book of the Dead*.

At the first stage, grief was displayed publicly through emotional displays, and preparations of the body were undertaken, supposedly lasting up to seventy days. This number was probably an ideal, or possibly even magical (Baines and Lacovara 2002). For the deceased, the body and personality were preserved, while they were transformed in order to attain the next level of being. Through ritual activity the *ḥk3*, personal magic, was activated. This extended period may have enabled family and friends to adjust and reintegrate the deceased into the group in a new social form; from another perspective the living social group is reintegrated in altered roles now that the deceased is no longer present. The recovery stage was marked by the funeral, operative on a community level, after the process of mummification was completed. When there was mummification, the embalmers employed the materiality of the body to make a lifelike, lasting image that could be revived and act as a vehicle for the transfigured person at any time (Hornung 1992: 168). Many bodies were not fully embalmed, even those from Deir el Medina. A form of revival occurred at the funeral, which encompassed rituals of transformation such as the Opening of the Mouth ceremony, which sought to reanimate the bodily functions, especially speech, leading to rebirth. The ability for the dead to speak was important, because the transitions they had to undergo before transfiguration often revolved around speaking the correct formula at the right moment. After passing through the postmortem transitions successfully, it was hoped that the deceased would *become an Osiris*—as both women and men are designated on such funerary equipment as coffins and shabtis. To maintain the deceased in the afterworld, social support was required, in the form of continuing rituals performed by family and community members after death. This could include meals taken in the tomb chapel, and the recitation of an offering formula that would provide *every vital thing* (*ḫt nbt nfrt*) to sustain the person.

For a full afterlife the body had to be physically intact, and there is a surfeit of textual references to fear about bodily destruction (Zandee 1960: 14–19). Terror and disgust were evoked by confrontation with the dead body, and spells like those in the *Book of the Dead* could be invoked to maintain the transitional state of the corpse. There was an explicit concern over bodily fluids, such as sweat, and with the dead body's loss of integrity through the presence of maggots. Sensual descriptions of death are common, and the Egyptians were not inhibited to write about the smell of the decaying body, the disintegration by parasites, the rotting of flesh, mutilation, the eyes perishing, and so on. This horror was reconciled, even remedied, by practices such as embalming and evisceration, which sought to overcome the natural processes of degradation. Even at Deir el Medina where written evidence is so extensive, we still do not know who performed these preparations on the corpse or where they took place. This apparent reticence may arise from ideas about pollution and taboo; perhaps it was thought inauspicious to write about the dead when they were at a dangerous liminal stage. But it could also be that we are not looking at the written data in the right way. Accounts of expenditure on linen that do not indicate a specific purpose could be related to the funerary industry. Linen was a potent whole-body protection against decomposition: it would enable the deceased to be cyclically resurrected in a perfect and vital form. Fear and acknowledgment of decomposition were juxtaposed with claims of godlike preservation and perfection. The *Tale of Sinuhe* is a reminder that the Egyptians respected death but also feared its horror and its blessing, and the uncertainty about what comes after it.

A night vigil will be assigned to you, with holy oils
and wrappings from the hands of Tayet.

A funeral procession will be made for you on the day of joining the earth,
with a mummy case of gold,
a mask of lapis lazuli,
a heaven over you, and you placed in a hearse,
with oxen dragging you,
and singers before you.
The dance of the Oblivious ones will be done at the mouth of your tomb-chamber
and the offering-invocation recited for you;
sacrifices will be made at the mouth of your offering-chapel,
and your pillars will be built of white stone.[5]

Egyptian thinking deemed that the corporeal self should have integrity in death. The body wrappings and coffins were regenerative casings that would allow the transfigured body to emerge free from earthly imperfections (Hornung 1992: 169; Willems 1988). At Deir el Medina, from Ramesside times onwards, we can see how the coffin became the primary focus of funerary wealth and elaboration (Meskell 1997, 1999b). This process of resurrection did not occur on one occasion, but took place every night, when dead individuals took control over their bodies. Existence formed a continuum that was only slightly interrupted by the experience of death. The needs of the body also extended into the afterlife, including sexual and material pleasures. The physical body could only really attain divine status through confronting the ultimate challenge to its integrity—death itself. The notion of human divinity is mirrored materially in Ramesside bodily practices, specifically evisceration and embalming, which only became characteristic at Deir el Medina in this period. Religious systems and social ideology allowed for the possibility for a "good burial" in ancient Egypt. Bloch and Parry (1982: 15–16) refer cross-culturally to notions of the good death as being reserved for the pious and dutiful persons who underwent the proper burial ritual—a scenario parallel with ancient Egyptian conceptions. A good death promises rebirth for the individual, while a bad death represents the loss of regenerative powers. In the course of life, one could internalize these meanings and thus transcend life's contingencies (Shilling 1993: 179).

The mortuary practices of pharaonic Egypt could be described as forming a "mausoleum culture;" given the powerful associations of the tomb, this would seem a particularly apt description. However, such expensive constructions were only possible for a small section of society, and poorer burial options leave little trace in the archaeological record. Tombs were constructed ideally during the tomb owner's lifetime and as such were very much part of life—the superstructure being a visible and tangible reminder of one's death and the hereafter. In principle, the tomb formed a material, yet liminal, installation for maintaining the deceased in life, where the world of

FIGURE 7.2. Pyramid Tomb of Sennedjem, TT 1, Deir el Medina. (Photo courtesy of the author)

the living and dead could overlap. The preservation of the deceased's mummified body, the grave goods, and the integrity of the tomb itself were fundamental (Baines and Lacovara 2002). Tombs fulfilled the double function of hiding the body of the deceased and leaving a sign of the deceased within the world of the living. In the tomb culture of the Egyptians, both these foci were widely extended (Assmann 1996: 61). The tomb operated as visualized

FIGURE 7.3. Tomb of Neferenpet, TT 336, Western Necropolis, Deir el Medina. (Photo courtesy of IFAO, Cairo)

memory. In addition, the associated chapel, which might be visited by the family at certain feast days, was the locus for the offering cult, which was crucial to the maintenance of the deceased. But despite a well-developed ideology concerning death and the hereafter, some literary texts reveal a profound skepticism about mortuary provision, the survival of monuments, and bodily destruction. And there was good reason to be skeptical, if we look at tombs such as the wealthy Nineteenth Dynasty burial of Neferenpet in the Western Necropolis at Deir el Medina (see Figure 7.3). The tomb was violated in the Third Intermediate period and in Graeco-Roman times when intrusive burials were placed there among the family of Neferenpet. At the time of excavation, there were more than seventy-four bodies retrieved dating to various periods of history (Bruyère 1926: 80–113).

Harpists' songs proclaim that people should live for the day, because *no one who has gone has come back*, suggesting that all these elaborate earthly preparations were futile, and the visible decay of the tomb itself was a potent reminder. A story copied at Deir el Medina tells how the spirit of an official, Nebusemekh, was unquiet because his burial, with its complement of ritual equipment, had fallen into disrepair. Nebusemekh was propitiated when the living restored the burial *with a coffin of gold and zizyphus-wood*.[6] John Baines comments (1991: 129) that, in general, the Egyptians had far more contact with the dead than they did with the gods. This is certainly true: in Egyptian thought, the life of the deceased resembles that of the living, and it is integrated within daily life and practices, such as rituals, oracles, magic, and intervention. In this way the material constructions (tombs, chapels, shrines, tomb goods), preparations (mummification), practices (domestic, mortuary, and commemorative rituals), and beliefs (about the individual, death, afterlife, cosmology), combined to produce the Egyptian experience of death with a particular focus upon the individual. However, it is also important to remember that the funeral served to *separate* the living from the dead, and that the boundaries between their worlds were only breached at specific times: festivals, for instance, or moments of trouble when recourse might be made to the power of the dead to intervene with the gods—hence the written requests to the dead. Illiterate individuals, who made up the bulk of the population, must have relied upon oral requests to the deceased.

SEX, DEATH, AND (RE)BIRTH

The leitmotif of rebirth in funerary rituals and the linkage between life and death have long been a focus in both anthropology and archaeology. This has immediate relevance to Egyptian afterlife beliefs, the changing focus of tomb goods, and the preparation of bodies themselves. Indeed, fertility, rebirth, sexual potency, revivification, and appetite are all aspects of the association between sex and death (Behrens 1982). As a striking illustration, Coffin Text spell 576 states *my phallus is Baba (?) . . . there is sperm in my mouth . . . . NN has the disposal of his desire . . .* [7] This linkage reinforces the idea that the body transcends death and maintains its fundamental character beyond the boundaries of mortality. In the Nineteenth Dynasty Ptah-Sokar chapel of Seti I at Abydos we see two scenes of Sokar-Osiris in a phallic state: one showing him holding his phallus, the other depicting him impregnating Isis in the form of a kite (Hare 1999: 120–21). In the *Book of the Earth*, represented in the tomb of Ramesses VI, a procreative god is depicted with his phallus bound to the goddesses of the hours (Hornung 1990: 85), linking sexuality and rejuvenation. Osiris also appears in his phallic form in the tomb of Ramesses IX. This sexual association could demonstrate a reluctance to accept the consequences of death that is manifest in the elaborate treatments of bodies in an attempt to sustain life, in the inclusion of artefacts from the world of the living, and also in pictorial representations of the living world with people in their alive state. These motifs and artefacts are evident in Eighteenth Dynasty tombs, although we witness a shift in emphasis in the Ramesside period and later (Meskell 1999b). As early as the Middle Kingdom, some funerary texts stressed sexuality; for example the *ba* of the deceased is described as being free to have sex with both goddesses and earthly women alike. The *ba's* sexual abilities had the purpose of guaranteeing a full life for the deceased (Willems 1994: 311). The connections between life, death, and sexuality were fundamentally important, and ritual practice was the medium through which they were most often united.

As discussed elsewhere (Meskell 1999a), anthropologists since the nineteenth century have sought to identify and comprehend this phenomenon cross-culturally. Central to many of these interpretations was the double aspect of funerals, first proposed by Hertz (1960). Many studies cited for the dual nature of the funeral also document communal fear surrounding the state of the deceased, as a spirit, throughout this liminal phase. Van Gennep ([1909] 1960) developed the notion of liminality, elaborated upon by Victor Turner (1967), positing that one could expect rites of separation, transition, and incorporation. The transference of the soul from one domain to the other involves a dangerous period when spirits are malevolent and socially uncontrollable. Thus, the funeral acts for the living in perpetuating the status quo, not just for the deceased (Bloch and Parry 1982). Related to this in Egypt were notions of the dangerous dead, previously mentioned, who figure strongly in texts and in personal letters (Pinch 1994: 45, 148). The deceased individual could threaten or bless the living long after the period of death, preparation, and burial. For the Egyptians, the deceased was incorporated into the realm of the living and continued to be a potent force, unlike cultural groups for whom the deceased is put to rest after a second burial.

Cross-culturally, the treatment of the dead often employs metaphors of life and death: change entails the death of the former self, and the birth of a new one. The anthropologist Maurice Bloch (1982) explains the linkage between birth and death by stating that both negate the notion of eternal unchangingness. Death rites are often filled with the symbolism of birth or accession into other new life stages, and this is true of the Egyptian data. A trope of Egyptian literary texts is the emphasis on being buried where one had been born and could be protected by the local gods, to whom one owed special duty. In the *Tale of Sinuhe*, the protagonist says: *What matters more than being buried in the land where I was born?*[8] Moreover, the recitations in the *Book of the Dead* frequently refer to the deceased being under the protection of their city gods, who are invoked at some of the most crucial moments of the death ritual. Thus in Chapter 23, the recitation at the Opening of the Mouth ritual runs: *My mouth is opened by Ptah, my mouth's bonds are loosed by my city god, Thoth has come fully equipped with my spells.*[9] The Opening of the Mouth ritual demonstrates some of the closest associations between death and (re)birth. Ann Macy Roth (1993) suggests that this ritual mimicked the birth and maturation of a child, and its purpose was to take the newly reborn deceased through the transitions of birth and childhood, so that he or she could be nourished by the (adult) food amply provided in the Egyptian mortuary cult. The ritual implements used in the opening of the mouth may also have underscored links with practices at the moment of birth, when the child's mouth was opened to help with breathing.

The moment of death is not simply related to the transition of the afterlife but indelibly linked to life experience and to concepts surrounding aging, maturation, life stages, and reproduction. Death relates inextricably to life, specifically the recent life of the deceased and the lives of their offspring (Metcalf and Huntingdon 1991: 108). Consider the New Kingdom tomb scenes of naked servants and dancing girls painted with erotic motifs (Derchain 1975: 66–69), the depictions of the goddess of sexuality Hathor, and the fishing and fowling scenes replete with sexual puns, which are a material reflection of continuing sexuality. These images were set up permanently in the tomb, not passing enactments, and demonstrate their continued importance for the deceased. A sexual being with sexual needs and desires, the deceased was tacitly male and no comparable tomb scenes cater specifically to female sexuality: heterosexual roles were also tacitly assumed.

Mourning the Dead

Tied to the idea of sex and death was a linking of women with the sphere of death and funerals. Though women were associated with fertility and sexuality in ancient Egypt, the emotive dances of mourning were also assigned to them. Grieving was subject to a sexed difference: compared to the quiet attitudes of men in tomb iconography, women's mourning gestures are vehement (Milde 1988: 18). In many cultures weeping at funerals is not only tolerated but required by custom (e.g., Metcalf and Huntingdon 1991: 44). Weeping also occurs on cue. In New Kingdom Egypt, this performance was largely delegated to women, like the wailing women in the tomb of Neferhotep (Zandee 1960: 45) or Minnakht, and it could be a hereditary role (Tosi and Roccati 1972: 88). If some women were paid for these displays, the institution would be mediated by class or status prerogatives: many could not have afforded such performances. This is not to say that people—men, women, and children—were not individually moved to tears by the passing of a loved one at the point of burial. But textual evidence suggests that emotionality was not prized in general by the scribal elite; rather coolheadedness and reservation seem to have been rewarded. And the silent one was always opposed to, and privileged above, the heated one (Assmann 1999c: 32).

Tomb iconography and accompanying texts reiterate the gendering of mourning practices. In the Eighteenth Dynasty tomb of Renni at el Kab (see Lüddeckens 1943), one can see the bodily rendering of grief and read the laments of his three daughters. One daughter cries, *Where are you going my father?* His wife asks, *Where should I go oh my master, for eternity.*[10] Loss and despair were expressed more frequently by female family members and participants: *I am your sister Meritre, oh great one do not leave Meritre . . . going away, how can you do it to me? I go alone and look I am behind you. You who loved to speak with me, you are (now) silent, and you do not speak.*[11] Mourning rituals may also have been hierarchically ordered, as seen in a Memphite relief from an official's tomb. It depicts General Horemheb followed by a series of individuals in groups. They are shown in order of ranked status: the two viziers of Egypt, scribes, and priests followed by female mourners. One of these women turns her head from the action in distress. The relief attempts to show emotion and movement, capturing the experiential dimension of the moment. In this highly dramatic and emotive scene it is striking that both men and women are depicted in distress—although they were not the highest ranked individuals. The accompanying register shows scenes akin to those common for festivals, where preparations are being made and drinking jars are positioned on stands in a canopy shaded by palm fronds. A similar scene is found in the Memphite tomb of Horemheb (Martin 1989: Plates 123, 125) showing elaborate funerary preparations, the smashing of pots, and visual displays of grief by both men and women. Several roughly carved images of male mourners have been added to the upper registers by unskilled hands. Again these scenes show parallels between funerals and festival activities as set out in Chapter 6: huts, sometimes referred to as tabernacles, with food

FIGURE 7.4. Stela Showing Mourners. (Photo courtesy of the Detroit Institute of Art, Inv. 24.98)

and drink offerings, incense burners, small wickerwork stands with jars, bouquets of flowers, and so on.

Cross-culturally, the display of emotion is often designated a female domain, as in the ritual lamentation in Greece (ancient and modern), the Bara of Madagascar, the Nyakyusa and Kuranko of Africa (Metcalf and Huntingdon 1991: 47; Jackson 1989: 69), or in modern Egypt (Abu-Lughod 1993). In Egypt today grief is usually portrayed as a shared emotional experience, and such communal sentiments enhance the sense of identification that underpins social bonds. The grief that women share is not merely a means of expressing sympathy but a reliving of their own grief and pain over the loss of a loved one (Abu-Lughod 1986: 69). There are obviously exceptions, and I do not advocate an essentialist position in terms of emotive responses. Other groups do not display strong emotional responses at funerals, as Geertz (1973: 153–62) has documented in Java. Attitudes to death across time are characterized by diverse emotions—fear, sorrow, anger, despair, resentment, resignation, defiance, pity, avarice, triumph, helplessness—and can manifest in a complex conflicting attitude for any individual (Whaley 1981: 9). Today we are faced with both the strange and the familiar in our own world. Such a mixture must also be considered for antiquity.

So far I have concentrated on the body of the deceased and its transmutations during death, burial, and beyond. However, the bodies of relatives and mourners were also transformed through the experience of death. Baring of the breasts was a sign of emotional distress, and was not normal dress for elite women. One vignette in the papyrus of Ani shows his grieving wife kneeling next to his coffin, wearing a dress of dark linen that exposes her breasts. Mourners were said to be "head-upon-knee." In some New Kingdom tomb scenes mourning women wear strips of blue cloth tied around their heads that mark the immediate household of the deceased, a custom with analogues in modern times. Other transient practices that formed part of the mourning displays were scratching the face, heaping dust or earth on the head, and rending the hair and garments (D'Auria et al. 1988: 56). The classical writer Diodorus Siculus (I 91.1–2) reported that *whenever anyone dies among them, all the family and friends cover their heads with mud and go about town making lamentation, until it is the time for the body to be treated. Furthermore, during this time they allow themselves neither baths, wine, or any expensive foods, nor do they wear brightly-coloured clothing.*[12] This statement closely parallels the New Kingdom iconographic data and evidence from the *Book of the Dead* spells, suggesting a significant lineage to these discursive practices. That the living, grieving body is modified might suggest a parallel to the dead body, in its transitional phase. The disheveling of the hair, face, and body may relate to general concepts of disorder, denial of bodily existence, and the inevitability of the death of the physical body in this world. Such an open display of what would normally be perceived as antisocial behavior may have enhanced the experiential, emotive, or even eroticized state of the mourners: it made grief embodied and palpable. Parallelism may have further been at work in abstinence from food, wine, and bathing, since all of these functions are about earthly pleasure, but irrelevant in death.

FAMILIES IN DEATH

Death left serious gaps in the social fabric. There are written references to the social dislocations this caused for individual people, such as the workman Userhet who was part of the gang at Deir el Medina. His main concern was that, as a widower, his three daughters should not be taken from him, and he swore an oath to that effect. He also paid for the long-term assistance of a wet nurse, as well as the service of a doctor.[13] The untimely death of the mother meant the possible breakup of the family. Perhaps a single man was not considered able to care adequately for his children. The death of a child would have also impacted on the family. As discussed in Chapter 3, it is often assumed that child deaths were not mourned in premodern cultures with high infant mortality rates, but the Egyptian evidence suggests otherwise.

The death of an individual caused social and emotional upheaval in other ways. Apart from the elaborate preparations for burial and the emotional needs of grief-stricken family members and friends, a set of socioeconomic exchanges surrounded those events. Houses and sometimes rooms within them might be redistributed among people, as were household furniture and other objects, foodstuffs, and commodities. One household may have been using such items one day and have had them removed and reassigned the next, causing serious disruptions and some recriminations. We cannot be sure if all family members were aware of a will before a person's death, or whether it became known after the event. The latter situation would obviously cause the most upheaval. People's future lives as well as their economic position could be greatly enhanced or, in some cases, reduced.

Women living outside of a male-centered family were most at risk in Egyptian society. Without the provisioning that men could offer, both in this life and in the next, women were vulnerable. Yet not all of them were powerless. As we have seen in Chapter 3, the will of Naunakhte shows how a woman chose to record and reward those children who provided for her while disavowing and disinheriting those who failed her. Naunakhte had been married twice, first to the scribe Qenherkhopishef, who was much

older than she and left her property including land, and then to the
workman Khaemnun, to whom she bore eight children (McDowell 1999:
38–39). Following custom she could dispose only of the property that she
brought into the second marriage and one third of the property she and
Khaemnun had accumulated together. Despite her efforts to denounce her
negligent children, she was aware that they would still inherit from their
father, as was customary.

> *List of the men and women to whom she gave:*
>
> > *the workman Maanakhtef*
> > *the workman Qenherkhopishef. She said: "I will give him a bronze washing-bowl as
> > a bonus over and above his fellows, (worth) 10 sacks of emmer."*
> > *the workman Amennakhte*
> > *the lady Wasetnakhte*
> > *the lady Menetnakhte.*
>
> *As for the lady Menetnakhte, she said regarding her, "She will share in the division of
> all my property, except for the oipe of emmer that my three male children and the lady
> Wasetnakhte gave me or my hin of oil that they gave to me in the same fashion."*
> *List of her children of whom she said, "They will not share in the division of my
> one-third, but only in the two-thirds (share) of their father."*
>
> > *the workman Neferhotep*
> > *the lady Menetnakhte*
> > *the lady Henutsenu*
> > *the lady Khatanebu*
>
> *As for these four children of mine, they will <not> share in the division of all my
> property. Now as for all the property of the scribe Qenherkhopishef, my (first)
> husband, and also his immovable property and the storehouse of my father, and also
> this oipe of emmer that I collected with my husband, they will not share in them. But
> these 8 children of mine will share in the division of the property of their father on
> equal terms.*[14]

It was the responsibility of children to repay their parents in old age for
raising them, especially the mother, who did the most for infants. Naunakhte's
children Neferhotep, Menetnakhte, Henutsenu, and Khatanebu somehow
failed to do this for her during her life, and she could not rely on them to
provide for her at the point of burial or for her mortuary cult. These were
primary concerns; perhaps by drawing up her will she similarly safeguarded
the loyalty of her good children after her death. One can imagine the
repercussions of such a legal statement and the attendant tensions between
the siblings that followed its pronouncement: in the case of Naunakhte this
probably occurred before her death.

Disputes over property could span the generations, as in the saga of the will of a woman named Tgemy who was married to the workman Huynefer.[15] In her will she stated that she wanted their son Huy to be given the entire inheritance, since he was the only child who would take care of her burial. This responsibility traditionally fell to the eldest son (e.g., Eyre 1992). When Huy died and left part of the property he inherited in this way to his son Hay, the other children of Tgemy came forward to collect their share, hoping that the first will might have been forgotten. The wrangling continued and was even brought before the village oracle in front of court officials, only for the challenge to be overthrown. It is likely that the surviving documents relating to this case resulted from legal challenges, rather than being wills in a modern sense. Although few of these documents have been preserved, those that survive suggest it was necessary to assign property to specific people, and the family members who were purposely ignored often proved litigious. Some children also made clear their contribution to the cost of burials, stressing that they had not been aided by their siblings.[16] As in many societies, family bonds may have been close, but when property or even household items were at stake, relations often became strained.

Other individuals took different precautions to ensure their long-term protection and commemoration after death. In the time of Ramesses II a Theban man named Kyky transferred his property to the temple of Mut while he was alive, in order to ensure a proper burial and the maintenance of his mortuary cult. Inscribed in his tomb was a biography that records making Mut his patron, further spelling out that he had no son to arrange his burial:

> I am a weak one of her town,
> a poor one and a pilgrim of her city
> I disposed of my possessions in her favour,
> in exchange for the breath of life.
> No one of my household will have a share in this,
> but to her ka shall belong everything in peace.[17]

MORTUARY ARCHAEOLOGY

Egyptologists know more about the realm of death and the afterlife than they do about many aspects of lived experience. There are more texts, more funerary objects, and more bodies and tombs amassed and studied than there are objects related to living communities. But what bearing has archaeology had on the sociological study of Egyptian mortuary behavior? Such a study would go beyond the boundaries of pure description, whether it be of embalming or tomb reliefs, and examine the individual at the point of burial and passage into the next life. How was he or she prepared? How were bodies treated through time? How were goods apportioned according to status or sentiment? How was one's own biography mirrored in the next world? These questions are difficult to answer without a coherent data set, such as would come from a cemetery that yields relevant personal information. For the New Kingdom, only the Deir el Medina cemeteries are well represented and recorded and can offer that picture of life beyond the grave.

The techniques of embalming are well known. The body was packed in natron and desiccated, the organs removed and preserved separately, the dried body washed and wrapped in strips of old linen and soaked with oils and resins (Quirke 1992: 144; Ikram and Dodson 1998). It was then placed in a coffin and surrounded by the canopic jars and material paraphernalia of death and rebirth. Analysis of the cemeteries of Deir el Medina shows that this was not the treatment that most people received in the New Kingdom (Meskell 1999b: 199). Throughout the Eighteenth Dynasty, irrespective of economic and status differentials, the vast majority of villagers were not embalmed in the ways described. Most bodies, like those of Kha and Merit as well as the poorer people buried in the Eastern Necropolis, were simply wrapped in linen without evisceration. Virtually no canopic jars have been found in pre-Ramesside tombs at the site. We cannot tell why full mummification was not chosen: for individuals like Kha or Sennefer, cost cannot have been an impediment (Meskell 1999a: 192). Some have surmised that such preparations would have taken place in the village itself. When the workman Harmose died, Piay and Mehy went to verify the situation, and his body was subsequently brought to the chief workman Neferhotep, so that he could *take proper care of him*.[18]

It appears that after the Amarna period both religious and mortuary practices changed. This development is not directly attributable to the religious upheaval, but was part of a much longer sociohistorical process that can shed light on private life as well. Prior to the Nineteenth Dynasty tomb assemblages and tomb decoration focus on the living world: indeed bodies more closely resembled the living body (Meskell 1999b: 188–90). Items such as foodstuffs (Ikram 1995: 209), ordinary pottery, clothes, furniture, and toiletry objects predominate in assemblages. It is as if the afterworld was to mirror a perfect life on earth and all its lavish accoutrements, a prime example being the tomb of Kha and Merit (Meskell 1998c). But from the Nineteenth Dynasty onward radical changes were marked upon bodies themselves, which became the focus of ritual and regenerative strategies, being eviscerated, embalmed, and transformed into another type of being altogether. Unlike its Eighteenth Dynasty predecessor it no longer resembled the living body. In the corresponding tomb assemblages there is a sharp

FIGURE 7.5. Coffin and Mummy-Cover of Iyneferti (TT 1), Western Necropolis, Deir el Medina. (Photo courtesy of the Metropolitan Museum of Art, Purchase, funds from various donors, 1886, 86.1.5abc)

FIGURE 7.6. Food from the Tomb. (Photo courtesy of the British Museum, EA 5340, 5341, 35939, 36292)

increase in the ritual paraphernalia of death and rebirth: shabtis, amulets, canopic jars, Opening of the Mouth tools, copies of the *Book of the Dead*. The world of the afterlife became of paramount concern. This development was counterbalanced by a marked reduction in food, unguents, linen, household furniture, and ceramics, which were taken directly from daily life. Though the change between periods is not immediate, the shift from a focus on the living world gradually to a focus on death and the afterlife is generally observable.

The composition of the cemeteries and individual tombs also changed. At Deir el Medina in the Eighteenth Dynasty there were two cemeteries in operation, the Eastern and Western Necropoleis. The former was primarily for poorer burials and those of children, whereas the latter was for wealthier, higher-status individuals. In the Eastern Necropolis there was a noticeable degree of equality in expenditure on burials of men, women, and adolescents, and although very young children were often buried more economically they were still interred with items of jewelry and burial goods otherwise typical of adult burials (Meskell 1994b). Conversely, in the Ramesside Period the entire community was buried in the Western Necropolis. Bodies tended to be buried

FIGURE 7.7. Tomb Painting of Sennedjem, TT 1, Deir el Medina. (Photo courtesy of IFAO, Cairo)

in pyramid-topped tombs with underground vaults—many of which were elaborately decorated. The location of the Western Necropolis made it the prime location, and its rock was more suited to the cutting of tombs with underground chambers. Here there was enormous individual variation in overall expenditure, with males receiving the greatest wealth, women considerably less, and children given comparatively meager burials.

At Deir el Medina there were significant changes in the burials of higher-status individuals during the transition from the Eighteenth to the Nineteenth Dynasties that are evident in the architecture of the Western Necropolis. Whereas the majority of the Eighteenth Dynasty tombs consisted of a shaft with single (approximately 105 or 72 percent) or multiple vaults (approximately 40 or 28 percent), those of the Nineteenth and Twentieth tended to develop into a full tomb complex with vaults, chapels, a courtyard, and often a pyramidion. Such an association of features was not completely absent in the Eighteenth Dynasty, since we have the fine example of Kha. About five Eighteenth Dynasty tombs had multiple vaults and a chapel, and perhaps only four of them have a full complex including pyramidia. Individuals like Kha could be perceived as exceptional cases, given that he was chief workman during the reigns of three pharaohs. However, it may be that other tomb markers were in place during the early New Kingdom but later obliterated by the continued reuse and remodeling of tombs. Given the large numbers of stelae and decorative architectural fragments uncovered in the region, the possibility of tomb markers should not be dismissed. In support of this, Davies (1938: 26) cited Theban tomb paintings that depict a mummy before a stela, with neither mortuary chapel nor pyramid, such as TT 13 and TT 273.

Here we witness a diachronic variability in the social inequality of death. In the Eighteenth Dynasty substantial inequality existed in the burials of men, women, and children, with the first group taking priority in tomb wealth and burial expenditure. In the Western Necropolis difference is constituted around sex and to a lesser degree age. At the same time, for the less affluent individuals in the Eastern Necropolis the major criteria were age and perhaps marital status. For instance, young females such as the one buried in tomb 1381 could be buried alone, perhaps suggesting that they were not married at the time of death or were too young for marriage (see Figure 7.9). The primary social divide, then, was really based upon wealth, followed by inequalities based on age or sex, depending on cemetery context. Intact Eighteenth Dynasty tombs from the richer Western Necropolis suggest that as wealth and status increased, the relative wealth of wives or female partners declined significantly in the mortuary sphere. In contrast, the situation for children appeared to be basically consistent across the social strata. The situation in the Ramesside Period was markedly different, exhibiting a move to generational tombs encompassing many individuals. While the visibility of women and children increases and the number of Eastern Necropolis burials declines, there is still a material discrepancy in favor of elite men and their male relatives. The increase in numbers of individuals present, and generally the more favorable treatment of women and children, continues and peaks in the Graeco-Roman period.

Tombs of the Eighteenth Dynasty tended to house individuals, couples, or small family groups. Ramesside tomb complexes contained larger numbers of individuals, presumably several generations of the same family (as in the case of Sennedjem, tomb 1), and exhibit slightly more balanced outlays of expense, at least between men and women. While these patterns demonstrate that material inequalities between individuals extended into the sphere of death, it is also likely that they are analogous with specific patterns of social difference during life. Private life in the New Kingdom was marked

FIGURE 7.8. Plan of Deir el Medina. (After G. Castel, *Deir el-Medineb 1970, fasc. I. Gournet Mar ei Nord* FIFAO 12, 1, Cairo, 1980)

N

10 20 30 40 50 m

FIGURE 7.9. Tomb Assemblage from TT 1381, Eastern Necropolis, Deir el Medina. (Photo courtesy of IFAO, Cairo)

publicly by social, economic, legal, and material inequalities. Women, children, and lower-status groups were unsurprisingly discriminated against in those spheres. Egypt was a highly cultured and also unequal and often uncompromising society that favored elite males over all others.

Social Memory

The Theban West Bank was invested with meaning because of its mortuary associations, its vast temples, and the festivals that processed through it on a yearly schedule. It remained important because it contained the sites of sacred events, such as the Beautiful Festival of the Wadi, invested with cosmological and mythic significance, enacted by humans making reference to symbolically potent features of the natural topography within which these sites were embedded. It was a dynamic locale, and memories of mythic, cosmological, ritual, and funerary significance fused together to create a set of shared memories and experiences for the people of pharaonic Egypt. It was a sacred geography.

The concept of memory has recently attracted Egyptologists' attention, but the degree to which "social memory" was a pervasive theme is debatable. Jan Assmann has argued (e.g., 1999b: 396) that memory was the social sense par excellence. The decay of memory is one of the symptoms of social disintegration: if the past is forgotten, people can no longer form relationships or ensure justice or order. In theory, the world would be out of kilter and would dissolve into an arena of fighting and chaos. In the Egyptian view, the responsible and dutiful person remembers, while those without memory are deemed socially irresponsible. Memory and love were two connective virtues. Together they allowed an individual to be reintegrated and sustained after death through the processes of remembrance (1999b: 398, 401). The individual's personal coherence was predicated more broadly upon order and social coherence. These beliefs were linked to *Maat*, which ensured social harmony, mutual love, and memory. *Maat* creates a social space by conjoining people through social time that links past, present, and future. This was the desired state of human affairs, yet it may have played out in significantly different ways.

Texts and iconography demonstrate that the community at Deir el Medina had a very limited sense of the past and could remember scarcely more than two generations back for their own commemorative family practices. There were few written references to events even as recent as twenty years in the past. Yet the Egyptians had a strong "sense" of the past, and they were surrounded by its materiality, only it did not always evoke feelings of reverence. At Deir el Medina, the villagers incorporated older funerary monuments into new constructions and regularly robbed tombs in the process of burial preparations. In the vital area of the world of the dead, they inhabited a doubly dead landscape in which the funerary monuments around them provided a model of achievement, even in their decayed form, as well as a physical environment into which they awkwardly inserted their current passage to a deceased status through destruction, usurpation, and reuse of older burial structures. I think it is important in this contextual setting not to conflate *social memory*, which suggests the long term, with *commemoration*, which refers to short-term practices operating only over a few generations.

In Egyptian culture death was not considered as the end of one's existence nor of one's effectiveness on earth. The dead were powerful beings who could intervene in the world of the living in both benevolent and malevolent ways. Ancestor busts and stelae provided a focus for interaction and attest to the dead person's willingness to intercede (see Figure 4.4). It is often said that the dead kept the living in line. The tomb culture of Egypt, with its associated mortuary cult, involved numerous ongoing practices including offerings and invocations to the deceased, thus creating and sustaining a reflexive relationship between living and dead. In

FIGURE 7.10. Stela of the Stonemason Bakenmin. (Photo courtesy of the Petrie Museum, UC14362)

nonroyal contexts, most of those involved would have been related in some way, so that this was a means of uniting the generations. But we have to question how long this process of commemoration lasted and how grounded these memories really were. Andrea McDowell (1992b) has found that in the highly literate village of Deir el Medina the recording of ancestors only stretched back a generation or two at most. This means that real social memory was short-lived. This seems to be confirmed by evidence from other periods of Egyptian history, including Roman times.

Some scholars have suggested that during this period it was customary to keep some mummies displayed in funerary chapels, where they were the object of cultic attention (see Borg 1997).

A salient example of commemorative practice was the setting up of stelae for deceased relatives, which served as a lasting reminder of family, both living and long deceased. Here the inscribed stela of the stonemason Bakenmin is an illustrative case (Figure 7.10). Bakenmin probably came from Memphis, since he is shown adoring the Memphite god Ptah, and he was probably dead when the commemorative stela was erected. From four of the registers of named individuals it is possible to reconstruct a genealogy that includes some four generations (Stewart 1976: 32). In the second register we see the owner of the stela and his wife Tameret sitting before an offering table, smelling lotus flowers. As described before, this action was inflected with symbolic meanings about beauty, perfection, and communing with the deceased and the deified in the afterworld. Minmose, whom Egyptologists interpret as the eldest son, pours a libation. Behind him are the couple's other sons Tusa, Iyerniutef, Taia, and Nakhy, each of whom holds a lotus flower. The next register shows Bakenmin's own parents Minmose and Tapakhentet, who must have been deceased at the time. Libating for them is their son Bakenmin (owner of the stela) and their daughter Nefertity, followed by another six kneeling individuals belonging to the family of Minmose. They are named as his sons Akhpet, Bakenmin, and Aa, his daughter Bakmin and her daughter Nedjemmennefer, and his other daughter, Henuttanebu. This proliferation of figures may recall the earlier suggestion in Chapter 2 that Egyptian families were large. The next register shows the owner's grandparents, Bakenmin and Nefertiry, who we can assume were also deceased at this time. In turn they receive a libation from their son Minmose. To the right of the scene, Minmose, Tapakhentet, and "her son" Bakenmin are shown again, but this time drinking from a vessel offered by Hathor, goddess of the sycamore tree, with a *ba* bird in attendance. The *ba* bird depicted is most likely to be the *ba* of one of the individuals shown, probably Bakenmin himself. In the final register we see the deceased Djaary and his wife Wernero receiving offerings from "her daughter" Tapakhentet and "his son" Tjanefer, "his daughter" Henuttanebt, and "his son" Minkha. The significance of this gendered pattern of naming remains unknown. Stewart (1976: 32) suggests on the basis of the similarity of names that the scene represents Bakenmin's maternal grandparents and their family. We can deduce that many of the individuals depicted, including the pivotal figure of Bakenmin, were deceased when the stela was carved and that those who commissioned it had gone to some lengths to incorporate the entire family. It is not indicated and it cannot be known whether particular people were omitted or how many other offspring failed to reach maturity: no young children are shown. Despite these gaps in the picture the stela confirms the general rule at Deir el Medina, in which remembering back two generations was often the extent of social memory. Nevertheless, these concerns with memorializing and remembering were part of a fundamental Egyptian desire, evidenced by the single text on this man's stela: *Breath shall belong to him. The name will not be forgotten of the Osiris, the stone-mason, Bakenmin.*[19]

It is probably safe to say that the dead were sustained through ongoing reflexive practices conducted by family members for a generation or two at most. These took place in the mortuary sphere, whether in chapels or in the vicinity of the tomb, as well as in the domestic sphere. Visits to the chapel involved an exchange of favors. The tomb owner received visits and allegiance, and offering formulas were said on his behalf; visitors received the protection of the tomb owner, who interceded on their behalf (Nordh 1996: 12). This practice of exchange was multidimensional, encompassing what we would term religious, emotional, and behavioral aspects. The important idea of a living memorial could be embodied in the construction of a tomb with a visible pyramid, chapel, and courtyard like those at Deir el Medina. The tomb was a testimony to the deceased, his life history, and his achievements: women could not be included in this specific construction of the "biography" because they did not hold official positions. The necropolis was the most potent locale where the dead held the greatest influence. Letters to the dead were left there, and it was also the place where magical texts were believed to have the greatest efficacy. The necropolis was the obvious and optimum zone for contact between the two worlds.

The tomb has often been portrayed as sacred ground, an impermeable structure respected by Egyptians that was perhaps even feared as the repository of danger and destructive spells. Yet we know that tombs were vandalized and desecrated throughout pharaonic times. Moreover, priests as well as ordinary workmen were capable of breaking into the royal tombs and stealing the possessions of the deceased. As a deterrent, there may have been a perceived threat from the deceased, and there were certainly the severest punishments here on earth for those who were caught. There was tomb robbery also at sites where graves were more meager and goods less numerous, such as cemeteries for middle- and lower-status individuals. Another related process was the reuse of older tombs, which is widely attested at sites such as Deir el Medina. Ostracon BM 5624 illustrates the practice of officially regulated tomb reuse, usually after a family line had died out, although reallocation did not always proceed smoothly. Amenemope retells how he asked, *direct (me) to a tomb among the ancestors! He gave me the tomb of Khay through a writing and I began to work in it.*[20] The reuse of tombs was significant because of the associations with their symbolic significance and location, not to mention the overall reduction in labor and expense. Despite this seeming disregard for the realm of the dead, the Egyptians had an ability, like those of many modern societies, to assimilate conflicting, or opposing, conceptions that enabled them to maintain both idealizing and rationalizing views of death and the dead (Baines and Lacovara 2002).

The Egyptian evidence suggests that events and rituals surrounding an individual's death involved significant numbers of people in the deceased person's community. Individual family members grieved for, mourned, and buried their dead. Additionally, female mourners may have been employed for more elaborate funerary displays (Bleeker 1967: 130). But before those steps were taken, workers had constructed the tomb, scribes and painters had decorated it, artisans had created shrines, statues, and the material culture of death itself, and others had embalmed the dead. An array of individuals were inextricably involved, some emotionally linked, others by social and economic forces. Women played significant roles in the social drama of death, not only in funerary preparations and grieving, but conceptually in the revivification process itself, at least for men. A successful burial and afterlife was ensured through the invocation of sexualized practices. Whether it be mythological, iconographic, or ideological, the connection between sex and death was integral. At sites such as Deir el Medina, individual tombs encircled the village in constant view of the living community, encroaching on the very edge of their existence and reminding them that the ancestors were ever present in living experiences and negotiations. Mortuary practices extended beyond interment. Commemoration and memorialization through venerating one's ancestors were fundamental both for a successful afterlife for the dead and for a prosperous earthly existence for the living. Georges Bataille (1993: 223) encapsulated well their particular vision of death and memory:

> In the eyes of the Egyptians, the pyramid was an image of solar radiation. In the person of the dead king, death was changed into a radiance, changed into an indefinite being. The pyramid is not only the most lasting monument, it is also the equivalency of the monument and absence of a monument, of passage and obliterated traces, of being and the *absence* of being. There death is no longer anything but death's inability to maintain an icy little horror, which is the projected shadow of individual anguish. Horror is the limit of the individual. What it proclaims is man's reduction into thinghood. It announces the world of practice. The intent of the world of practice is to banish, once and for all, the horror that cannot be separated from it by any means. But at the foot of the pyramid, the world of practice has disappeared; its limit is no longer perceptible.

Postscript

MANY BOOKS focus on the unique articulation and convergence of death and the afterlife in ancient Egypt: very few speak to the conditions of living. I hope that this book makes a contribution to discussions of life experience and embodied being in the New Kingdom—not in the guise of total recovery, which is itself a form of narrative fiction, but rather as a fragmentary mosaic. We can also choose to celebrate the disjunctures and heterogeneous nature of the material, which reminds us of the unknowability of the past, the constant linear narratives we construct (White 1987), and the multiplicity of accounts we could reasonably offer. Perhaps the lacunae keep us in line.

This project has drawn on a variety of scholarly traditions: the *Annales* historians, third wave feminism, the postprocessual school of archaeology, and a host of disciplines such as anthropology, social theory, and literary studies. Crucial insights from those fields allow us to view Egypt from a postcolonial perspective, to deconstruct the layered preoccupations of older scholarship, and to expose our own preconceptions, thereby reenvisioning Egypt for a new millennium. Using the archaeological, iconographic, and documentary sources dialogically allows us to highlight the contingencies and contradictions of the record as it survives. Each source may provide a different window onto the past. A salient example of this process revolves around discussion of women's lives in the New Kingdom. Legal texts, economic transactions, love poetry, tomb assemblages, domestic space, material culture, and wall paintings all offer very different expressions of women's lives and the inequalities they faced. Prior unilinear or monolithic views have been further problematized by the recognition that women cannot be treated uniformly, since their life experiences were inflected with all the other markers of difference, such as their life stage, social grouping, marital status, ethnicity, and occupation. As in contemporary culture, we must allow for a multiplicity of biographies.

The questions asked throughout the book are very much of the moment, dealing with the construction of communities, identity, and authenticity and with the material conditions of living. The importance of place was interlaced with notions of self and of belonging, something we see strongly articulated in narrative accounts of Egyptians traveling to lands beyond the nation's borders. Time and space is another unifying theme detailed at the outset: the Egyptians had multilayered conceptions of time that were both cyclical and linear. As Hornung (1992: 69–70) eloquently remarks, compared with the vast expanses of time, the individual's life on earth seemed nothing more than a passing dream. Yet while the Egyptians recognized life's brevity, they also knew that ultimately what mattered was not the "quantity" of a person's lifetime. Meaningfully filled time was ultimately of far greater importance than empty duration. Moreover, the supply of time was not unlimited, and there were always anxieties that, at some future moment, it would all come to an end. At the end of this wide-ranging review of the material within the book, it is evident that this anxious desire lies at the nexus of the Egyptian formulation of eternity.

Other questions focused on the constitution of personhood, kinship, individual life stages, and the concomitant social organization following that progression. This included sensual and sexual life, the erotics of representation and the persistence of signs that marked Egyptian sexuality. At the outset I talked about the dynamics of category, and I hope to have demonstrated that the taxonomies traditionally used to describe the New Kingdom are both limiting and inadequate. We would do better to refigure domains conventionally viewed as natural and discrete—kinship, sexuality, domesticity, ritual—as overlapping and permeable (Meskell 2000b). I have attempted to demonstrate that sexuality pervaded other spheres of life in a manner very different from contemporary societies, and I suggest that we need to rethink sexual life in ancient Egypt. On the other hand, Egyptologists have long recognized the interconnectedness of the themes of life and death in literary texts, mythological accounts, iconography, and to a lesser degree in mortuary archaeology. Sex, death, and rebirth were also inextricably entwined, another example of the dynamics of Egyptian cultural categories. Egyptian festivals provide another set of performative spaces in which the symbols, associations, and practices mirrored those of funerals, invoking both the living and the dead while simultaneously communing with the gods. Reformulating Egyptian experience through the lens of these new hybrid domains and dynamic categories may provide an alternative way of interpreting the evocative materials left to us.

Throughout I have argued that the life cycle forms the template for accessing Egyptian life, rather than our nomothetic classifications or the familiar trope of rites of passage. The project attempts to follow those structures and experiences of the cycle, from conception through maturity and beyond. Those structures are not necessarily commensurate with our own ingrained ones, and there are other ways of knowing, or being enculturated into, a specific society—what I have described as embodied knowledge. In the New Kingdom there was a rich repertoire of corporeal symbols that encoded sensual life—the tastes, aromas, tactile sensations, sounds, textures, and aesthetic pleasures of life. These conjoined in love poetry, festivals, and funerals and find their archaeological traces in pictorial forms and in items of material culture. As a counterbalance the texts provide sobering images of the hardships of life and the horrors of death, invoked by oppressive sights and smells. Reinstating the sensory dimension of ancient life has been another explicit aim of this book.

Ancient Egyptian cycles of life and death were always in dialogue and were as complex as those of any modern culture. Death did not mean a step out of time into eternity—it represented the transition to a new existence or what might be termed an interstitial realm. The deceased remained within time and experienced new lifetimes in the underworld. The fortunate individual participated in the daily orbit of the sun, which formed a temporal and spatial link between this life and the hereafter (Hornung 1992: 66). But the passage to the hereafter was fraught with uncertainties. The underworld, so vividly described in the *Book of the Dead*, could prove to be a place of nightmarish destruction for the unworthy person. It was talked of as *completely deep, completely dark*, and *completely unending*. It was a place inhabited by forces that destroyed everything on entry and that knew no bounds in their destructive imagination. Decapitation was only one of the bodily tortures inflicted upon the damned (Hornung 1992: 99–101). As discussed, the destruction of the body similarly meant the dissolution of the *ba* and all possibilities for eternity. Those individuals faced oblivion and nonexistence. In one scene from the *Book of Gates*, the ninth hour, we encounter the serpent that breathed fire upon the condemned (Hornung 1999: 41), while other scenes illustrated fire-filled pits or the Lake of Fire, filled with burning red liquid. In the *Book of Caverns*, also reproduced on the walls of royal tombs, we see knife-wielding demons heating cauldrons in which the deceased were dissolved, physically and spiritually, resulting in a state of nonbeing that the Egyptians considered as anathema. Bodies were frequently inverted in this realm of chaos or were dismembered: into burning cauldrons were placed human heads, hearts, and flesh. Judgment after death is first known from Egypt, a concept depicted in the weighing of the individual's heart on the scales against the concept of right order, personified as the goddess Maat. These scenes of judgment and the hellish moments afterward were first represented iconographically in the Eighteenth Dynasty. This elite vision of the abyss and of torture in the royal tombs was somehow set against the common images of the life hereafter in the chapels of private tombs showing scenes of drinking, dancing, feasting, and all the signs of luxury and indulgence. Both worlds featured strongly in the Egyptian imaginary. One looked forward optimistically to an existence better than its earthly counterpart, while the alternative can only be described as the ancient precursor to Dante's *Inferno*. There are potent elements of familiarity between ancient and modern cultures, even in the final, existential moments of an individual's life, and again we see the enormity of our inheritance. The specter that is Egypt has resounding longevity and offers endless inspiration.

Notes

CHAPTER TWO
LOCALES AND COMMUNITIES

1. O. Varille 13, trated by McDowell (1999: 66).
2. From the *Hymn to the Aten*, translated by Lichtheim (1976: 98).
3. From the *Tale of Sinuhe*, translated by Parkinson (1997: 33).
4. From the *Tale of the Shipwrecked Sailor* (Parkinson 1997: 97).
5. BM EA 10085, translated by Leitz (1999: 89–90).
6. LRL No. 35, Twentieth Dynasty, translated by Wente (1990: 183).
7. LRL No. 50, Twentieth Dynasty, translated by Wente (1990: 189).
8. From the *Tale of Sinuhe* (Parkinson 1997: 38).
9. P. Anastasi 1, translated by Parkinson (1999: 70).
10. The inscription dates to the early Middle Kingdom, V48–12, K. Sethe (1959).
11. I thank Roland Enmarch for this translation and for all his help on the concepts of locality and identity.
12. O. Petrie 39, translated by McDowell (1999: 157).
13. From McDowell's translation (1999: 158).
14. From the *Tale of the Shipwrecked Sailor* (Parkinson 1997: 92).
15. From the Report of Wenamun, translated by Lichtheim (1976: 227).
16. From McDowell's translation (1999: 51–52).

CHAPTER THREE
SOCIAL SELVES

1. Ebers 956h, in Nunn (1996: 48).
2. Pyramid Texts 1248a–d, translated by Hare (1999: 111).
3. O. Berlin 10627, Twentieth Dynasty: Ramesses III–IV, translated by Wente (1990: 149).
4. P. Ebers 832, cited in Wilfong (1999: 423).
5. Wrezinski Incantation 42, translated by Leitz (1999: 70).
6. P. BM 10059, 13, translated by Borghouts (1978: 24).
7. P. Leiden I 348, translated by Borghouts (1978: 39).
8. O. Cairo 25517 verses 4–7, translated by McDowell (1999: 35).
9. Turin 50058, translated by Lichtheim (1976: 107–8).
10. O. Michaelides 48 rto. cited in Wilfong (1999: 423).
11. From the *Instruction of Ani* (7, 17–18, 1), translated by McDowell (1999: 38).
12. P. Berlin 3027, translated by Borghouts (1978: 41–42).
13. From the stela of Isemkheb (Leiden Museum V 55), perhaps dating to the Twenty-first Dynasty. Translation from Lichtheim (1980: 58–59).
14. O. Letellier, Nineteenth Dynasty, translated by Wente (1990: 141).
15. O. DeM 438, translated in McDowell (1999: 130).

16. I thank Gay Robins for informing me of these connections.
17. O. Ägyptisches Museum, Berlin 23676, Nineteenth Dynasty.
18. O. Oriental Institute Museum 13512, excavated at Medinet Habu, although probably deriving from Deir el Medina; translated by Wilfong (1999: 420).
19. Translated by McDowell (1999: 39).

CHAPTER FOUR
FOUNDING A HOUSE

1. Translations of the *Teachings of Ptahhotep* from Parkinson (1999: 257).
2. P. DeM 27 translated by McDowell (1999: 48–49).
3. O. Prague 1826, Nineteenth Dynasty, translated by Wente (1990: 147–8).
4. O. Nash 6 in McDowell (1999: 45–46).
5. The *Instruction of Ptahhotep*, translated by Parkinson (1997: 255).
6. O. UCL 19614 , translated by McDowell (1999: 43).
7. HO 64, 2 = O Bodleian Library 253, translated by McDowell (1999: 33).
8. O. Petrie 61, translated by Wente (1990: 147).
9. O. Ashmolean 1945: 39, translated by McDowell (1999: 34–35).
10. P. Salt 124, translated by Černý (1929: 245).
11. From P. BM 10052, translated by Ward (1986: 67).
12. P. Bankes I, Twentieth Dynasty, translated by Wente (1990: 129–30).
13. Translated by Lichtheim (1976: 13).
14. e.g. O. Gardiner 72, 3; O. DM 189, II, 2.
15. e.g. O. IFAO 1106, 5; O. Gardiner 123, 1.
16. O. Turin 6361, Černý (1973: 180).
17. From Berlin Papyrus 9784, 1–10, in Loprieno (1997: 204).
18. O. DM 439, Twentieth Dynasty, translated by Wente (1990: 148); see also Borghouts (1981).
19. P. Cairo 65 739, translated by Eyre (1998: 178).
20. P. BM 10 052, 13, 10–26, Twentieth Dynasty.
21. O. IFAO 556, O. IFAO 884, & O. Gard, translated by McDowell (1999: 109).
22. P. British Museum 9994: 10, translated by Lichtheim (1976: 173).

CHAPTER FIVE
LOVE, EROTICISM, AND THE SEXUAL SELF

1. I would like to thank Richard Parkinson for his discussions with me concerning lyric genres.
2. Translation from McDowell (1999: 154–55).
3. Translation from McDowell (1999: 153–54).
4. Translation from Fox (1985: 37).
5. From the Cairo Love Songs, translation from McDowell (1999: 153).
6. From the Cairo Love Songs, translation from McDowell (1999: 154–55).
7. From the Cairo Love Songs, translation from McDowell (1999: 156).
8. From the Cairo Love Songs, translation from McDowell (1999: 153–54).
9. Translation from Fox (1985: 74).
10. P. Chester Beatty I, translation from Fox (1985: 75).

11. From P. Chester Beatty I, no. 34, translation from Fox (1985: 53).
12. Translation after Omlin (1973: 71).
13. Ebers 783, translation from Nunn (1996: 196).
14. Translated from H. Grapow et al. (1958: 211–12). See also Riddle (1992: 72).
15. BM EA 10902, translated by Leitz (1999: 93).
16. P. Chester Beatty X rto I, 9. Leitz (1999: 93).
17. Translation from Parkinson (1999: 260).
18. Translation from Parkinson (1995: 70).
19. Translation from Parkinson (1995: 71).
20. Translation from Parkinson (1995: 72).

CHAPTER SIX
EMBODIED KNOWLEDGE

1. Translation from Manniche (1999: 104).
2. I thank Roland Enmarch for his discussion of the relevant terms.
3. I thank Tom Hardwick for this suggestion.
4. From the Cairo Love Song, translated by McDowell (1999: 152).
5. *Deben* refers to a weight in copper, about 91 grams.
6. From P. Harris 500, translated by Fox (1985: 15, 17).
7. From P. Chester Beatty I, translation from Fox (1985: 71).
8. From the *Dialogue of a Man and his Ba*, translated by Parkinson (1997: 160).
9. BM EA 10085, translated by Leitz (1999: 90).
10. Translation from Parkinson (1997: 158).
11. Translation from Fox (1985: 73).
12. Translation from Parkinson (1997: 287).
13. O. DeM 312, Nineteenth Dynasty, translated by Wente (1990: 157).
14. O. Černý 19, Nineteenth Dynasty, translated by Wente (1990: 153).
15. O. Vienna 1 and O. IFAO 628, translated by McDowell (1999: 69–71).
16. P. Nevill, late Twentieth Dynasty, translated by Wente (1990: 219).
17. I am grateful to Hubertus Meunch for many stimulating discussions about festivals.
18. I would like to thank Dominic Montserrat for this information.
19. Hieratic inscription from Deir el Bahri, translated by Marciniak (1971: 59). I owe this reference to Dominic Montserrat.
20. O. DeM 551, translated by McDowell (1999: 97).
21. O. Cairo 25234, translated by McDowell (1999: 96).
22. O. IFAO. 1322 and O. Varille 38 and O. Cairo 25705, translated by Janssen (1997: 56–57).
23. This information was supplied by Mark Depaw and Mark Smith.
24. Tomb 359 at Deir el Medina, translated by McDowell (1999: 125–26).

CHAPTER SEVEN
CYCLES OF DEATH AND LIFE

1. Translation from Lichtheim (1976: 12).
2. Translated by Parkinson (1997: 250).

3. Translated by McDowell (1999: 104).

4. O. Louvre 698 verso 12–22, translation from McDowell (1999: 106); see also Frandsen (1992).

5. From the *Tale of Sinuhe*, translated by Parkinson (1997: 151).

6. O. Gardiner 306, translated in Simpson, Faulkner, and Wente (1972: 138).

7. NN indicates that the name of a specific individual was inserted into a standardized text. Baba is the baboon god who has a phallic aspect (Pinch 1993: 239).

8. Translated by Parkinson (1997: 34).

9. Translation from Lichtheim (1976: 120).

10. From the tomb of Renni at el Kab (Lüddeckens 1943: 37–38), translation by Roland Enmarch.

11. From the Theban tomb of Neferhotep (Lüddeckens 1943: 109–10), translation by Roland Enmarch.

12. Translation from Montserrat (1997: 33–44).

13. P. Turin 1880 (Turin Strike Papyrus) vs. 5, 2–6, discussed by McDowell (1999: 36) and Janssen and Janssen (1990).

14. P. Ashmolean Museum, 1945.95, 97, translation from McDowell (1999: 38–39).

15. P. Boulaq X, recto, translated by Janssen and Pestman (1968).

16. O. Petrie 16 (Hier. Ostr. 21, 1) tells of Siwadjy being the only child to help in the burial of his mother Tenhasy and of the personal expense he incurred.

17. Translation from the tomb of Samut-kyky in Assmann (1999c: 34).

18. O. DeM 126, Dynasty 19, translated by Wente (1990: 143).

19. Translation of UC 14362, from Stewart (1976: 32).

20. Translated by McDowell (1999: 68).

Bibliography

Abu-Lughod, L. 1986. *Veiled sentiments: Honor and poetry in a Bedouin society*. Berkeley and Los Angeles: University of California Press.
———. 1993. Islam and the gendered discourse of death. *International Journal of Middle Eastern Studies* 25: 187–205.
Aldred, C. 1980. *Egyptian art in the age of the pharaohs*. New York: Thames and Hudson.
Andreu, G. 1997. *Egypt in the age of the pyramids*. Ithaca: Cornell University Press.
Anthes, R. 1943. Die deutschen Grabungen auf der Westseite von Theben in den Jahren 1911–1913. *Mitteilungen des Deutschen Instituts für Ägyptische Altertumskunde in Kairo* 12(1): 1–72.
Appadurai, A., ed. 1986. *The social life of things: Commodities in cultural perspective*. Cambridge: Cambridge University Press.
———. 1997. *Modernity at large: Cultural dimensions of globalization*. Minneapolis: University of Minnesota Press.
Ariès, P. 1962. *Centuries of childhood*. New York: Knopf.
———. 1974. *Western attitudes to death: From the Middle Ages to the present*. Baltimore: Johns Hopkins University Press.
Arnold, D. 1996. *The royal women of Amarna: Images of beauty from ancient Egypt*. New York: Metropolitan Museum of Art.
Assmann, J. 1982. Persönlichkeitsbegriff und -bewusstsein. *Lexikon der Ägyptologie*, ed. W. Helck and E. Otto. Wiesbaden: Otto Harrassowitz.
———. 1989. Der Schöne Tag. Sinnlichkeit und Vergänglichkeit im altägyptichen Fest. *Das Fest*, ed. W. Haug and R. Warning. Munich: Wilhelm Fink.
———. 1993. Literatur und Karneval im alten Ägypten. *Karnevaleske Phänomene in antiken und nachantiken Kulturen und Literaturen*, ed. S. Döpp. Trier: Verlag Trier.
———. 1996. Preservation and presentation of self in ancient Egyptian portraiture. In *Studies in Honor of William Kelly Simpson*, ed. P. De Manuelian. Boston: Museum of Fine Arts.
———. 1999a. Cultural and literary texts. In *Definitely: Egyptian literature*, ed. G. Moers. Göttingen: Seminar für Ägyptologie und Koptologie.
———. 1999b. A dialogue between self and soul: Papyrus Berlin 3024. In *Self, soul, and body in religious experience*, ed. A. I. Baumgarten, J. Assmann, G. A. G. Stroumsa. Leiden: Brill.
———. 1999c. Conversion, piety, and loyalism in ancient Egypt. In *Transformations of the inner self in ancient religions*, ed. J. Assmann, A. I. Baumgarten, and G. G. Stroumsa. Leiden: Brill.
Atiya, N. 1984. *Khul-khal: Five Egyptian women tell their stories*. Cairo: American University in Cairo Press.
Atkinson, C. 1983. Precious balsam in a fragile glass: The ideology of virginity in the later Middle Ages. *Journal of Family History* 8(2): 131–43.

Attir, M. O. 1985. Ideology, value changes, and women's social position in Libyan society. In *Women and the Family in the Middle East: New Voices of Change*, ed. E. W. Fernea. Austin: University of Texas Press.

Bagnall, R. S., and B. W. Frier. 1994. *The demography of Roman Egypt*. Cambridge: Cambridge University Press.

Bahrani, Z. 1998. Conjuring Mesopotamia: Imaginative geography and a world past. In *Archaeology under Fire*, ed. L. M. Meskell. London: Routledge.

Bailey, E. 1996. Circumcision in ancient Egypt. *Bulletin of the Australian Centre for Egyptology* 7: 15–28.

Baines, J. 1983. Literacy and ancient Egyptian society. *Man* 18: 572–99.

———. 1987. Practical religion and piety. *Journal of Egyptian Archaeology* 73: 79–98.

———. 1988. Literacy, social organisation, and the archaeological record: The case of early Egypt. In *State and society: The emergence and development of social hierarchy and political centralization*, ed. J. Gledhill, B. Bender, and M. T. Larsen. London: Unwin Hyman.

———. 1991. Society, morality, and religious practice. In *Religion in ancient Egypt*, ed. B. E. Shafer. London: Routledge.

———. 1996. Contextualizing Egyptian representations of society and ethnicity. In *The study of the ancient Near East in the twenty-first century*, ed. J. S. Cooper and G. M. Schwartz. Eisenbrauns, Ind: Winona Lake.

———. 1999. Forerunners of narrative biographies. In *Studies in honour of H. S. Smith*, ed. J. Tait and A. Leahy. London: EES Occasional Publications, Egypt Exploration Society.

———. 2001. Egyptian letters of the New Kingdom as evidence for religious participation and practice. *Journal of Ancient Near Eastern Religions*.

Baines, J., and P. Lacovara. 2002. Burial and the dead in ancient Egyptian society: Respect, formalism, neglect. *Journal of Social Archaeology* (2)1.

Baines, J., and J. Málek. 2000. *Cultural atlas of ancient Egypt*. New York: Checkmark Books.

Bakhtin, M. 1984. *Rabelais and his world*. Bloomington: Indiana University Press.

Bakir, A. 1952. *Slavery in pharaonic Egypt*. Cairo: Imprimerie de l'Institut Français d'Archéologie Orientale.

Bass, G. F. 1987. Oldest known shipwreck reveals splendors of the Bronze Age. *National Geographic Magazine* 172 (6): 692–733.

Bataille, G. 1993. *The accursed share*. Vols. 2 and 3. New York: Zone Books.

Becker, W. 1895. *Illustrations of the private life of the ancient Greeks*. London: Longmans.

Behrens, P. 1982. Phallus. *Lexikon der Ägyptologie*, vol. 4, ed. W. Helck and E. Otto. Wiesbaden: Otto Harrassowitz.

Bell, M. R. 1982. Preliminary report on the Mycenaean pottery from Deir el Medina (1979–1980). *Annales du Service des Antiquities de Egypte* 68: 143–63.

Bierbrier, M. L. 1975. *The late New Kingdom in Egypt*. Warminster: Aris and Phillips.

———. 1980. Terms of relationship at Deir el-Medina. *Journal of Egyptian Archaeology* 66: 100–107.

Bietak, M. 1979. Urban archaeology and the "town problem" in ancient Egypt. In *Egyptology and the Social Sciences*, ed. K. Weeks. Cairo: American University in Cairo Press.

———.1995. *Avaris: the capital of the Hyksos—Recent excavations at Tell el-Daba*. London: British Museum Press.

Bleeker, C. J. 1967. *Egyptian festivals: Enactments of religious renewal*. Leiden: E. J. Brill.

Bloch, M. 1982. Death, women, and power. In *Death and the regeneration of life*, ed. M. Bloch and J. Parry. Cambridge: Cambridge University Press.

Bloch, M., and J. Parry. 1982. Introduction: Death and the regeneration of life. In *Death and the regeneration of life*. Cambridge: Cambridge University Press.

Bochi, P. A. 1994. Images of time in ancient Egyptian art. *Journal of the American Research Center in Egypt* 31: 55–62.

Bolshakov, A. O. 1997. *Man and his double in Egyptian ideology of the Old Kingdom*. Wiesbaden: Harrassowitz.

Bomann, A. H. 1991. *The private chapel in ancient Egypt*. London and New York: Kegan Paul International.

Bonnet, C., and D. Valbelle. 1976. Le village de Deir el Médineh. *Bulletin de l'Institut Français d'Archéologie Orientale* 76: 317–42.

Borchardt, L., and H. Ricke. 1980. *Die Wohnhäuser in Tell el-Amarna*. Berlin: Gebr. Mann Verlag.

Borg, B. 1997. The dead as a guest at table? Continuity and change in the Egyptian cult of the dead. In *Portraits and masks: Burial customs in Roman Egypt*, ed. M. L. Bierbrier. London: British Museum Press.

Borghouts, J. F. 1971. *The magical texts of Papyrus Leiden I 348*. Leiden: E. J. Brill.

———. 1978. *Ancient Egyptian magical texts*. Leiden: E. J. Brill.

———. 1981. Monthu and matrimonial squabbles. *Revue d'Égyptologie* 33: 11–22.

Bosse-Griffiths, K. 1980. Two lute-players of the Amarna era. *Journal of Egyptian Archaeology* 66: 70–82.

Boswell, J. 1994. *The marriage of likeness: Same-sex unions in premodern Europe*. New York: Villard Books.

Bourdieu, P. 1977. *Outline of a theory of practice*. Cambridge: Cambridge University Press.

Bourriau, J. 1991. The Memphis pottery project. *Cambridge Archaeological Journal* 2: 263–8.

Bowman, A. K., and E. Rogan. 1999. Agriculture in Egypt from pharaonic to modern times. In *Agriculture in Egypt: From pharaonic to modern times*, ed. A. K. Bowman and E. Rogan. Oxford: Oxford University Press.

Brewer, D. J., and E. Teeter. 1999. *Egypt and the Egyptians*. Cambridge: Cambridge University Press.

Brookes, I. A. 1989. Early Holocene basinal sediments of the Dakhleh Oasis region, south central Egypt. *Quaternary Research* 32(2): 139–52.

Brooten, B. 1996. *Love between women: Early Christian responses to female homoeroticism*. Chicago: University of Chicago Press.

Brovarski, W., S. K. Doll, and R. Freed, eds. 1982. *Egypt's golden age: The art of living in the New Kingdom 1558–1085 B.C.* Boston: Museum of Fine Arts.

Brunner-Traut, E. 1955. Die Wochenlaube. *Mitteilungen des Instituts für Orientforschung* 3: 11–30.

Bruyère, B. 1926. *Rapport sur les Fouilles de Deir el Médineh (1924–1925), Troisième Partie*. Cairo: Imprimerie de l'Institut Français d'Archéologie Orientale.

Bruyère, B. 1930. *Rapport sur les Fouilles de Deir el Médineh (1929), Deuxième Partie.* Cairo: Imprimerie de l'Institut Français d'Archéologie Orientale.

———. 1937. *Rapport sur les Fouilles de Deir el Médineh (1934–1935), Deuxième Partie FIFAO 15.* Cairo: Imprimerie de l'Institut Français d'Archéologie Orientale.

———. 1939. *Rapport sur les Fouilles de Deir el Médineh (1934–1935), Troisième Partie FIFAO 16.* Cairo: Imprimerie de l'Institut Français d'Archéologie Orientale.

Budge, E. A. W. 1891. *Dwellers on the Nile: Chapters on the life, literature, history, and customs of the ancient Egyptians.* London: Religious Tract Society.

Butler, J. 1993. *Bodies that matter: On the discursive limits of "sex."* New York: Routledge.

Butzer, K. 1976. *Early hydraulic civilization in Egypt: A study in cultural ecology.* Chicago: University of Chicago Press.

Cameron, A., and A. Kuhrt, eds. 1993. *Images of women in antiquity.* London: Routledge.

Caminos, R. A. 1997. Peasants. In *The Egyptians*, ed. S. Donadoni. Chicago: University of Chicago Press.

Capel, A. K., and G. E. Markoe, eds. 1996. *Mistress of the house, mistress of heaven: Women in ancient Egypt.* New York: Hudson Hills Press.

Carrithers, M., S. Collins, and S. Lukes, eds. 1985. *The category of the person: Anthropology, philosophy, history.* Cambridge: Cambridge University Press.

Černý, J. 1929. Papyrus Salt 124 (Brit. Mus. 10055). *Journal of Egyptian Archaeology* 15: 243–58.

———. 1954. Consanguineous marriages in pharaonic Egypt. *Journal of Egyptian Archaeology* 40: 23–29.

———. 1973. *A community of workmen at Thebes in the Ramesside period.* Cairo, BdE 50, Institut Français d'Archéologie Orientale.

Černý, J., and T. E. Peet. 1927. A marriage settlement of the Twentieth Dynasty. *Journal of Egyptian Archaeology* 13: 30–39.

Chartier, R., ed. 1989. *A history of private life: Passions of the Renaissance.* Cambridge, Mass.: Harvard University Press, Belknap Press.

Cherpion, N. 1994. Le cône d'onguent, gage de survie. *Bulletin de l'Institut Français d'Archéologie Orientale* 94: 79–106.

Classen, C., D. Howes, and D. Synott. 1994. *Aroma: The cultural history of smell.* London: Routledge.

Cohen, A. P. 1994. *Self consciousness: An alternative anthropology of identity.* London: Routledge.

Crocker, P. T. 1985. Status symbols in the architecture of el-'Amarna. *Journal of Egyptian Archaeology* 71: 52–65.

Curto, S., and M. Mancini. 1968. News of Khaʿ and Meryt. *Journal of Egyptian Archaeology* 54: 77–81.

D'Auria, S., and P. Lacovara, eds. 1988. *Mummies and magic: The funerary arts of ancient Egypt.* Boston and Dallas: Boston Museum of Fine Arts and Dallas Museum of Art.

Davies, B. G. 1999. *Who's who at Deir el Medina: A prosopographic study of the royal workmen's community.* Leiden: Nederlands Instituut voor het Nabije Oosten.

Davies, B. G., and J. Toivari. 1997. Misuse of a maidservant's services. *Studien zur Altagyptischen Kultur* 24: 69–80.

Davies, N. M. 1938. Some representations of tombs from the Theban necropolis. *Journal of Egyptian Archaeology* 24: 25–40.

Davies, W. V., and L. Schofield, eds. 1995. *Egypt, the Aegean, and the Levant.* London: British Museum Press.

de Lauretis, T., ed. 1984. *Alice doesn't: Feminism, semiotics, cinema.* Bloomington: Indiana University Press.

De Mause, L., ed. 1974. *The history of childhood.* New York: Psychohistory Press.

de Wit, C. 1972. La circoncision chez les anciens Egyptiens. *Zeitschrift für Ägyptische Sprache und Altertumskunde* 99: 41–48.

Dean-Jones, L. 1994. *Women's bodies in classical Greek science.* Oxford: Oxford University Press.

Demarée, R. J. 1983. *The 3 ḫ I ḳr n Rʿ-stelae: On ancestor worship in ancient Egypt.* Leiden: Nederlands Instituut voor het Nabije Oosten.

Depuydt, L. 1997. *Civil calendar and lunar calendar in ancient Egypt.* Leuven: Peeters and Departement Oosterse Studies.

Derchain, P. 1975. La perruque et le cristal. *Studien zur Altägyptischen Kultur* 2: 55–74.

Desroches-Noblecourt, C. 1954. Poissons, tabous et transformation du mort. Nouvelles considérations sur les pèlerinages aux villes saintes. *Kêmi* 13: 32–42.

Dolgin, J. L. 1995. Family law and the facts of family. In *Naturalizing Power: Essays in feminist cultural analysis,* ed. S. Yanagisako and C. Delaney. New York: Routledge.

Donadoni, S., ed. 1997. *The Egyptians.* Chicago: University of Chicago Press.

Douglas, M., 1966. *Purity and danger: An analysis of the concepts of pollution and taboo.* London: Routledge.

Douglas, M., and S. Ney. 1998. *Missing persons: A critique of personhood in the social sciences.* Berkeley: University of California Press.

Duby, G. 1987. Foreword. In *A history of private life: From pagan Rome to Byzantium,* ed. P. Veyne. Cambridge, Mass.: Harvard University Press, Belknap Press.

———, ed. 1988. *A history of private life: Revelations of the medieval world.* Cambridge, Mass.: Harvard University Press, Belknap Press.

Eilberg-Schwartz, H., and W. Doniger, eds. 1995. *Off with her head: The denial of women's identity in myth, religion, and culture.* Berkeley: University of California Press.

El Mahdy, C. 1987. *Exploring the world of the pharaohs.* London: Thames and Hudson.

Emboden, W. 1981. Transcultural use of narcotic water lilies in ancient Egyptian and Maya drug ritual. *Journal of Ethnopharmacology* 3(1): 39–83.

———. 1989. The sacred journey in dynastic Egypt: Shamanistic trance in the context of the narcotic water lily and the mandrake. *Journal of Psychoactive Drugs* 21(1): 61–75.

Eriksen, T. H. 1993. *Ethnicity and Nationalism.* London: Pluto Press.

Erman, A. 1894. *Life in ancient Egypt.* London: Macmillan.

Eyre, C. J. 1979. A "strike" text from the Theban necropolis. In *Glimpses of ancient Egypt: Studies in honour of H. W. Fairman,* ed. J. Ruffle, G. A. Gaballa, and K. A. Kitchen. Warminster: Aris Phillips.

———. 1984. Crime and adultery in ancient Egypt. *Journal of Egyptian Archaeology* 70: 92–105.

———. 1992. The adoption papyrus in social context. *Journal of Egyptian Archaeology* 78: 207–21.

Eyre, C. J. 1998. The market women of pharaonic Egypt. In *Le commerce en Égypte anciene*, ed. N. Grimal and P. Menu. Cairo: Imprimerie de l'Institut Français d'Archéologie Orientale.

———. 1999. The village economy in ancient Egypt. In *Agriculture in Egypt: From pharaonic to modern times*, ed. A. K. Bowman and E. Rogan. Oxford: Oxford University Press.

Fantham, E., H. P. Foley, N. B. Kanpen, S. B. Pomeroy, and A. A. Shapiro, eds. 1994. *Women in the classical world*. Oxford: Oxford University Press.

Featherstone, M. 1999. Love and eroticism: An introduction. In *Love and eroticism*, ed. M. Featherstone. London: Sage Publications.

Feher, M., R. Naddolf, and N. Tazi, eds. 1989. *Fragments for a history of the human body*. New York: Zone Books.

Fernandez, J. W. 2000. Peripheral wisdom. In *Signifying identities: Anthropological perspectives on boundaries and contested values*, ed. A. Cohen. London: Routledge.

Feucht, E. 1995. *Das Kind im alten Ägypten*. Frankfurt and New York: Campus Verlag.

———. 1997. Women. In *The Egyptians*, ed. S. Donadoni. Chicago: University of Chicago Press.

Foertmeyer, V. A. 1989. Tourism in Graeco-Roman Egypt. Ph.D. diss., Princeton University.

Foucault, M. 1972. *The archaeology of knowledge*. London: Routledge.

———. 1978. *The history of sexuality*. London: Routledge.

———. 1985. *The history of sexuality: The use of pleasure*. London: Penguin.

Fox, M. V. 1985. *The song of songs and the ancient Egyptian love songs*. Madison: University of Wisconsin Press.

Frandsen, P. J. 1990. Editing reality: The Turin Strike papyrus. In *Studies in Egyptology presented to Miriam Lichtheim*, vol. 1, ed. S. Israelit-Groll. Jerusalem: Magnes Press.

———. 1992. The letter to Ikhtay's coffin: O. Louvre INV. no. 698. In *Village voices*, ed. R. J. Demarée and A. Egberts. Leiden: Centre for Non-Western Studies.

Frankfort, H. 1927. Preliminary report on the excavations at Tell El-'Amarnah 1926–1927. *Journal of Egyptian Archaeology* 13: 209–18.

Freed, R. E., S. D'Auria, and Y. Markowitz, eds. 1999. *Pharaohs of the sun: Akhenaten, Nefertiti, Tutankhamun*. Boston: Museum of Fine Arts.

Friedl, E. 1994. Sex and the invisible. *American Anthropologist* 96(4): 833–44.

Friedman, F. A. 1985. On the meaning of some anthropoid busts from Deir el Medina. *Journal of Egyptian Archaeology* 71: 82–97.

———. 1994. Aspects of domestic life and religion. In *Pharaoh's workers. The villagers of Deir el Medina*, ed. L. H. Lesko. New York: Cornell University Press.

Gadfelter, B. G. 1990. Geomorphic setting of Upper Paleolithic sites in Wadi el Sheikh, southern Sinai. *Geoarchaeology* 5(2): 99–119.

Gatens, M. 1996. *Imaginary bodies*. Routledge: London.

Geary, P. 1994. *Poor women and children in the European past*. London: Routledge.

Geertz, C. 1966. The impact of culture on the concept of man. In *New Views on the Nature of Man*, ed. J. Platt. Chicago: University of Chicago Press.

———. 1973. *The interpretation of culture*. New York: Basic.

Gero, J. M., and M. W. Conkey, eds. 1991. *Engendering archaeology: Women and prehistory.* Oxford: Blackwell.

Ghosh, A. 1992. *In an antique land.* London: Granta.

Giddens, A. 1991. *Modernity and self-identity: Self and society in the late modern age.* Cambridge: Polity Press.

Giddy, L. 1987. *Egyptian oases: Bahariya, Dakhla, Farafra, and Kharga during pharaonic times.* Warminster, U. K.: Aris and Phillips.

———. 1999. *The survey of Memphis II—Kom Rabi'a: The New Kingdom and post-New Kingdom objects.* London: Egypt Exploration Society.

Gies, F. 1987. *Marriage and the family in the Middle Ages.* New York: Harper and Row.

Grapow, H., H. von Deines, and W. Westendorf. 1958. *Grundriss der Medizin der alten Ägypter.* 9 vols. Berlin: Akademie-Verlag.

Grimal, N. 1992. *A history of ancient Egypt.* Oxford: Blackwell.

Halperin, D. 1990. *One hundred years of homosexuality and other essays on Greek love.* New York: Routledge.

Hare, T. 1999. *ReMembering Osiris: Number, gender, and the word in ancient Egyptian representational systems.* Stanford: Stanford University Press.

Harer, W. B. 1985. Pharmacological and biological properties of the Egyptian lotus. *Journal of the American Research Center in Egypt* 22: 49–54.

Harré, R. 1998. *The singular self: An introduction to the psychology of personhood.* London: Sage.

Hassan, F. A. 1997. The dynamics of a riverine civilization: A geoarchaeological perspective on the Nile valley, Egypt. *World Archaeology* 29(1): 51–74.

Herdt, G., ed. 1993. *Third sex, third gender.* New York: Zone Books.

Herlihy, D. 1995. *Women of the English nobility and gentry, 1066–1500.* Manchester: Manchester Unversity Press.

Hertz, R. 1960. A contribution to the study of the collective representation of death. In *Death and the right hand.* London: Cohen and West.

Hoch, J. E. 1994. *Semitic words in Egyptian texts of the New Kingdom and Third Intermediate period.* Princeton: Princeton University Press.

Hodder, I. 1999. *The archaeological process: An introduction.* Oxford: Blackwell.

Hodel-Hoenes, S. 2000. *Life and death in ancient Egypt: Scenes from private tombs in New Kingdom Thebes.* Ithaca and London: Cornell University Press.

Hornung, E. 1990. *The Valley of the Kings: Horizon of eternity.* New York: Timken.

———. 1992. *Idea into image: Essays on ancient Egyptian thought.* New York: Timken.

———. 1999. *The ancient Egyptian books of the afterlife.* Ithaca: Cornell University Press.

Hufton, O. 1984. Women without men: Widows and spinsters in Britain and France in the 18th century. *Journal of Family History* 9(4): 355–76.

Hunt, L., ed. 1993. *The invention of pornography: Obscenity and the origins of modernity 1500–1800.* New York: Zone Books.

Ikram, S. 1995. *Choice cuts: Meat production in ancient Egypt.* Leuven: Peeters and Departement Oosterse Studies.

Ikram, S., and A. Dodson. 1998. *The mummy in ancient Egypt: Equipping the dead for eternity.* London: Thames and Hudson.

Jackson, M. 1989. *Paths toward a clearing: Radical empiricism and ethnographic inquiry.* Bloomington: Indiana University Press.

James, T.G.H. 1962. *The Hekanakhte papers and other Early Middle Kingdom documents*. New York: Metropolitan Museum of Art Egyptian Expedition.

———. *Pharaoh's people: Scenes from life in imperial Egypt*. London: Bodley Head.

Janssen, J. J. 1975. *Commodity prices from the Ramessid Period*. Leiden: E. J. Brill.

———. 1988. Marriage problems and public reactions (P. BM 10416). In *Pyramid studies and other essays presented to I. E. S. Edwards*, ed. J. Baines, T.G.H. James, A. Leahy, and A. F. Shore. London: Egypt Exploration Society.

———. 1997. *Village Varia: Ten studies on the history and administration of Deir el-Medina*. Leiden: Nederlands Insituut voor het Nabije Oosten.

Janssen, J. J., and P. W. Pestman. 1968. Burial and inheritance in the community of the necropolis workmen at Thebes. *Journal of the Economic and Social History of the Orient* 11: 137–70.

Janssen, R., and J. J. Janssen 1990. *Growing up in ancient Egypt*. London: Rubicon Press.

———. 1996. *Getting old in ancient Egypt*. London: Rubicon Press.

Jeffreys, D., and A. Tavares. 1994. The historic landscape of early dynastic Memphis. *Mitteilungen des Deutschen Archäologischen Instituts, Abteilung Kairo* 50: 142–73.

Johnston, H. 1903. *The private life of the Romans*. Freeport, New York: Books for Libraries Press.

Keimer, L. 1941. *Études d'Égyptologie. Fasc. III*. Cairo: Imprimerie de l'Institut Français d'Archéologie Orientale.

Kemp, B. J. 1977a. The city of el Amarna as a source for the study of urban society in ancient Egypt. *World Archaeology* 9: 124–39.

———. 1977b. The early development of towns in Egypt. *Antiquity*: 185–200.

———. 1979. Wall paintings from the workmen's village at el-Amarna. *Journal of Egyptian Archaeology* 65: 47–53.

———. 1980. Preliminary report on the El-'Amarna expedition 1979. *Journal of Egyptian Archaeology* 66: 5–16.

———. 1984a. In the shadow of the texts: Archaeology in Egypt. *Archaeological Review from Cambridge* 3(2): 19–28.

———. ed. 1984b. *Amarna Reports I*. London: Egypt Exploration Society.

———. ed. 1985. *Amarna Reports II*. London: Egypt Exploration Society.

———. 1987a. The Amarna workmen's village in retrospect. *Journal of Egyptian Archaeology* 7(3): 21–50.

———. ed. 1987b. *Amarna Reports IV*. London: Egypt Exploration Society.

———. 1989. *Ancient Egypt: Anatomy of a civilization*. London: Routledge.

Kemp, B. J., and R. S. Merrillees. 1980. *Minoan pottery in second millenium Egypt*. Mainz am Rhein: Philipp von Zabern.

Klingshirn, W. 1994. *Changing face of friendship*. South Bend: Notre Dame University Press.

Knapp, A. B. 1996. Archaeology without gravity: Postmodernism and the past. *Journal of Archaeological Method and Theory* 3(2).

Kozloff, A. P., and B. Bryan. 1992. *Egypt's dazzling sun: Amenhotep III and his world*. Cleveland: Cleveland Museum of Art.

Kritzman, L. D. 1988. *Michel Foucault—Politics, philosophy, culture: Interviews and other writings, 1977–1984*. New York: Routledge.

Kuhrt, A. 1995. *The ancient Near East, c. 3000–330 B.C.* London: Routledge.

Kulick, D. 1997. The gender of Brazilian transgendered prostitutes. *American Anthropologist* 99(3): 574–85.

La Fontaine, J. S. 1985. Person and individual in anthropology. In *The category of the person*, ed. M. Carrithers, S. Collins, and S. Lukes. Cambridge: Cambridge University Press.

Lacovara, P. 1993. State and settlement: Deir el Ballas and the development, structure and function of the New Kingdom royal city. In *Near Eastern languages and civilizations*. Chicago: University of Chicago.

———. 1994. *The New Kingdom royal city.* London: Kegan Paul International.

Lancaster, R. N., and M. di Leonardo, eds. 1997. *The gender/sexuality reader: Culture, history, political economy.* New York: Routledge.

Lane, E. W. [1836] 1989. *Manners and customs of the modern Egyptians.* The Hague & London: East-West Publications.

Laslett, P. 1995. Necessary knowledge: Age and aging in the societies of the past. In *Aging in the past: Demography, society and old age*, ed. D. I. Kertzer and P. Laslett. Berkeley: University of California Press.

Le Roy Ladurie, E. 1980. *Montaillou: Cathars and Catholics in a French village, 1294–1324.* London: Penguin.

Leitz, C. 1994. *Tagewählerei: Das Buch ḥȝt nḥḥ pḥwy dt und verwandte Texte.* Wiesbaden: Harrassowitz Verlag.

———. 1999. *Hieratic papyri in the British Museum VII: Magical and medical papyri of the New Kingdom.* London: British Museum Press.

Lepper, V. 1998. Die Schreiberstatuetten der späten 18. Dynastie. Studien Persönlichen Frömmigkeit in Amarna. Master's thesis, Department of Egyptology, University of Bonn.

Lesko, B. S. 1999. *The great goddesses of Egypt.* Norman: University of Oklahoma Press.

Leyser, H. 1995. *Medieval women: A social history of women in England, 450–1500.* London: Weidenfeld and Nicolson.

Lichtheim, M. 1976. *Ancient Egyptian literature.* Vol. 2, *The New Kingdom.* Berkeley: University of California Press.

———. 1980. *Ancient Egyptian literature.* Vol. 3, *The late period.* Berkeley: University of California Press.

Lindholm, C. 1999. Love and structure. In *Love and eroticism*, ed. M. Featherstone. London: Sage.

Lingis, A. 1994. *Foreign bodies.* New York: Routledge.

Lloyd, A. B. 1989. Psychology and society in the ancient Egyptian cult of the dead. In *Religion and philosophy in ancient Egypt*, ed. W. K. Simpson. New Haven: Yale Egyptological Studies.

Loose, A. A. 1992. Woonhuizen in Amarna en het domein van de vrouwen. *Phoenix* 38(2): 16–29.

Loprieno, A. 1996. Defining Egyptian literature: Ancient texts and modern theories. In *Ancient Egyptian literature: History and forms.* Leiden: E. J. Brill.

———. 1997. Slaves. In *The Egyptians*, ed. S. Donadoni. Chicago: University of Chicago Press.

Lüddeckens, E. 1943. Untersuchungen über religiösen gehalt, sprache und form der Ägyptischen totenklagen. *Mitteilungen des Deutschen Instituts für Ägyptische Altertumskunde in Kairo* 11: 1–188.

Mahmoud, A. 1999. Ii-neferti, a poor woman. *Mitteilungen des Deutschen Archäologischen Instituts, Abteilung Kairo* 55: 315–23.

Manniche, L. 1987. *Sexual life in ancient Egypt.* London and New York: Kegan Paul.

———. 1988. *Lost tombs: A study of certain Eighteenth Dynasty monuments in the Theban necropolis.* London and New York: Kegan Paul.

———. 1999. *Sacred luxuries: Fragrance, aromatherapy, and cosmetics in ancient Egypt.* Ithaca: Cornell University Press.

Marciniak, M. 1971. Encore sur la Belle Fête de la Vallée. *Etudes et travaux* 5: 54–71.

Martin, G. T. 1989. *The Memphite tomb of Horemheb commander-in-chief of Tut'ankhamun.* London: Egypt Exploration Society.

Mathieu, B. 1996. *La poesie amoureuse de l'Égypte ancienne: Recherches sur un genre litteraire au Nouvel Empire.* Cairo: Institut Français d'Archéologie Orientale.

Mauss, M. [1938] 1985. A category of the human mind: The notion of person, the notion of self. In *The category of the person,* ed. M. Carrithers, S. Collins, and S. Lukes. Cambridge: Cambridge University Press: 1–25.

McDaniel, W. [1871] 1963. *Roman private life and its survivals.* New York: Cooper Square Publishers.

McDowell, A. G. 1990. Jurisdiction in the workmen's community of Deir el Medina. Leiden: Nederlands Instituut voor het Nabije Oosten.

———. 1992a. Agricultural activity by the workmen of Deir el Medina. *Journal of Egyptian Archaeology* 78: 195–206.

———. 1992b. Awareness of the past in Deir el-Medina. In *Village voices,* ed. R. J. Demarée and A. Egberts. Leiden: Centre of Non-Western Studies. 95–109.

———. 1994. Contact with the outside world. In *Pharaoh's workers: The villagers of Deir el Medina,* ed. L. H. Lesko. New York: Cornell University Press.

———. 1999. *Village life in ancient Egypt: Laundry lists and love songs.* Oxford: Oxford University Press.

McKinnon, S. 1995. American kinship / American incest: Asymmetries in a scientific discourse. In *Naturalizing power: Essays in feminist cultural analysis,* ed. S. Yanagisako and C. Delaney. New York: Routledge.

Merleau-Ponty, M. 1962. *The phenomenology of perception.* London: Routledge and Kegan Paul.

Meskell, L. M. 1994a. Deir el Medina in hyperreality: Seeking the people of pharaonic Egypt. *Journal of Mediterranean Archaeology* 7(2): 193–216.

———. 1994b. Dying young: The experience of death at Deir el Medina. *Archaeological Review from Cambridge* 13(2): 35–45.

———. 1996. The somatisation of archaeology: Institutions, discourses, corporeality. *Norwegian Archaeological Review* 29(1): 1–16.

———. 1997. Egyptian social dynamics: The evidence of age, sex, and class in domestic and mortuary contexts. Ph.D. diss., Cambridge University.

———. 1998a. Size matters: Sex, gender, and status in Egyptian iconography. *Redefining archaeology: Feminist perspectives,* ed. M. Casey, D. Donlon, J. Hope, and S. Welfare. Canberra: Australian National University: 175–81.

———. 1998b. An archaeology of social relations in an Egyptian village. *Journal of Archaeological Method and Theory* 5(3): 209–43.

———. 1998c. Intimate archaeologies: the case of Kha and Merit. *World Archaeology* 29(3): 363–79.

———. 1999a. *Archaeologies of social life: Age, sex, class et cetera in ancient Egypt.* Oxford: Blackwell.

———. 1999b. Archaeologies of life and death. *American Journal of Archaeology* 103: 181–99.

———. 2000a. Cycles of life: Narrative homology and archaeological realities. *World Archaeology: Lifecycles* 31(3): 423–41.

———. 2000b. Re-embedding sex: Domesticity, sexuality, and ritual in New Kingdom Egypt. In *Archaeologies of sexuality,* ed. R. Schmidt and B. Voss. London: Routledge.

———. 2001. Archaeologies of identity. In *Archaeological theory: Breaking the boundaries,* ed. I. Hodder. Cambridge: Polity.

Metcalf, P., and R. Huntingdon. 1991. *Celebrations of death: The anthropology of mortuary ritual.* Cambridge: Cambridge University Press.

Midgley, M. 1984. Sex and personal identity: The Western individualistic tradition. *Encounter* 63(1): 50–55.

Milde, H. 1988. "Going out into the day:" Ancient Egyptian beliefs and practices concerning death. In *Hidden futures: Death and immortality in ancient Egypt, Anatolia, the classical, biblical, and Arabic-Islamic world,* ed. J. M. Bremer, T. P. van den Hour, and R. Peters. Amsterdam: University of Amsterdam Press: 15–35.

Millard, A. 1986. *The position of women in the family and in society in ancient Egypt, with special reference to the Middle Kingdom.* Department of Egyptology. London: University College London.

Miller, E., and R. B. Parkinson. 2001. Reflections on a gilded eye in "Fowling in the marshes" (British Museum EA 37977). In *Colour and Painting in Ancient Egypt,* ed. W. V. Davies. London: British Museum Press.

Miller, R. L. 1990. Hogs and hygiene. *Journal of Egyptian Archaeology* 76: 125–40.

———. 1991. Counting calories in Egyptian ration texts. *Journal of the Economic and Social History of the Orient* 34: 257–69.

Millet, N. B., G. D. Hart, T. A. Reyman, M. R. Zimmerman, and P. K. Lewin. 1998. ROM I: mummification for the common people. *Mummies, disease, and ancient cultures,* 2d ed., ed. A. Cockburn, E. Cockburn, and T. A. Reyman. Cambridge: Cambridge University Press.

Mitchell, T. 1990. The invention and reinvention of the Egyptian peasant. *International Journal of Middle Eastern Studies* 22: 129–50.

Mitterauer, M., and R. Sieder. 1982. *The European family.* Oxford: Blackwell.

Moers, G. 1999. Travel as a narrative in Egyptian literature. In *Definitely: Egyptian literature,* ed. G. Moers. Göttingen: Seminar für Ägyptologie und Koptologie.

Montserrat, D. 1997. Death and funerals in the Roman Fayyum. In *Portraits and masks,* ed. M. Bierbrier. London: British Museum Press.

———. 2000. *Akhenaten: History, fantasy, and ancient Egypt.* London: Routledge.

———. ed. 1998. *Changing bodies, changing meanings: Studies on the human body in antiquity.* London: Routledge.

Montserrat, D., and L. M. Meskell. 1997. Mortuary archaeology and religious landscape at Graeco-Roman Deir el Medina. *Journal of Egyptian Archaeology* 84: 179–98.

Moreno Garcia, J. C. 1999. *Hwt et le milieu rural égyptien du IIIe millénaire: Économie, administration et organisation territoriale.* Paris: H. Champion.

Morris, B. 1991. *Western conceptions of the individual*. Oxford: Berg.

———. 1994. *Anthropology of the self: The individual in cultural perspective*. London: Pluto Press.

Murnane, W. J. 1995. *Texts from the Amarna period in Egypt*. Scholars Press: Atlanta.

Nicholas, D. 1985. *The domestic life of a medieval city: Women, children, and the family in fourteenth century Ghent*. Lincoln: University of Nebraska Press.

Nicholson, L. J., ed. 1997. *The second wave: A reader in feminist theory*. New York: Routledge.

Nicholson, S. 1996. Environmental changes within the historic period. In *The physical geography of Africa*. Oxford: Oxford University Press: 60–87.

Nordh, K. 1996. Aspects of ancient Egyptian curses and blessings. *Egyptology*. Uppsala, Sweden: Boreas, Acta Universitatis Upsaliensis.

Nunn, J. F. 1996. *Ancient Egyptian medicine*. London: British Museum Press.

O'Connor, D. 1993. *Ancient Nubia: Egypt's rival in Africa*. Philadelphia: University of Pennsylvania.

———. 1995. The social and economic organisation of ancient Egyptian temples. In *Civilizations of the ancient Near East*, ed. J. M. Sasson. New York: Charles Scribner's Sons.

———. 1997. Ancient Egypt: Egyptological and anthropological perspectives. In *Anthropology and Egyptology: A developing dialogue*, ed. J. Lustig. Sheffield, U.K.: Sheffield Academic Press.

Omlin, J. A. 1973. *Der Papyrus 55001 und seine satirisch-erotischen Zeichnungen und Inschriften*. Turin: Museo Egizio di Torino.

Ortner, S. B. 1981. Gender and sexuality in hierarchical societies: The case of Polynesia and some comparative implications. In *Sexual meanings: The cultural construction of gender and sexuality*, ed. S. B. Ortner and H. Whitehead. Cambridge: Cambridge University Press.

Osburn, W. 1854. *The monumental history of Egypt as recorded on the ruins of her temples, palaces, and tombs*. London: Trübner.

Osing, J. 1976. Ächtungstexte aus dem Alten Reich II. *Mitteilungen des Deutschen Archäologischen Instituts, Abteilung Kairo* 32: 133–85.

Pantel, P. S., ed. 1992. *A history of women: From ancient goddesses to Christian saints*. Cambridge, Mass.: Harvard University Press, Belknap Press.

Parkinson, R. B. 1995. "Homosexual" desire in Middle Kingdom literature. *Journal of Egyptian Archaeology* 81: 57–76.

———. 1997. *The Tale of Sinuhe and Other Ancient Egyptian Poems*. Oxford: Clarendon Press.

———. 1998. Invisible cities: Landscape and urban life in ancient Egypt. Paper presented to the Friends of the Oriental Museum, Durham, United Kingdom.

———. 1999. The dream and the knot: Contextualising Middle Kingdom literature. In *Definitely: Egyptian literature*, ed. G. Moers. Göttingen: Seminar für Ägyptologie und Koptologie.

Paz, O. 1995. *The double flame: Love and eroticism*. New York: Harcourt Brace & Co.

Peet, T. E., and C. L. Woolley. 1923. *City of Akhenaten*. London: Egypt Exploration Society.

Pestman, P. W. 1961. *Marriage and matrimonial property in ancient Egypt: A contribution to establishing the legal position of the woman.* Leiden: NINO/ Papyrologica Lugduno-Batava IX.

Peters, J. 1988. Palaeoenvironment of the Gilf Kebir-Jebel Uweinat area during the first half of the Holocene: The latest evidence. *Sahara* 1: 73–76.

Pinch, G. 1983. Childbirth and female figurines at Deir el-Medina and el-'Amarna. *Orientalia* 52: 405–14.

———. 1993. *Votive offerings to Hathor.* Oxford: Griffith Institute.

———. 1994. *Magic in ancient Egypt.* London: British Museum Press.

Pomeroy, S. B. 1975. *Goddesses, whores, wives, and slaves: Women in classical antiquity.* New York: Schocken Books.

Porter, R., ed. 1997. *Rewriting the self: Histories from the Renaissance to the present.* London: Routledge.

Prost, A. 1991. Public and private spheres in France. In *A history of private life: Riddles of identity in modern times,* ed. P. Ariès and G. Duby. Cambridge, Mass.: Harvard University Press, Belknap Press.

Prost, A., and G. Vincent, eds. 1991. *A history of private life: Riddles of identity in modern times.* Cambridge, Mass.: Harvard University Press, Belknap Press.

Quirke, S. 1992. *Ancient Egyptian religion.* London: British Museum Press.

Reeder, G. 2000. Same sex desire, conjugal constructs, and the tomb of Niankhkhnum and Khnumhotep, *World Archaeology* 32(2): 193–208.

Reyman, T. A., and W. H. Peck. 1998. Egyptian mummification with evisceration per ano. In *Mummies, disease and ancient cultures,* 2d ed., ed. A. Cockburn, E. Cockburn, and T. A. Reyman. Cambridge: Cambridge University Press.

Richlin, A., ed. 1992. *Pornography and representation in Greece and Rome.* Oxford: Oxford University Press.

Riddle, J. 1992. *Contraception and abortion from the ancient world to the Renaissance.* Cambridge, Mass.: Yale University Press.

Robins, G. 1979. The relationships specified by Egyptian kinship terms of the Middle and New Kingdoms. *Chronique d'Égypte* 54(107): 197–217.

———. 1993a. Review of "The family in the Eighteenth Dynasty of Egypt," by Sheila Whale. *Journal of Egyptian Archaeology* 79: 294–97.

———. 1993b. *Women in ancient Egypt.* London: British Museum Press.

———. 1994–95. Women and children in peril: Pregnancy, birth, and infant mortality in ancient Egypt. *KMT* 5(4): 24–35.

———. 1994a. Some principles of compositional dominance and gender hierarchy in Egyptian art. *Journal of the American Research Center in Egypt* 31: 33–40.

———. 1994b. Review of *Growing up in ancient Egypt* by R. M. and J. J. Janssen. *Journal of Egyptian Archaeology* 80: 232–5.

———. 1996. Dress, undress, and the representation of fertility and potency in New Kingdom Egyptian Art. In *Sexuality in ancient art,* ed. N. Boymel Kampen. Cambridge: Cambridge University Press.

———. 1999. Hair and the construction of identity in ancient Egypt, c. 1480–1350 B.C. *Journal of the American Research Center in Egypt* 36: 55–69.

Rosenthal, J. 1996. *Old age in late medieval England.* Philadelphia: University of Pennsylvania Press.

Ross, E., and R. Rapp. 1997. Sex and society: A research note from social history and anthropology. In *The gender/sexuality reader: Culture, history, political economy*, ed. R. N. Lancaster and M. di Leonardo. New York: Routledge.

Roth, A. M. 1991. *Egyptian phyles in the Old Kingdom*. Chicago: Oriental Institute.

———. 1993. Fingers, stars, and the "Opening of the Mouth": The nature and function of the *ntrwj*-blades. *Journal of Egyptian Archaeology* 79: 57–79.

———. 2000. Father earth, mother sky: Ancient Egyptian beliefs about conception and fertility. In *Reading the body*, ed. A. Rautman. Philadelphia: University of Pennsylvania Press.

Said, E. 1979. *Orientalism*. New York: Vintage.

Sameh, W. 1964. *Daily life in ancient Egypt*. New York: McGraw Hill.

Samuel, D. 1993. Ancient Egyptian cereal processing: Beyond the artistic record. *Cambridge Archaeological Journal* 3(2): 271–83.

———. 1994. An archaeological study of baking and bread in New Kingdom Egypt. Ph.D. diss., Cambridge University.

———. 1999. Bread making and social interactions at the Amarna workmen's village, Egypt. *World Archaeology* 31(1): 121–44.

Schiaparelli, E. 1927. *La tomba intatta dell'architetto Cha*. Turin: Museo di Antichità.

Scott, N. E. 1944. *The home life of the ancient Egyptians*. New York: The Metropolitan Museum of Art.

Sears, E. 1986. *The ages of man: Medieval interpretations of the life cycle*. Princeton: Princeton University Press.

Sethe, K. 1959. *Ägyptische Lesestücke*. Hildesheim, Germany: Georg Olms Verlagsbuchhandlung.

Shafer, B. E. 1997. Temples, priests, and rituals: An overview. In *Temples in ancient Egypt*, ed. B. E. Shafer. Ithaca: Cornell University Press.

Shanks, M., and C. Tilley. 1987a. *Social theory and archaeology*. Cambridge: Polity Press.

———. 1987b. *Reconstructing archaeology: Theory and practice*. London: Routledge.

Shaw, I.M.E. 1988. A statistical analysis of artefacts at el 'Amarna, Egypt. Ph.D. diss., Cambridge University.

———. 1991. *Egyptian warfare and weapons*. London: Shire Egyptology.

———. 1992. Ideal homes in ancient Egypt. *Cambridge Archaeological Journal* 2(2): 147–66.

———. 1996. Akhetaten Tell el-Amarna. In *Royal cities of the biblical world*, ed. J. G. Westenholz. Jerusalem: Bible Lands Museum.

Sherratt, A. 1995. Alcohol and its alternatives: Symbol and substance in pre-industrial cultures. In *Consuming habits: Drugs in history and anthropology*, ed. J. Goodman, P. E. Lovejoy, and A. Sherratt. London: Routledge.

Shilling, C. 1993. *The body and social theory*. London: Sage Publications.

Shortland, A. J. 2000. *Vitreous materials at Amarna*. Oxford: British Archaeological Reports.

Simpson, W. K., E. F. Faulkner, and E. F. Wente. 1972. *The literature of ancient Egypt*. New Haven: Yale University Press.

Somerville, S. 1997. Scientific racism and the invention of the homosexual body. In *The gender/sexuality reader: Culture, history, political economy*, ed. R. N. Lancaster and M. di Leonardo. New York: Routledge.

Stead, M. 1986. *Egyptian life*. London: British Museum Press.

Stewart, H. M. 1976. *Egyptian stelae, reliefs, and paintings from the Petrie Collection*. Warminster, U.K.: Aris and Phillips.

Stone, L. 1977. *The family, sex and marriage in England, 1500–1800*. New York: Harper and Row.

Strathern, M. 1988. *The gender of the gift: Problems with women and problems with society in Melanesia*. Berkeley: University of Califorina Press.

———. 1992. *After nature: English kinship in the late twentieth century*. Cambridge: Cambridge University Press.

Strouhal, E. 1992. *Life in ancient Egypt*. Cambridge: Cambridge University Press.

Strouhal, E., and L. Vyhnánek. 1980. *Egyptian mummies in Czechoslovak collections*. Prague: Narodní Museum.

Sweeney, D. 1993. Women's correspondence from Deir el-Medineh. In *Sesto Congresso Internazionale di Egittologia. Atti. II.*, ed. G. M. Zaccone and T. R. di Nero. Turin, Comitato Organizzativo del Congresso.

te Velde, H. 1990. Some remarks on the concept "Person" in the ancient Egyptian culture. In *Concepts of person in religion and thought*, ed. H. G. Kippenberg, Y. B. Kuiper, and A. F. Sanders. Berlin: Mouton de Gruyter.

Thomas, A. P. 1981. *Gurob*. Warminster, U.K.: Aris and Phillips.

Tietze, C. 1986. Amarna Teil II: analyse der ökonomischen Beziehungen der Stadtbewohner. *Zeitschrift für Ägyptische Sprache und Altertumskunde* 113: 55–78.

Toivari, J. 1998. Marriage at Deir el Medina. In *Proceedings of the Seventh International Congress of Egyptologists*, ed. C. J. Eyre. Leuven: Uitgeverij Peeters.

———. 2000. Women at Deir el-Medina: A study of the status and roles of the female inhabitants in the workmen's community during the Ramesside period. Ph.D. diss., University of Leiden.

Tosi, M., and A. Roccati. 1972. *Stele e altre epigrafi di Deir el Medina. N. 50001–N. 50262*. Torino: Edizioni d'Arte Fratelli Pozzo.

Traunecker, C. 1979. Manifestations de piété personnelle a Karnak. *Bulletin de la Société française d'Egyptologie* 85: 22–31.

Trigger, B. G. 1981. Akhenaten and Durkheim. *Bulletin de l'Institut Français d'Archéologie Orientale* 81(supplement): 165–84.

Trigger, B. G., B. J. Kemp, D. O'Connor, and A. B. Lloyd. 1983. *Ancient Egypt: A social history*. Cambridge: Cambridge University Press.

Troy, L. 1984. Good and bad women: Maxim 18/284–88 of the Instructions of Ptahhotep. *Gottinger Miszellen* 80: 77–81.

Turner, B. S. 1984. *The body and society*. Oxford: Basil Blackwell.

Turner, V. 1967. *The forest of symbols*. Ithaca: Cornell University Press.

Tyldesley, J. 1994. *Daughters of Isis: Women of ancient Egypt*. London: Penguin Books.

Tylor, J. J., and F. L. Griffith, eds. 1894. *The tomb of Paheri at El Kab*. Ahnas el Medineh (Heracleopolis Magna). London: Egypt Exploration Fund.

Valbelle, D. 1972. Le naos de Kasa au Musée de Turin. *Bulletin de l'Institut Français d'Archéologie Orientale* 72: 179–94.

———. 1981. *Satis et Anoukis*. Mainz, Germany: Philipp von Zabern.

230 · Bibliography

Valbelle, D. 1985. *"Les Ouvriers de la Tombe." Deir el Médineh à l'époque ramesside, BdE 96*. Cairo: Institut Français d'Archéologie Orientale.
———. 1997. Craftsmen. In *The Egyptians*, ed. S. Donadoni. Chicago: University of Chicago Press.
Van Gennep, A. [1909] 1960. *The rites of passage*. Chicago: University of Chicago Press.
van Nieuwkerk, K. 1995. *"A trade like any other:" Female singers and dancers in Egypt*. Austin: University of Texas Press.
Vandier d'Abbadie, J. 1937. *Ostraca figurés de Deir el Médineh*. Cairo: l'Institute Français d'Archéologie Orientale.
Veyne, P. 1978. La famille et l'amour sous le Haut-Empire romain. *Annales* 33: 35–63.
———. ed. 1987. *A history of private life: From pagan Rome to Byzantium*. Cambridge, Mass.: Harvard University Press, Belknap Press.
Vogelsang-Eastwood, G. 1993. *Pharaonic Egyptian clothing*. Leiden: E. J. Brill.
———. 1999. *Tutankhamun's wardrobe: Garments from the tomb of Tutankhamun*. Rotterdam: Barjesteh van Waalwijk van Doorn and Co.
Walker, J. H. 1996. *Studies in ancient Egyptian anatomical terminology*. Warminster, U.K.: Aris and Phillips.
Ward, W. A. 1986. *Essays on feminine titles of the Middle Kingdom and related subjects*. Beirut: American University of Beirut.
———. 1994. Foreigners living in the village. *Pharaoh's workers: The villagers of Deir el Medina*, ed. L. H. Lesko. Ithaca: Cornell University Press.
Watterson, B. 1991. *Women in ancient Egypt*. New York: St. Martin's Press.
———. 1997. *The Egyptians*. Oxford: Blackwell.
Weeks, J. 1997. *Sexuality*. London: Routledge.
———. 1999. The sexual citizen. In *Love and eroticism*, ed. M. Featherstone. London: Sage Publishing.
Wegner, J. 1998. Excavations at the town of Enduring-are-the-Places-of-Khakaure-Maa-Kheru-in-Abydos: A preliminary report of the 1994 and 1997 seasons. *Journal of the American Research Center in Egypt* 35: 1–44.
Wendorf, F., and R. Schild, eds. 1976. *Prehistory of the Nile Valley*. New York: Academic Press.
Wente, E. 1990. *Letters from ancient Egypt*. Atlanta: Scholars Press.
Weston, K. 1995. Naturalizing power. In *Naturalizing power: Essays in feminist cultural analysis*, ed. S. Yanagisako and C. Delaney. New York: Routledge.
Whale, S. 1989. *The family in the Eighteenth Dynasty of Egypt: A study of the representation of the family in the private tombs*. Sydney: Australian Center for Egyptology.
Whaley, E. J. 1981. Introduction. In *Mirrors of mortality: Studies in the social history of Death*. London: Europa Publications.
White, H. 1987. *The content of the form: Narrative discourse and historical representation*. Baltimore: Johns Hopkins University Press.
Wilfong, T. G. 1999. Menstrual synchrony and the "Place of women" in ancient Egypt. Oriental Institute Museum Hieratic Ostracon 13512. In *Gold of praise: Studies in honour of Professor Edward F. Wente*, ed. E. Teeter and J. A. Larson. Chicago: University of Chicago Press.

———. 2001. Friendship and physical desire: The discourse of female homoeroticism in fifth century C.E. Egypt. In *From the homosocial to the homoerotic: Women's relations to women in antiquity*, ed. N. S. Rabinowitz and L. Auanger. Austin: University of Texas Press.

———, ed. 1997. *Women and gender in ancient Egypt: From prehistory to late antiquity.* Ann Arbor: Kelsey Museum of Archaeology.

Wilkinson, J. G. 1841. *Manners and customs of the ancient Egyptians.* 3 vols. London: John Murray.

Willems, H. 1983. A description of Egyptian kinship terminology of the Middle Kingdom c. 2000–1650 B.C. *Bijdragen tot de Taal, Land–en Volkenkunde* 139: 152–68.

———. 1988. *Chests of life: A study of the typology and conceptual development of Middle Kingdom standard class coffins.* Leiden: Ex Oriente Lux.

———. 1994. *The coffin of Heqata (Cairo JdE 36418).* Leuven: Peeters and Departement Oriëntalistiek.

Wilson, H. 1997. *People of the pharaohs: From peasant to courtier.* London: Michael O'Mara Books.

Wilson, J. A. 1960. Egypt through the New Kingdom: Civilization without cities. In *City Invincible*, ed. C. H. Kraeling and R. M. Adams. Chicago: University of Chicago Press.

Wyke, M., ed. 1998. *Gender and the body in the ancient Mediterranean.* Special Issue of *Gender and History.* London: Blackwell.

Yanagisako, S., and C. Delaney, eds. 1995a. *Naturalizing power: Essays in feminist cultural analysis.* New York: Routledge.

Yanagisako, S., and C. Delaney 1995b. Naturalizing power. In *Naturalizing power: Essays in feminist cultural analysis*, ed. S. Yanagisako and C. Delaney. New York: Routledge.

Zandee, J. 1960. *Death as an enemy according to ancient Egyptian conceptions.* Leiden: E. J. Brill.

Index

Numbers in italics refer to illustrations.